God Is a Woman: Dating Disasters

Comedian Ian Coburn

Cover layout and design by Rich Mohr
Cover photograph by Ian Coburn

Women snapshots of Danielle G., Jennifer S., Jenni S.

Edited by Margaret Shake

Published by Firefly Glow Publishing, Chicago, IL

Printed in the United States of America

ISBN 0-9787979-5-7
EAN 978-0-9787979-5-9

First Edition 2006

Library of Congress Control Number 2006933907

In memory of Dan Flatly, who—when I started doing open mics—was the only comedian who took the time to give me advice. His untimely demise left the world a little less funny and minus one true talent.

Special thanks to Paul, Heather, Greg, and Margaret Shake for editing and opinions. Special thanks to Steve for web hosting. And a very special thanks to Denise, for her constant, vehement encouragement to write this book.

Contents

Why I Wrote This Book

When I first started to date, I was the same as everyone when they start to date—confused and scared. Like most guys, I looked to magazines and movies for advice. Both sucked. Magazines told me all I needed were some cool clothes, a hot car, and the right cologne, along with a few million dollars to pay for all that crap. The articles were nothing more than guys on ego trips bragging about their sexual conquests; I learned nothing. Movies skipped the most important scenes, where the guy says all the right things to the girl. Instead, movies showed the guy meeting the girl, then cut to them in bed together; big fucking help. To make matters worse, my mom gave me a book about chickens laying eggs and lambs suckling. *Someone shoot me*, I thought.

What I needed was a book with honest, adult advice—which wasn't afraid to get graphic when necessary—that taught me what to say, what actions to take, and how to read women. My sisters seemed to need similar information about guys. It would help if the stories were funny so I didn't feel so alone and self-conscious. Better yet, if some of them included celebrities, they'd be even more entertaining and really put me at ease. (If I knew celebrities struggled with sex and dating, I'd feel better about my own problems with them.)

No such book was ever published. Much to my surprise, as I got older I found I could use such a book even more. Then one day I woke up and realized: I could write the needed book. I had the celebrity stories. I had learned about sex and dating the hard way. I could tell guys how to get women. And I could tell women what men were thinking, as well as how to identify the good guys from the creeps. And I could do it all through stories of my funny failures.

God

GOD IS A WOMAN.

No discussion, no debate, no denial. She's a woman. That people challenge this notion is ridiculous. The proof is all around. If God were a man, He'd be the only one. There would not be another man anywhere. The entire planet would be full of no one but beautiful women. Blondes, brunettes, green eyes, brown eyes, big breasts, medium breasts (no small breasts), full rotund butts, and small tight asses; whatever was needed to fulfill His passing fancy. And none of them would have names; that way He wouldn't have to worry about forgetting them. If God were a man, there would be no STD's and women wouldn't get pregnant.

The only time there'd be another man is on the rare occasion when God created one, so that He could hike the guy up to the top of a mountain to brag. God would point at all the beautiful women and tell him, "See all them? I sleep with them all, whenever I want."

"Bullshit! You do not."

"The blonde over there rode me all night long. The redhead there woke me up with a hummer while the blonde was still sleeping beside me. And you know what? I never have to wear a condom… close your mouth."

Then God would kill the guy, hike down the mountain, and bang a brunette. Yup, God is a woman, no doubt about it.

Many women would be thrilled to hear a guy concede that God is female. Why, I have no idea. Think of all the crap women go through: age lines, split ends, bleeding, swollen feet, cramps… Why would a female God put women through all this? Because She is female.

For all their complaining about how badly they are treated by men, no one treats women worse than other women. They borrow and ruin each other's clothes, then rationalize it. They steal each other's boyfriends. If they're not dating anyone, they'll give their best friend bad relationship advice simply to keep her single, too. Women are catty and God is no exception.

Consider four guys grabbing grub at a steakhouse. The bill arrives. One guy picks it up. He looks at it and thinks *Fuck...math.* One of two things happens: He says, "Split it four ways?"

"Sure."

"Sounds good."

"Yeah."

They add in the tip, round it up to the next number divisible by four and they're done. Or, the guy who picked up the bill says, "I'll get this one, you guys get the next one?"

The guys agree, knowing that it will all even out at some point.

Four women paying a bill should be an Olympic event. When the bill arrives, one of them pushes it into the middle of the table. All four hover over it like angels hovering over Baby Jesus. They think things like *All right, Tracy had three bites of my salad. There's like twenty-four bites in the salad total. It's $8.00 for a salad. Tracy owes me one dollar, I'll deduct that from my bill. Last week I took a cab with Jen and it was $7.00. I paid four, she paid three. She owes me fifty cents, I'm deducting that.* In an instant all four whip out their cells and busily type away (it's the only time a cell's calculator feature is used). They throw their money into a heap, one counts it up, and then informs the others, "We're short."

They each throw a little more in, and she retorts, "We're still short."

They go through this several times, baffled at how they could be short, until one finally puts in significantly more money than the others. Her friends bat their innocent eyes, "Are you sure?"

"Yeah, that's too much. You shouldn't have to put in that much."

She pretends she doesn't care, even though inside she is seething.

"Oh, it's okay; don't worry about it. I'm fine."

If She were God, She'd be thinking *Fine, I'll pay more. Just wait until you all wake up tomorrow morning with feet that are three shoe-sizes bigger than they are now.* And that's why women have so many issues. Because God is a woman.

Now, as much as God enjoys punishing Her daughters, She takes far greater pleasure in using them to frustrate her sons... especially me. In ten years on the road as a comedian and six as a resident of Chicago's Lincoln Park neighborhood—teeming with pretty women—She's had ample opportunities to do so, which she's used to craft some of Her best work. Here, then, are stories of women frustrating me with near successes in dating or sleeping with them.

Hold the phone; why would I want to embarrass myself with stories of near successes with women? Why not share the successful stories? Sure, I could do that. I could recall the time I worked with Brian Regan in Atlanta. After the show, I met a pair of hot twenty-two-year-old identical twins, Southern Belles complete with accents and flowing, long blonde hair. They wore the same yellow summer dresses, which clung to their perfectly formed bodies, and smiled at me with their matching blue eyes. We wound up back at their place, me sandwiched between the two of them in the shower. Sure, I could tell that story.

The problem is, except for making me look like a god to men and an ass to women, the story serves no purpose. I didn't learn anything from the experience. I had an incredible time that has left me with a wonderful memory, but I didn't learn anything. My near successes taught me much more than any successes ever taught me. Plus, sadly, there are more of them and they're much funnier stories.

After each storytelling, I cover what I learned then give an example of how I put my newfound knowledge to work on a future date. I've also inserted "quickies"—little pieces of advice for men or women—between chapters. It is my hope that both men and women will find my stories entertaining and insightful. That you will be able to find more enjoyment in each other's company, whether it be for a long-term relationship or a quick roll in the hay. Life is too short for anything else. Enjoy!

The Women's Names

I HAVE CHANGED THE NAMES OF THE WOMEN IN THESE STORIES TO PROTECT their identities, which was easy to do, since I don't remember most of the names to begin with. Of course, knowing my luck, it's possible that I may have inadvertently chosen the actual name of one of these women. If so, it's purely accidental. Please accept my apology in advance.

I suppose I could have avoided the possibility of choosing a correct name by selecting unattractive names for the women, like Elvira or Trudy; but those names sound ridiculous and no one would ever believe the women were attractive. Certain names always yield attractive women. Like Heather. Or Veronica. Other names, like Gwendomeire, never have attractive owners. That's why, if I ever have the pleasure of being a father, my daughters will have names like Bertha and Gertrude…better yet, Bubba. Sure, they'll be doomed to a life of celibacy, but hey, I'll sleep much better. Just to be certain, they'll also wear clothes made from potato sacks and get a bowl haircut every two weeks.

While I'm at it, note that while these entertaining stories provide good dating tips, success cannot be guaranteed. Also, I'm not a lawyer, so nothing here is legal advice. I'm also not a doctor. Actually, there are a lot of things I'm not—like a racecar driver or a senator—but those are the only two I have to point out in a disclaimer.

Too Much Is No Good

I ADORE WOMEN. THAT'S DIFFERENT THAN ADORING SEX. ALL MEN WHO adore women adore sex; but, all men who adore sex do not adore women. Written as a Venn diagram, it would look like this:

Okay, that was completely unnecessary; but in college I took this logic class and all we did was draw these stupid Venn diagrams. I've never used one in real life and have been determined to do so, just to keep the class from being a complete waste. Mission accomplished.

Some men who adore sex actually detest women. It's almost like the sex is a conquest instead of a shared moment. They take pride in "tricking" women into bed. I've worked with lots of comedians that fit this mold. (Often, a comedy club will rent a condo for the comedians to stay in while they play the club for the week. We learn a lot about each other while roomies.)

One particular comedian who adored sex but not women stuck in my mind. There was one day in which he had sex with three different women at different times of the day, one of whom was married. And he was still on the prowl!

I learned that sex can become a drug for a lot of these guys. They had to have more and more sex to get that exciting, fulfilling feeling. I decided early on not to become one of these guys. I never wanted sex

7

to be like eating a donut or sipping a beer. So I guess my first lesson about sex didn't come from a woman; it came from horny comedians. Too much empty sex—sex for the sake of simply having sex—leads to nothing but empty sex; highly undesirable.

Grand Prix Fiancée

EXCEPT FOR ITS SPELLING, ALBUQUERQUE IS A PRETTY COOL CITY; BETTER than a lot of other U.S. cities. I've played there several times and all the visits have merged together in my mind. With the exception of the first one—that trip I'll never forget.

I was featuring at Laffs Comedy Corner. Sonya White, a talented comedienne with whom I had worked before in Wisconsin, was the headliner. (The headliner is the main act, who closes the show with forty-five minutes or more of material. The feature act performs a thirty-minute set just before the headliner. The emcee opens the show and introduces the other acts.)

I was pleased to be working with Sonya, as she was a lot of fun and offered lots of advice about the business. I was just out of college and this was one of my first big road tours. Sonya was maybe ten or twelve years older than me and from South Carolina. She was very friendly; working with her was like having a cool big sister around.

The first show of the week went great. I couldn't have had a better set. After a show, it was customary for me to stand near the exit and mingle with the crowd as they left. I was always flattered to get requests for an autograph. I stood just outside the door and shook hands with customers on their way out.

"Great show; really funny."

"Very, very funny."

Abruptly, a blonde with more curves than the Autobahn stepped out of the club. She and her friend, who I can't describe at all because I was looking at the blonde so intently, walked up to me.

"Hi, I'm Lori." She pointed across the street, "We're going over there to sing some karaoke; you should definitely come."

They walked away while I and the rest of the men watched Lori's shapely nineteen-year-old ass try to wiggle out of her skintight jeans. She was around 5'7" with long legs, long hair, and green eyes.

About ten minutes later Sonya came out of the club.

"Hey Ian, before I forget, this sweet young blonde girl wanted me to tell you she was going across the street to sing some karaoke. And she is hot."

If a woman says another woman is hot...she's hot. I was getting all kinds of good signs. Lori made a point of telling me where she was going and hinted that if I followed, I would reap rewards. The fact that she made a point of asking Sonya to be sure to let me know where she was going was huge. It was obvious she wanted badly for me to follow. Sonya and I headed over to the karaoke bar to see what would unfold.

My first concern was locating Lori. Would the bar be too crowded to find her? Would she forget who I was by the time I did find her? Most likely, I'd find her in a mob of guys. I decided that was the best place to start looking for her—in a mob of guys.

I needn't have worried. Despite the huge size of the karaoke bar, when we entered we discovered that there were only a few patrons scattered about. No one was singing. In fact, there wasn't even any music playing, an interesting strategy for a karaoke bar.

Not only that, but Lori was sitting near the entrance with her friend, staring at the door. Before I could say anything, she raised her hand. "Hey, Mr. Comedian Guy, over here!"

Good thing she told me; otherwise, I never would have found her. If a woman is 5'7" with long legs, has straw blonde hair that drapes over her shoulders, along with a tight rotund butt, and taut, mouthwatering breasts, she doesn't need to tell men where she's sitting; we already know. Sonya and I joined them at their table.

"Wait, let's not sit here; there's a better table over there." Lori and her friend got up and we followed them to a table smack in the middle of the bar, away from everyone else.

All right, things just kept looking better. She was sitting at the door only to make sure I found her; gotta like that. We all sat down.

"I'm Lori. What's your name again?"

"Ian."

"Ian, that's right. I just love that name so much."

"Thank you. So, I thought you'd be singing something when I came in. I'm kind of disappointed."

She smiled. "I don't sing, except in the shower."

"That's kind of an odd place to hold a concert, but if you give me some tickets, I can sell 'em at the show tomorrow."

She laughed and placed a hand on my shoulder. "You're so funny."

She ran her fingers all the way down my arm and over my hand. Wow, getting all kinds of great signals here. She over laughed at the flirting then made a point of touching me for a few seconds. Touching? Scratch that; more like stroking me for a few seconds. We looked into each others eyes for a moment and suddenly I didn't know what to say. Sonya knew something was up and quickly interjected, "I love to sing. I'll sing a song, but only if you two promise to dance."

Gotta love Sonya; how come I couldn't work with her every week? Sonya got up and sang some slow song. I was impressed with her voice. Lori and I danced by our table for about one minute. After that, I thought I was going to have to track down a local dentist in the morning to replace all the fillings she was sucking out. She was a very good kisser and knew just how to press against a guy and pull away, so as to get him all worked up and thirsty. She was also quite a talent with whispering in the ear, "Oh, baby, I want you so bad. Do you like the way my breasts feel against you? Are they nice and firm?"

All I could do was manage a nod. She giggled and began to probe my mouth again with her tongue. We continued to make out long after Sonya finished singing. Suddenly, Lori pulled away and exclaimed, "Let's go dancing!"

"We are dancing." I tried to kiss her some more.

She laughed, "This is not dancing."

She stepped back and turned to her friend, who was long gone. She looked around the bar. "Oh…I guess my friend left."

Meanwhile, I located Sonya. She was sitting at the bar with some of the staff from Laffs, who had since closed up the club and come over to hang out. Lori grabbed her purse and took my hand. "Come on, let's go dancing."

Now this was an odd request. We were having a perfectly good time and suddenly she wanted to go dancing? I'd noticed this before with women; when things start to progress quickly with someone they've just met, they'll suddenly change gears all together, in fear of being labeled a slut. So it wasn't unexpected and I could understand her sudden concern, although completely unnecessary in my case. I was only in town for the week and knew none of her friends. What was I going to do? Spread rumors?

I walked over to Sonya and informed her Lori and I were going dancing. Several of the staff decided to join us, while Sonya resolved to retire to the condo. We left for the most popular dance club in town. When we stepped out of the bar, Lori led me to her large 4X4. She opened her purse, took her keys out, unlocked the truck, and tossed her purse inside. Then she handed me her keys. "Here, hold onto these for me."

This was unbelievable. It kept getting better and better! I had her keys, so she wasn't going anywhere without me and I no longer had to concern myself with her purse. Guys, always know where the woman's purse is because she sometimes forgets. More than one night has ended tragically for me when a girl and I got back to my hotel room. We'd kiss a little more, I'd unlock the door and start to open it when suddenly she'd shriek, "Oh my God! My purse! Where is my purse?"

Next thing I know, instead of a night of being naked together, I'm driving her all over town trying to locate her purse.

"I think I had it when we are at the second bar. Did I? Maybe I left it at the first bar."

When the purse is finally located, or worse, chalked up as lost, the moment is gone and her mood is completely changed. In fact, many a woman will blame the guy for not making sure she picked up her purse before leaving an establishment.

"I can't believe you let me leave my purse there!"

Let her. Yes, I did; because, believe me, running around town all night looking for a purse is so much better than having sex over and over and over, until the sun comes up. What's going on tomorrow night? I say we lose the purse and do this all over again, it was such a blast! Best time of my life! But this particular night in Albuquerque, I didn't have to worry about the purse.

I drove my car around the dance club's crammed parking lot for about ten minutes before a spot finally opened up. There was a long line outside the club.

"Shoo, I hate it when there's a line. We're never gonna get in."

I smiled. "Don't worry about it."

We stood near the main entrance and waited. The staff from Laffs showed up and then I headed for the doorman. My fate was in his hands. If we had to wait in line, things would fade away and Lori would start to lose interest. She wanted to dance and dance now damn it, not wait in line to dance! I wasn't worried, though; I didn't even give it a thought.

"Hey man, how's it going? Busy night, eh?"

"No more than usual; it's cool."

"Good deal. Hey, I'm the comedian at Laffs this week. These guys are the staff over there—"

He unhooked the velvet rope without me even having to ask. No line, no waiting. Plus, I looked like an important dignitary all of a sudden. She had already been into me before; she was into me double that now.

"Thanks, man. What's your name? I'll leave it at the club with some comp tickets for ya."

The club was mobbed inside. Lori led us to an area that was somewhat open, where, of course, we ran into a bunch of guys she knew, all of whom wanted to fuck her. The Laffs staff went their own way and it was just me, Lori, and the wolf pack.

I was a lone wolf dangerously trekking through their territory, and they weren't about to have any of it. They used every trick in the book to cut me off from her. Two would step between us and ask me questions about comedy while another led her away and bought her a drink. Another would point out other women in the club to me.

"Damn, she's hot. You should be talking to her. Do you want something to drink? They have some cool stuff here. Let's go over to the bar and check it out."

Yawn. I simply grabbed a stool and sat down. My only need was to keep Lori in my sight. I had to know where she was, that was all. What about a drink? Of course, at some point, the wolves slipped up by buying them for me.

For the next hour I just sat there. The guys thought they had me out of the picture. I just sat and smiled. This was perfect. I didn't like the music, so I didn't want to dance. Didn't have to; they were dancing with Lori for me. I didn't spend a dime on alcohol; they bought my drinks and hers all night. I just sat on my stool, smiling while they hi-fived each other over their victory. I still had Lori's keys. And they say what people don't know can't hurt them.

At one point, I did run into trouble. I had to pee badly. If I left the area, the guys would try to move her to another part of the club, or, if they could manage, out of the club entirely. I wasn't about to be ditched and even if Lori no longer wanted anything to do with me, I didn't want to leave her without keys. What to do? Think, damn it. I looked around the club. Ah, yes. I walked over to a couple guys I recognized from the comedy club. They had shaken my hand after the show.

"Hey, it's the comedian. What's up, man?"

"Hey guys, how are you doing?"

"Having a good time, man; just enjoying the scenery, you know?"

"I hear ya, man. Speaking of scenery, see that woman over there?"

I explained my predicament.

"No problem, dude. We gotcha."

I walked my "comedy boys" over to the wolf pack and introduced them; then I headed for the bathroom. When I returned, it was just as I suspected. The pack had relocated; but, one of my comedy boys had stayed behind, while his buddies stayed with the pack. He beckoned for me to follow him to them.

Now, it was not enough for me to just relocate. I would have looked like a candy ass. So, I walked up to Lori and said, "Hey, there you are. Can't take my eyes off you for a second; I go to the restroom, come back and you're gone."

She smiled and kissed me. I led her back to our original spot. The pack and the comedy boys followed. I sat back down on my stool. Lori resumed dancing with the pack, soaking up the attention. She loved it. One of the comedy boys walked up to me, "Dude, aren't you worried? Why are you letting them in there? You need to knock that shit off."

I shrugged. "I have her keys."

The guy spilled his beer all over himself as he let out a guffaw. He told his buddies and they nearly peed themselves, they laughed so hard. The club thinned out as the night went on and my comedy boys went home. Still, the wolf pack was strong. I decided it was time to leave. I stood up and walked over to Lori, pushing my way through the pack as they tried to block me.

"Hey, let's get going. Ya ready?"

She seductively replied, "Yeah."

I took her hand and started to lead her away when the pack converged.

"Where ya going, Lori?"

"I thought you were coming back to our place? We're having an after-hours party."

"Oh, that's right. They're having an after-hours party, Ian. Do you want to go?"

Yes, I want to go. Instead of heading some place where we can be alone, I want go to a place with you and a bunch of drunken guys. Woo hoo!

"Na, he's not invited; just you, Lori."

This was getting out of hand. Lori was wavering and in about ten seconds she was going to ask me for her keys. I did the only thing a 5'10" 120 lb. guy could do in that situation. I bent over, picked up Lori, and slung her over my shoulder. I turned away from the pack and headed for the exit.

Lori looked back at them and waved, "I guess we're leaving! Bye!"

I glanced back at the bewildered faces of the wolves: I had made such a bold and original move they didn't know how to react.

Back in my car, Lori couldn't keep herself off me. I wanted to head back to the comedy condo or to her place, but she insisted that we stay in the car. As we made out, she started with the questions.

"Am I the prettiest girl you've ever kissed?"

"Am I the sexiest girl you've met in all the cities you've been to?"

I have no idea why some women ask such questions. I suspect it's a self-esteem issue. I would never ask a woman if I was the biggest guy she ever had or the hottest. These questions just aren't pertinent. Besides, what idiot is going to answer them "No," even if that's the honest answer? A murmured "Yes" and "Mmhm" here and there satisfied her. One question she asked, I did fully answer.

"What's the best part about meeting me?"

That was easy.

"That it happened on the first night. We have the whole week to hang out together. We can grab dinner at a nice restaurant, maybe hit a museum."

Typically, when a comedian is fortunate enough to meet a woman, it happens on the last night he's in town. There's no time to spend together. This...this could be like dating someone for a week, something road warrior comedians don't get to experience. She liked that answer.

I kept trying to get Lori to head back to the condo with me, but she insisted on staying where we were. I was awfully worked up and couldn't handle it anymore. While people filed out of the closing club, I took off her shirt and bra.

She had the second best pair of breasts I've ever had the pleasure of seeing. (At the time, they were the best.) They were nice and large but very taut. They didn't drop even slightly when the bra came off. The ratio of breast to nipple was perfect. I was extremely pleased by this.

Usually large breasts have surprisingly small nipples, while small breasts may unexpectedly be almost all nipples. That's the best part of getting to a woman's breasts for the first time for guys; we've been wondering what they look like and having that answered is always extremely fulfilling and erotic.

"Do you like my breasts?"

All I could do was nod and gasp. She smiled. "Show me how much you like them."

I started to reach for them when the catcalls began from the scores of people leaving the club. She quickly threw on her shirt, "Let's get out of here."

Now I was the one reluctant to leave. I had just seen the best breasts ever for only a moment and now they were gone. I managed to start the car and pull out. "Back to the condo it is."

She shook her head, "No. I know a place."

I listened to her directions intently, switching back and forth between driving too fast in anticipation, and too slow for fear a cop would pull us over and put an end to it all. I had to see those breasts again! Remember, I hadn't even had a chance to touch them, yet.

"How much further?"

"Not far."

I felt like a kid—Are we there yet? Are we there yet? Are we there yet? Every now and then she let out a laugh; she knew full well what she was doing to me and it made her hotter and hotter. We drove for what felt like forever–four minutes–when we came to the back of an empty warehouse.

"Pull in here."

I parked in privacy behind the warehouse. Loving the build-up to things myself, I slowly began the process again, instead of just going straight for the breasts. We made out for a while. I teased her every now and then by starting to remove her shirt, then stopping. Eventually neither one of us could take it anymore. I took off her shirt.

We were parked right under a light. Thank God, because I loved those beautiful breasts and I could see them perfectly clearly in the spotlight that rained down on her. It was like a light from Heaven was shining on her half-naked body, while I sat right beside her in darkness.

"Now, where were we?" she asked.

"I think right about here."

I began to caress her breasts and then went to town on them with my mouth and tongue, which I only mention because I didn't know such action was acceptable until the third or fourth time I got off a woman's top. (Think about it; it doesn't exactly come up in sex ed. How's a guy or girl to know?) I was careful to give each breast equal time. I'd had enough candid conversations with waitresses to learn that women notice when guys favor a breast, which we typically do. It freaks them out some, so try not to do it.

She went crazy, "Oh, God, Ian, baby, Jesus! Oh God, I love it when you suck my tits. Jesus Christ! Ahh! Mmmm. God, if my fiancé knew what I was doing right now, he'd be pissed."

What?!

"You have a fiancé?"

"Mmm, yeah." She shoved my head back to her breast.

Well, this was an interesting turn of events. My engine had long since started, though, and I really couldn't even consider what she said beyond being momentarily surprised. I felt I had to say something, though. I think I managed a "That's cool" and went back to the breasts.

"I have to pee."

Finally! She had to go back to the condo now; even Taco Bell was closed at this time of night. She put her bra and shirt back on as I drove to the condo.

"Do you want to just sleep with me?"

"No. If we don't have sex tonight, that's fine. I'm actually looking forward more to getting together for some dinners and hanging out... if your fiancé doesn't mind."

"He's huge. He's like six-two and really built. He'd come to the comedy club and kill you if he ever found out."

"That's nice."

Back at the condo I was surprised to find Sonya still awake. She was chatting in the living room with another comedian who was passing through town. He had been given permission by the club to crash in the condo for the night. (The emcee was a local act, so the third bedroom was open.)

Lori politely said "Hello" and headed into the bathroom. Our guest made a beeline and accosted me just outside the bathroom door. "Whoa, she is smoking hot. Did you fuck her, yet? God...mind if I do?"

"Actually, I'm thrilled I met her on the first night. We have the whole week to hang out."

I led him away from the door, as he continued to rant and rave about how hot Lori was. I shushed him, I told him to be quiet; he simply wouldn't shut up. Obviously, God had brought him here for the sole purpose of screwing me over.

Lori came out of the bathroom. She was not happy. Surprisingly, the bathroom door was not made of three-inch thick steel. Furthermore, the bathroom itself was not soundproof. Huh; who would have thought it? She heard what was said.

"I want to leave. My keys, please."

I could see there was no talking her out of it, so we headed back out to my car. I fished out her keys and handed them to her. On the way back to her truck, which was still parked in the comedy lot, I smoothed things over. She massaged my lap the last few blocks. I barely pulled into the lot and threw the car in park. In an instant, I had her top off again.

"Oh, God. It's going to be so hard to date you. I just don't think it would work. Do you?"

Date me? What the hell was she talking about? Before long there was a lot less fooling around and a lot more talk from her about us dating.

I don't lie to women; it's unnecessary and disrespectful. I never understood how someone could fool around with someone they didn't respect.

"Look, we're not going to date. You live in New Mexico, I live in Chicago. I travel all over the place. You're engaged. But we have this week and I think we could have a really great time that we'll remember for a long time."

Surely she realized that she was being unreasonable and would be as happy as me that we had a whole week together. She was not.

"You don't want to date, huh? That's because you probably have a girl in every city."

She put her bra and top back on. I told her I didn't have a girl in every city; that I rarely hooked up with anyone, which was the truth. She kept insisting that I did. The more I refuted it, the more she insisted I had a woman stashed in every city.

"Look, I'm flattered that you think I'm this stud, but I don't have a woman in every city. We have a chance to have a really special week here. Don't you want that?"

We argued for a while longer. Abruptly, she stopped. She began to kiss me again.

"Sorry, Ian. I don't know what came over me."

We necked for a few minutes then she decided it was time to call it a night.

"Walk me back to my truck?"

"I'll just drive you over there."

"No, I want you to walk me. It's more romantic."

I smiled; we were back on track. We got out of my car and walked toward her truck. After a few steps, she took my hand. This was nice, really nice. We reached her truck and she gave me one final long kiss goodnight.

"Let me write down my number for you. I have a pen in my purse."

She opened the truck and climbed inside. She started it. She rolled down her window and looked me square in the eyes, "Save your lies for all your women in other cities!"

She threw the truck into gear, floored it, and started to drive away. I called after her, "Lori! Lori! Come on, Lori! What are you doing?"

I stood there for a moment, wondering what the hell had just happened; but, I didn't have much time to think about it. Lori's truck was heading right for me. She wasn't driving very fast, but she did aim the truck right at me. At that point I thought to myself *You know, it's quite possible this woman's not entirely stable.*

I jumped out of the way and she spun the truck around. She headed for me a second time. I looked to my car. Damn, it was still way on the other end of the parking lot. Where's KITT from *Knight Rider* when you need him? I didn't know what to do. No way could I outrun her to my car. If I tried, would she run me down? It suddenly occurred to me how little I knew about this girl. Was she psychotic? A criminal? Or just angry she cheated on her fiancé and taking it out on me? I decided to keep walking to my car, nonchalantly. At least I'd die with dignity.

She ran at me and veered away a few more times. Then she drove circles around me as, little by little, I worked my way closer to my car. It's funny, but even while freaking out and feeling my heart in my throat, I was still a comedian. I yelled to her, "Is this how they do foreplay in New Mexico?"

I have never been so happy to climb inside my car. I started it and threw it in drive. She ran at my car a few times. I drove slowly, turning my car around so I could get out onto the street. She made one last run at me then veered away. She flipped me off as she drove out of the lot.

I stopped my car and just watched, waiting until her taillights were barely a dot in the distance. What the hell had just happened? My hands were trembling. After a few minutes I relaxed.

I realized that I had just had a complete relationship in one night. We met, we had chemistry, we dated for a short time, I sucked some tit, we argued, we fought, she tried to run me over; a complete relationship in one night, Jerry Springer style.

I drove back to the condo and lay in bed, replaying the events to figure out where I went wrong.

I learned five things from Lori:
• Women just want to be right.

- Women assume that a guy they just met is lying about something and they'll analyze his comments to identify the lie.
- Women have to create an expectation they know is false in order to permit themselves to act on something they want to do.
- Don't directly confront a woman when she is wrong.
- No matter what, ALWAYS STAY IN THE CAR.

I heard, "You must have a girl in every town," or some variation of that phrase, from almost every woman I met after Lori.

"You have a girl in every state."

"You've probably slept with a hundred women."

"You have sex every night with a different woman, don't you?"

Some of them were women I was interested in; most weren't. I had learned from Lori that it was no good to refute the statement. These women all wanted to be right. They were wrong, but if I called them on it, they would simply get defensive and agitated. They were right; how dare I question them!

Instead, I decided to go in the opposite direction. I wouldn't refute their statements; I would diffuse them by agreeing with exaggeration.

"You must have a girl in every town."

"No."

She'd frown.

"I have three girls in every town. I'm going to need you to introduce me to two of your friends."

—OR—

"You've probably slept with a hundred women."

"No I haven't."

Again, a frown.

"I've slept with ten thousand...and three...wait, four...no, three... yeah, ten thousand and three. I've slept with ten thousand and three women. Wait, are we counting oral sex, too?"

In virtually every single case, my exaggeration got a laugh and the topic was dropped. I had shown them that their statements were wrong by pointing out how ridiculous they were. I did it, though, in an indirect, non-confrontational way. They still felt like they were right and I wasn't challenging them. I simply pointed out through humor that how many women I'd had or hadn't had didn't matter. Just to test my theory, every now and then I would refute them when they accused me of having a woman in every city. Sure enough, it got ugly every time.

I used the same approach when a woman started to create a false expectation. For example, consider a woman I met in Boise.

"I think it would be hard for us to date. Would you call me? Do you think it would work out?"

"Work out, are you kidding me? While you've been talking, know what I've been doing? Thinking up names for our kids. We should have three. Ooh, and a dog. Do you like the name Rex for a dog or is that too cliché?"

She laughed and punched me, "You're silly; we're not going to have kids and a dog. We'll probably never even talk again after this week."

Again, the topic was dropped. I don't know why, but for some reason indirectly pointing out the folly of their false expectations with exaggeration puts women at ease. It was like I was saying, "Yeah, I feel the same way you do. I'd like to date, too; but we both know it's not going to happen."

They needed to create an expectation of dating to allow themselves to have a level of intimacy with me; otherwise, they would feel like sluts. I told them I knew what they were doing by exaggerating it and that I understood; we were on the same wavelength. I couldn't say the actual words, "Yeah, I'd like to date, too; but, we both know it's not going to happen." Why not? Remember, women assume a guy they just met is lying about something. They'd assume I was lying and become insulted that I was trying to "humor" them by saying what I thought they wanted to hear.

Exaggeration worked great because it left them nowhere to go. They didn't have to ponder *Wait, I know he's lying. It sounds so good, though. He is lying, but where is the lie? Is he lying or not?* My exaggerations were so preposterous, there was nothing to analyze. Clearly, I was lying. It was an obvious lie, though, which made it not a lie.

My exaggerations also got the smallest part of them to worry *Oh my God; does he really think we're going to date? I better make sure he doesn't.* Suddenly, they had to make sure I had both of my feet on the ground, as opposed to me having to make sure they had both their feet on the ground. Sound complicated guys? Think of it this way: I switched them from defense to offense.

Also, I think they were flattered that I made the effort to be so elaborate in my exaggeration. Best of all, I stayed true to myself and respectful by not lying to a single woman. It's very important to stay true to oneself.

Of course, I never, ever, not even one time, walked a woman from my car to hers again. I always drove her…every single time.

 **QUICKIE**

A LOT OF GUYS COMPLAIN THAT THE HARDEST THING TO DO IS BREAK THE ICE with a woman. That's why many guys use lines. I'm not a fan of lines. They sound insincere, most are old and tried, and if a woman falls for them, I typically lose respect for her, followed by a loss of interest.

Instead, look for the common-denominator. The common-denominator is the thing the guy and girl have in common. There is always a common-denominator; it just has to be found.

For example, one night I was out with a buddy, waiting for a table at a pool hall. We set up shop near a table of three women playing, one who immediately caught my eye. I waited. On one of her shots, she ran the cue ball along the edge of the pool table. It nearly fell off but managed instead to fall onto the table and into a pocket. Bingo. I approached her after she and her friends laughed about the shot. I raised my beer in a toast.

"I've played a lot of pool, but that is the most original scratch I've ever seen."

She toasted me and laughed. Shortly thereafter, one of the ladies left and my friend and I paired up with the two remaining women for some team play. The one I liked took my number and called me the next day.

Look for the common-denominator; it's there and the conversation will flow much more naturally. By the way, it works just as well for a woman looking to break the ice with a guy.

Some common-denominators can be reused from time to time when nothing fresh comes to mind. My personal favorite standby has proven very effective for starting conversations on Friday nights.

Again, I use it only when nothing else comes to mind, in order to keep it sounding fresh. I walk up to a woman.

"So, are you out celebrating a good week or trying to forget a bad one?"

Starts a conversation every time, including the night I came up with it. (Hey, get a different standby; this one's mine!)

Don't Tell my mom

COMEDY CLUBS ARE CATEGORIZED. A-ROOMS BOOK A LOT OF BIG NAMES to headline—acts on the verge of getting a sitcom or who have been on TV frequently. They typically run shows five to seven nights a week. B-rooms don't headline big names much and typically run shows three to five nights a week. A lot of their headliners are just as funny as big-name acts; they just haven't met the right people. In entertainment, meeting the right people is Big. Both A- and B-rooms tend to be in larger cities.

One-nighters are just what they're named. They're one night gigs that can take place anywhere, but tend to be in towns and smaller cities. One-nighters that suck are called hell gigs. Most of the time, comedians have no idea they are working a hell gig until they're already at the gig. I once played a bowling alley, which is a bad gig to begin with; the other acts and I assumed the show would take place in a room separate from the bowling lanes, like maybe the bar. Nope. At show time the manager simply kicked customers off the center lane, and that became the stage. We each did our act standing halfway down the alley while people bowled in the lanes around us. Good times.

My first big A-room gig came when I was nineteen. I did open mic night at KJ Riddles, an A-room in a suburb south of Chicago. While I was onstage, comedian Jimmy Pardo and the owner, Ken, hung out in the back of the club. I had met Jimmy when we both made finalist status in a competition to appear on *The Tonight Show*.

Ken picked up a flyer advertising the acts for the next few months off a table. He pointed to a week and told Jimmy, "I need an emcee for this week. Any ideas?"

Jimmy pointed to me onstage and asked, "What about Ian?"

Timing is another big element in entertainment. Had Jimmy not been sitting with Ken at the moment I was onstage, and had Ken not brought up the week, it probably never would have occurred to Ken to consider me for the spot. Good ole Jimmy. Ken approached me with the flyer as I got offstage, "Hey kid, I need an opener this week; you free?"

I recognized the picture of the headliner. He'd been on *The Tonight Show* several times, as well as a bunch of other television shows. His name was Drew Carey.

At the time, I was going to school in DeKalb, Illinois, which was a good hour-and-a-half away from the club. I didn't have a car, and it was a week-long gig occurring in January, while school was in session. (Currently, I was on winter break.) I looked at Ken and without missing a beat replied, "Yeah, I can do that."

Immediate panic set in. What the hell was I saying? I couldn't do the gig; I had no way of getting to it. There wasn't any public transportation anywhere near the club and the friend who had driven me that night would be back at school in Iowa.

"Good. It pays four hundred dollars."

Four hundred dollars?! Four hundred dollars?! I might as well have been Whoopi Goldberg in *Ghost* yelling, "Four million dollars? Four million dollars?"

To a college student in 1991, four hundred dollars was like ten grand. Hell, I was writing checks for thirty-four cents...and they were bouncing. Four hundred dollars was a semester of work. It was fifteen minutes a show, eight shows total. That's four hundred bucks for two hours of work. At the time I was making four dollars an hour after taxes in my dorm's cafeteria. I was going to get paid one hundred hours of dish work for two hours of comedy work. Ken said a bunch of other things after "four hundred dollars," but I have no idea what they were. I didn't hear anything after four hundred dollars.

The day after I booked the week at Riddles, I started calling other comedy clubs to let them know I was working there and that I was opening for Drew Carey. It was the first big step toward full-time comedy. Doors that had been shut tight before were suddenly opened. I booked two months of emcee work in two days. I booked clubs in

Wisconsin, Indiana, Illinois and Iowa. All the gigs took place during the school session. And yes, I still didn't have a car.

Back at school, a week before my gig at Riddles, I began to freak out. I still didn't have a car. I had been unable to secure any rides to the show. My bank account boasted a lofty $54 and some odd cents. Not too many cars were going for that price (I checked). What to do? What to do? The answer hit me on my way to Japanese class (yeah, I don't know what I was thinking when I signed up for that course either, except that it would be nice to understand my math teacher for a change). There, at a table in the middle of the sidewalk leading up to the arts building was the sign—literally. It said "MasterCard."

In college banks give you credit cards like they are handing out candy to trick-or-treaters on Halloween. I had avoided them before, for fear of racking up bad credit, but now seemed like a good time to change my tune. Armed with MasterCard checks and a $2000 credit limit, I went to work finding a car. I bought one for $1600 the day before the gig started. It was a 1985 Buick Century. On the advice of the seller, I took it in immediately for an oil change.

The first night of the show went great. I was nervous as hell in front of a packed house of 450 people, but after my opening joke killed, I relaxed and just cruised through my material. I met Drew while the feature act was onstage. He gave me his intro. He was a very cool guy and made me feel at ease. I was surprised at how nervous he was. Every show, as it got closer and closer to his time to go up, he paced back and forth, back and forth, relentlessly.

He also couldn't talk to a pretty woman to save his life. Every time one of the cute waitresses approached him for an autograph or to chat, he could only manage to mumble and mutter in reply. He didn't go out after any of the shows; he just went back to his motel room and read a book. I later learned that he preferred to frequent strip clubs. I found that surprising, given that it was very easy for even me to meet women after a show. There weren't any strip clubs near KJ Riddles.

On my way back to school after opening night, my brand-new secondhand car died. I restarted it and continued to drive…with the engine light on. (Needless to say, I knew very little about cars at the time.) After a few miles the car died again and would not restart, despite my begging, cursing, and eventual pounding on the steering wheel. Luckily my roommate's parents lived close to where I broke down, so I was able to spend the night with them. In the morning AAA towed my car to a shop. (AAA is the wisest investment I ever made. They saved my butt many, many times. Anyone with a car should join; go with AAA-Plus.) Apparently the mechanics who changed my oil had stripped the oil pan (they over-tightened the drain bolt). Oil had been slowly leaking out of my car as I drove. My engine light went on because I was driving without any oil.

What an exciting turn of events. A day ago I owned my first car; now I owned my first two-ton paperweight. A new engine would cost more than I spent for the car, so I cut my losses and junked it. I was now in worse shape than my original dilemma. I had two months of gigs—one of which I was in the middle of—no car, and only $400 of credit left on my MasterCard. I was also standing, bewildered, in an auto repair shop while I was supposed to be eighty miles away, taking a test in Japanese. Everyone who's been to college knows that tests are huge. College classes only give two or three tests each semester and each one accounts for like forty percent of the final grade. I did the only thing I could do…I called my mommy.

I felt like an idiot for calling my mom, but I was glad I did. Although she didn't like the idea of her little boy performing in clubs with "drunk people, clouds of smoke, and loose women," she did have a solution: I would stay with her the rest of the week back home in Oak Park, a suburb just west of Chi-Town, and she would drive me to the shows for the rest of the week. This was a big sacrifice on her part, as I had never known my mom to spend any time at a bar or nightclub. She detested most of them.

Mom wore her favorite scarf the first night she drove me. It was hand-knitted for her by her favorite aunt or someone who had since passed away. She had had it for years and wore it everywhere. On the way to the club, she became too warm with it on and took it off, placing it between the driver's and passenger's seat.

My second night went just as well as my first. My mom sat in the back of the sold out club. I went up to her after the set. "Well, whad ya think?"

"Do you have to swear so much?"

"Mom, I swear like twice and all I say is hell and damn."

"Exactly."

Boy was she in for a surprise. Although Drew's standup was

squeaky clean on TV, his favorite adjective was "fuck" and he used it like a chef over-seasoning a meal. To make matters worse, his closer was a three-minute bit on masturbation. I decided not to be anywhere near her during his act. She liked the feature, as he spent a good portion of his show impersonating Bob Hope, who didn't use harsh words like "damn" or "hell."

Drew and I spent most of the feature's act talking about my car situation. He liked that I was willing to make stupid decisions just to get onstage. I decided to get another credit card and buy another car, which is what I eventually did. All the money I ended up making over the next two months paid for the cars and then was gone. But I got two months of experience onstage, which was priceless. (Yeah, my second card was a MasterCard, too.)

Years later, when Drew had his sitcom, I heard stories of him buying new cars for employees who owned clunkers. I had worked with Drew just before he shot his first sitcom, *The Good Life*, on which he was a sidekick. The show bombed and got canceled after a few episodes, but it was enough to get Drew his own show. It's a known fact in Hollywood that one of the best roles an act can land is the sidekick on a new sitcom. If the show flops, everybody blames the lead, not the sidekick. Plus, the sidekick has been seen and now networks can cast him in just the right role, as they've seen his work. The worst thing to be is the lead on a flop; no one wants to touch the actor after that with the proverbial ten-foot pole. (I guess it's true; Drew Carey landed a big successful sitcom after *The Good Life* flopped while John Caponera, the show's lead, fell off the radar. It's too bad because John is talented and, truthfully, most sitcoms fail because of just-awful, forced writing; not because of the lead.)

It's too bad I didn't work with Drew when he was buying people new cars. That's the kind of guy Drew was when I worked with him— genuine, grateful, and someone who felt it was important to spread his good fortune. It's always good to see people like that find great success, as they deserve it.

During Drew's set I headed out into the club's lobby, where I met Jennifer. She was standing in the lobby alone, looking at the pictures of comedians papering the walls.

"What are you doing out here?"

"Hey, you were the first guy. You're really funny."

"Thanks. So what are you doing out here?"

"Oh, I'm only eighteen and I got caught. They kicked me out of the show and now I have to wait for my friends. I'm bored to death."

"Oh, that sucks. I'm only nineteen and they let me stay in there."

"You're one of the acts."

"Exactly. So just go on and do some time."

She laughed, "Yeah, right; I could never do what you do. I'd be so nervous."

"Yeah? What can you do?"

"I can do some things."

"Yeah, like what?"

She smiled. She was really cute, with short brown hair, big brown eyes, and deep dimples. I was scared to death but I stepped into her as I asked again, "Tell me, what can you do?"

She grinned, "Stuff."

I kissed her. In a few moments we started to make out. She slid her hand down to my crotch and told me she had never seen a penis. I told her no girl had ever seen my penis. She asked, "Do you have a car?"

"Sure, just let me go get the keys; they're in my jacket."

Back in the showroom, my mom was pissed.

"This guy is filthy. I should have brought my earplugs. Why does he have to curse so much? You're not going to be like that, are you? 'Fuck this, fuck that'; I won't have it."

I grabbed the car keys.

"Hey, where are you going with those?"

"I left something in the car."

Inside the car, Jennifer changed her mind. We just kissed for a while. She kept rubbing my crotch, though.

"Are you sure you don't want to see it?"

She nodded, "I'm sure."

I touched her breasts over her shirt, which she wouldn't let me remove, even though I tried several times. After a while, as Jennifer kept talking about penises, I decided to be bold. I unzipped and released the beast. She freaked out. "Oh my God! Put it away!"

Not the reaction a guy hopes to get. I zipped up.

"Sorry."

She stared at my crotch, "Why did you do that?"

I shrugged, "Seems like you really want to see one and I'd like someone to see mine. I'd like the first to be you."

"Take it out again."

I was more than happy to oblige. Immediately, she recanted, "Okay, okay, put it away."

This went on a few more times. I was going crazy, sitting in my mom's car with Sybil. At her request, I took it out yet again. She looked at it. "What's it feel like?"

"Touch it."

She shook her head. I gently took her hand and moved it over.

"Wow. It feels so different than I imagined. It feels really good."

She tried touching me in different ways. "Does this feel good? Does this feel good? What if I do this?"

"It all feels good."

It felt amazing. I was her tutor; her practice tool. There was something especially fulfilling in that. Suddenly, she threw me a curve ball. "Do you have a condom?"

I stared at her, "Really?"

"Yeah…really."

I did not have a condom, as I had never needed one. What's more, I did not want to search the car for one. My parents had been divorced since I was six and I really didn't want to know if my mom had condoms in the car.

"Damn it; I don't have one."

"It's okay. Tell me what feels best."

When she hit a motion that made my eyes roll back in my skull, I nodded my head rapidly, "That's it; that's the one."

Suddenly, just as I was about to orgasm from my first hand job, I heard huge applause coming from inside the club. I looked at my watch. Oh my God! Drew was getting off. I had lost complete track of time.

Part of the emcee's job is to go up and close the show after the headliner finishes; tell the crowd to tip the staff, point to the exits, let them know who's appearing next week, that kind of thing. Here it was, the second night of my first big week and I was going to blow it! I knew from the first night that Drew got two big applauses at the end of his act. I had just heard the first one; the second would come in about thirty seconds. I had to get back inside! As every guy knows, though, at nineteen, there was no turning back. God was going to force me to stop now? To come this close and stop? Such cruelty!

"Oh God, Jennifer, hurry; I have to get back inside."

She finished. Now, it being my first time, I was especially excited. After all, I'd been imagining this moment since I was twelve and had seven years of pent-up anticipation. Stuff went everywhere; I mean everywhere: the steering wheel, the dashboard, the radio… Jennifer was impressed.

"Wow. Does it always happen like that?"

"No, not even close. That's all because of you. You were great."

She smiled, "Thanks."

In my extreme haste, I grabbed the only thing in sight big enough for this job…my mom's scarf. I mopped up everything, zipped up, then Jennifer and I sprinted for the club. I tossed the scarf into the trash along the way.

Even though Drew and I got off at the same time, the continuous applause from the crowd bought me some time. I made it back and brought him off the stage. No one was the wiser.

Strangely, I didn't see Jennifer again. She left without saying goodbye. I thought we would exchange numbers, but we didn't. Yet, I didn't mind. There was something satisfying about it, like a secret. It actually made the whole incident more exciting. We had shared something special in a car while everyone else was inside the club. No one knew but us. We gave each other something for the first time and we always had that. I couldn't explain it but I liked that feeling.

Years later, when I was headlining Riddles myself, a woman approached me after the show and told me she had seen me back when I was starting out, when I opened for Drew Carey.

"My friend gave you a hand job in your car."

That was awesome.

When my mom and I got in the car to go home, there was no reason for her to grab her scarf; the car was still warm from Jennifer and me. We had the heat on while we were in the car. It wasn't until we got home that she realized the scarf was gone.

Every night she made me ask each waitress if they had seen a hand-knitted scarf. Every night she bugged the club manager to look in the lost and found. Till this day, she still doesn't know what happened.

And as I don't expect she will be reading this book, please don't tell her. Thanks.

I learned five things from Jennifer:

- Always have quick, easy access to condoms.
- Actions speak louder than words.
- Observe; pay close attention.
- Take a risk; flirt.
- Anticipation and build up enhance sexual gratification for both people.

I was always a little disappointed that Jennifer and I weren't each other's first, mostly because it was due to my lack of preparedness. She had given me something really good and I would have liked to have repaid her…in spades, if possible. (Which was probably very unlikely at nineteen.)

From that day forward, I always carried some condoms. The decision has had many impacts that I never anticipated. For example, consider an occurrence at which I used all the knowledge I learned from Jennifer.

One night I was out with some friends, all guys, at a popular bar named John Barleycorn. Four women approached us, all attractive, the ringleader hot. She was young and had a great, tight little body. They had a list of items typed on a piece of paper. "Are you grocery shopping and you got really, really lost?"

The girls laughed at my joke. It turned out they were on a scavenger hunt as part of a bachelorette party. They needed to get a condom from a guy. Surprisingly, they were having a tough time. I was shocked to learn that none of my friends had a condom. I took one out and held it up. The ringleader, smiling at me, reached for it. I pulled it away, "Not so fast."

I paid close attention to her reaction. She smiled, "What?"

I had been given a green light to continue.

"What's in it for me?"

"What? Do you want like a dollar or something?"

I shook my head, "I don't want a dollar."

"Then what?"

"Well, ideally, I'd like to use his brother."

I pulled out another condom and the girls all laughed in dismay. My friends backed away, suddenly embarrassed to know me.

35

"But I'll settle for a kiss."

The ringleader asked, "Who do you want to kiss you?"

"Why you, of course."

"I'm not going to kiss you."

She closed her eyes, though, so she was obviously preparing for a kiss. Her actions spoke louder than her words. I leaned in and kissed her. We swapped spit for a good minute and then I gave her the condom. I got her number and we went out a few times.

My friends were amazed my approach worked, which baffled me; I thought it was common knowledge. Since then, after many candid conversations with guys and gals, I learned that it is not common knowledge; most guys don't know how to behave or read signals, and most women are frustrated with guys' poor interpretation skills. It's one of the reasons I decided to write this book. One woman I recently met went out with one guy several times who never made a move.

"Jesus, how many low-cut tops can a gal wear? I invite him up to my apartment, I'm wearing the lowest-cut shirt I own, nothing. Hello?!"

Some of my other friends had no idea that a girl twirling her hair while she talked to them was a sign of interest. One even thought it meant she was bored! I informed my friends of the need to pay close attention, to be prepared, and to take a risk and flirt. Sexual contact of any sort cannot be initiated without taking risk. Remember Jennifer. I risked making a move, we wound up in my mom's car, she said she didn't want me to take out my penis but clearly she did, and had I had a condom, Drew Carey would STILL be onstage at KJ Riddles... how's that for wishful thinking?

QUICKIE

"Ten percent of the guys date ninety percent of the women."

A friend told me that several years ago. I thought about it and realized he was right. That means that ninety percent of the women date ten percent of the guys; not very comforting to men.

There are a lot of clueless guys out there, which may be part of the reason why many women seem to be attracted to guys who are already dating someone. It may be an indicator that the guy indeed has a clue. Most guys need to be better at reading the signals and getting over their fear of taking a risk.

And why is it so many guys don't take a risk? Fear of rejection. Here's a little secret: Everybody gets rejected. Guess what? We're still breathing; still walking around. It's no big deal. The only way to become at ease with taking a risk is to develop a thick skin. The only way to develop a thick skin is to get lots of rejection. The only way to get rejected is to take a risk.

Like women, I thought that guys just got over the fear of rejection with age. Not true, it has nothing to do with age. It only has to do with two things: the amount of previous rejections, and alcohol. Unfortunately, being a drunken, babbling idiot isn't typically appealing to women.

Guys, get out there and get rejected! It will help you out immensely with women.

First Date

MANY PEOPLE MEET AT BARS, PARTIES, OR THROUGH DATING SERVICES. THESE places are designated pickup spots. People go to them just hoping to meet someone and, in some cases, pay top dollar to do so. They dress up, put on their best game face, and prepare for battle. Women, though, also surround themselves with friends, put up their guard, and set expectations.

Meeting a woman is tough when her guard is up, and God help me if she has expectations. I do not score high on lists of expectations. Since God is the one yanking my chain, I'm not going to get any help from Her; so, it's best for me to stay away from anyone with expectations.

Some of the best places to meet people are places that aren't designated pickup spots—a hockey game, the tennis court, a pickup game of volleyball. Women don't have expectations and their guards are down. People also don't have their game faces on; they're being their honest selves.

If people want to date, it is best for them to meet as their honest selves; if they're just looking to get laid, honesty is a moot point. That's why a lot of bar encounters don't work out as meaningful relationships; both people had their game faces on when they met, and when their real faces are revealed later, they're just not in sync.

Whenever I returned home from a big road tour, the first thing I did was go to my bank, TCF, which was still pretty small at the time (now they're in every Jewel across the Midwest). I can't buy a gallon of milk without worrying about my money. *How much money do I have in my accounts? That seems high; did I pay my rent?* I just want some milk! I can't eat without being reminded that I'm broke.

39

One particular Monday I went to my bank and noticed they had hired a new teller. She was very pretty. She had a tight little body, short auburn hair, blue eyes, full lips, stood around 5'3", and was my age, twenty-two. I had to meet her.

I counted my money while trying to prepare a strategy. Comedians get paid in cash and I had been on tour for three months, so I had a nice wad to deposit. Also, I had a bit in my act about wearing a glow'n-the-dark condom. Naturally, I sold glow'n-the-dark condoms on key chains after shows, for two dollars apiece. I had nearly $300 in singles to deposit along with the rest of my money.

I got in line and waited. I'd have to get pretty lucky with the timing. There were four tellers working the windows (something one doesn't see at all anymore), so the odds were good that when my turn came, she would not be the available teller. Sure enough, when it was my turn a different teller beckoned to me. I waved through the guy behind me and stayed at the head of the line. Sadly, the next available teller was not the one I wanted to meet either, so I waved through yet another person in line. Finally, before my intentions became too painfully obvious, her window opened and she beckoned me. I headed over to her.

"I thought you were just going to let everyone pass you by."

Great, she was on to me. I held up my wad of cash, "No, it's just that I was still counting all my money."

"Wow, that's a lot of singles."

"I'm a stripper. As you can tell from my deposit, I'm quite good."

"I thought you looked familiar. Do you have a tattoo of a Dragon?"

"No...gerbil."

We flirted a little more before I asked her out for later that week. To my surprise, she accepted. We decided to meet at a popular elegant restaurant. I quickly left the bank before she came to her senses. I didn't even exchange numbers; I didn't want to leave her an out.

The night of the date couldn't have gone better. Usually guys have to worry about how far to try and take things on a first date. We're not even always sure it is a date. *Is it okay to touch her hand? Should I try for the goodnight kiss? Is it too soon to ask her to move in with me?* There are lots of things to think about.

I didn't have to worry about such things with Gina, which was quite refreshing. She smiled pleasantly throughout dinner and occasionally touched my hand. She even played footsies. There wasn't any ambiguity; we were on a date and she was definitely interested.

We dined outside and after the meal she suggested we dance to the music. There wasn't a dance floor but almost everyone else had left, so we created one in the aisle. After keeping the staff half-an-hour past closing time, we decided to leave. We wound up in a nearly empty park, where we just sat and talked for a while. The conversation had been going well all night. In fact, it had been going too well. There were no pauses in which to steal a kiss or give a wink. I was beginning to long for one more and more as she spoke. She was very interesting and I liked her a lot.

It turned out Gina had a second job as a bikini shot-girl at a bar. This meant that she wore a skimpy bikini while she toted around a tray of shots. She recanted stories of men hitting on her and uttering stupid things. She couldn't have turned me on more if she was sitting there wearing only lingerie. For some reason it is a huge turn on for a guy to be out with someone who has many men after her. Dozens of guys hit on this girl daily and she didn't give them the time of day. Half of them went home and jerked off to her image after closing, and here she was, out with me. I guess it just makes a guy feel special to be out with a woman who so many guys ogle over regularly. That's part of the whole appeal of waitresses, bartenders, and models.

Eventually, one thing led to another and we started to make out. After a while things escalated and rampant groping began. Every now and then she pulled away at the end of a long kiss. "Mmm, I'm getting uncomfortable."

I'd simmer down but things steamed up again pretty quickly.

"Mmm, this is too far."

We'd slow down for a bit then we'd end up pushing the envelope even further. This went on for a while before it occurred to me that Gina was doing some things that she didn't really want to do. Perhaps she thought she needed to if she wanted to be sure I would call her. (We had exchanged numbers over dinner.) I really liked her a lot and decided that I needed to let her know that she didn't need to do anything she didn't want. I resolved to put her mind at ease if she got uncomfortable again. Which she did.

"I'm uncomfortable again. I'm sorry; I'm such an old fogy."

"Don't worry about it. It's only a first date…I didn't expect to get this far."

It is the stupidest thing I ever said to a woman. Of course I didn't mean it the way it sounded. It just came out horribly wrong. She was so classy, she didn't reply. She didn't call me an ass or anything. We hung out for a while longer and then we drove back to her car, where we made out some more.

I was such an idiot, I actually could not figure out for the life of me why Gina didn't return any of my calls. We had such a good date; why would she blow me off? About a month after the date, it finally hit me. I left a message apologizing and tried to explain but there was no way to fix it. My mouth and I blew it big time. I had become Gina's latest story of a guy uttering something stupid.

I learned four things from Gina:
- There is an effective way to pick up waitresses.
- Some mistakes just can't be fixed.
- Think carefully before speaking.
- I am a complete idiot.

Lots of guys fall for waitresses and bartenders. They tend to be very pretty, friendly, smile a lot, and typically have good dispositions. Plus they take orders. What guy doesn't want a woman who takes orders every now and then?

"Bring me a Corona, honey."

"Sure."

Of course, she brings the lime without even having to ask. The primary appeal of bar staff, though, is that they have to talk to a guy. They are sexy women who can't walk away. It's surprising how many guys will continually interpret waitresses' friendly demeanors and flirting as interest. The waitresses, on the other hand, are after tips, not guys.

Personally, I stay away from bar staff for several reasons. First, they get hit on relentlessly. Second, their guards are on overdrive. They know patrons have their game faces on, so they don't believe most of what guys tell them, even if they are swearing on a Bible.

Third, bar staff have heard it all. Whatever fresh angle a guy thinks he's laying on a waitress, there's a ninety percent chance she's heard it…more than once; which makes him just another guy hitting on her. Plus, the staff is working! How annoying is it for a waitress to be working hard at her job, smiling pleasantly, while eight guys at different tables hit on her?

And last, I'm past the point in my life where I'm looking for one-night stands, brief flings, or two-week "relationships." I prefer a real relationship that could go somewhere. Bar staff are not conducive to dating. They work horrible hours, usually just starting when other jobs finish; the weekends are the biggest moneymakers for them; frequently their bar gig is a second job; many are adult students; and they are often on call. Their social lives and friends frequently revolve around the bars at which they work.

In short, it's hard to schedule time together, and when plans are made, they are prone to last second cancellations. In an effort just to see them, their boyfriends often wind up hanging out with them and the rest of the bar staff after closing, when the staff spends most of the time reliving inside stories about working at the bar. I spent many nights chatting in such groups after comedy shows, watching poor boyfriends sit there with nothing to say.

If a guy wants to have a fighting chance with a waitress, the first thing he should do is make small talk with her. Find out where she likes to hang out when she's not working. Does she have another job? He should try to meet her at those places, where he won't be just another patron hitting on her. He also has the perfect icebreaker.

"Don't you work at that bar around the corner?"

"Yeah, I do."

"I thought you looked familiar. What's your name again?"

And so forth. If he can't ascertain such things, his next best move is to find out what slow nights she works at the bar. He can talk to her on one of those nights, when she actually has time to converse and isn't hurried. I've successfully picked up several waitresses using these approaches. It also helps if the guy is a good storyteller, so he can effectively breach the inside conversation when he's sitting with his girl and the rest of the bar staff after closing.

Some mistakes just can't be fixed. Cut your losses and move on; otherwise, obsession and bitterness may ensue, making you miss out on new opportunities. As much as I hated it, I blew it big time with Gina and there was no way to fix it. I cut my losses and moved on, determined not to be so stupid again.

Guys say stupid things all the time to women with only the best intentions at heart. I have a friend who was on a date with a guy who had gone out with a model. He told her, "You know, outside her picture, the model looked just like an average girl; like you."

My friend never spoke to him again. As a guy, I know he meant, "I've been out with a model and I have to tell you, you're just as pretty as she is."

Why do guys say stupid things? On the early dates we may be nervous or anxious. We're being so cautious not to say the wrong thing at key times during the date, we overlook a quick blurb that is hurtful to her. In a relationship, we get comfortable. Comfortable guys make the wrong comments every now and then to their friends and girlfriends alike. While our friends think little of poorly phrased comments, a girlfriend may interpret them as taking her for granted.

A guy just needs to take a moment and think about how a comment will be heard before he makes it. If something dumb is uttered, he needs to clarify or apologize right away. (If she replies with quietness or changes the subject by asking an unrelated question, something dumb was uttered.) Women, who are much better with phrasing, can help a guy out by being a little more understanding. They can also let a guy know he said something stupid, to give him a chance to both realize and correct it. If Gina and I had both done these things, we'd be at home right now, where she would be bringing me a beer... wearing only her teeny bikini.

QUICKIE

GUYS SAY STUPID THINGS ALL THE TIME. HOW CAN A WOMAN TELL THE difference between a good guy who has simply said something stupid versus a guy who's simply an ass?

Let the guy know he said something stupid. Does he apologize? Does he attempt to correct it? Does he choose his words more carefully in the future in order to express what he really means? If he does, he's a good guy and he's interested; cut him some slack.

If the guy continues to say stupid things, doesn't bother to correct them, and doesn't apologize, he's an ass. If he's been dating a girl for a while, says stupid things, she calls him on them, and his response is always a shrug and, "You know what I meant," he's an ass. Kick these guys to the curb.

Women need to be aware that there is only one guy in the world who says all the right things 24/7. He's the guy who's not interested in the woman, he's interested in getting into her pants. There's nothing wrong with that, but women should be aware of it, so they don't set themselves up to be hurt.

When a guy really likes a woman as a whole, he's going to say stupid things every now and then. We can't help it; it's simply how we're affected by women we like and there's no way around it.

Every guy is an ass to some women, because he's not interested in them. They don't affect him, so he says all the right things because he's not even slightly anxious; or, when he says the wrong things, he simply doesn't care.

This same guy is a good guy to other women, because he is interested in them. They do affect him, so he doesn't say all the right things because he is a little anxious, and when he says the wrong things, he does care.

Women would do themselves a great service by paying attention to these differences in a guy's behavior. They'll be able to tell if he's truly interested, uninterested, or just looking to get laid. This way they know what they're in for and can take care not to emotionally attach themselves to the wrong guy.

The Package

I ATTENDED NORTHERN ILLINOIS UNIVERSITY IN DEKALB, ILLINOIS, ABOUT sixty miles west of Chicago. DeKalb was popular for a while because it's the hometown of Cindy Crawford. DeKalb should be well-known because it's where barbed wire was invented. Think of all the places that use barbed wire: farms, prisons, battlefields, security fences; but, barbed wire didn't give DeKalb its fifteen minutes of fame, Cindy Crawford did. Such is the magnitude of T&A.

I chose NIU over the esteemed Northwestern University because I wanted to be a jazz trumpet player and NIU had arguably the best jazz program in the country. Northwestern's program? Let's move along. I soon learned that, while I was a good trumpet player in high school, I sucked in college. NIU recruited for jazz musicians like Texas recruits for football players. I was literally blown away by the competition. It is the hardest thing in the world to face the reality that a dream will not come true. It is also the most strengthening thing that can happen to a person. I had tried my hand at standup just before I entered my freshman year and, when jazz didn't pan out, I turned to comedy. Unlike jazz, I was exceptional in standup and, as it turned out, I enjoyed it more than the trumpet.

Of course, I owe my first credit card to comedy; I had to charge a car to get to my Drew Carey gig. My older sister did not have a credit card. She did, however, have a boyfriend and she strongly desired to purchase a few nice things for herself (for him) from the Frederick's of Hollywood catalog. She harassed me endlessly to use my card to place the order until I finally obliged.

Huge mistake. Immediately, I became an esteemed member of the Frederick's of Hollywood mailing list. Worse, I was friends with everyone who worked behind my dorm's front desk, the people responsible for placing mail into our mailboxes. I could no longer talk to coeds in the dorm lobby. Anytime I started a conversation with one, a friend from behind the front desk would yell, "Hey, Ian...Ian! You got the latest Frederick's of Hollywood catalog today!"

It didn't matter whether I had actually received the latest copy that day or not, they still yelled it out. God help me if the catalog actually did arrive that day. (Again, She's not going to help; She prefers to torture me.) One of them would hold it up and wave it at me. "Hey, here it is, Ian! Thought you might want it right away! Be sure to check out page 43! Grrroowl."

He would give me a thumb's up with a nod. Women scattered like roaches when the light goes on.

Frederick's of Hollywood doesn't like it when a member on its mailing list goes a long time without ordering anything. As I soon learned, the company takes dramatic measures to keep the customer's business.

My dorm, named Grant North, had twelve floors. (I should be clear that NIU insists their dorms are not dorms; they are residence halls. Ha! When the walls are so paper thin that the sound of your neighbor having an idea wakes you up, it's a dorm.)

Different floors had different rules. I lived on five, which along with three was the least regulated floor. Anyone could get on the floor at anytime. It was coed by room. Girls and guys walked around in towels and students did not need to make an effort to be quiet until 11 P.M., 1 A.M. on the weekends. Every weekend students sprayed the fire extinguisher in the hallway, punched holes in the walls, glued condoms to someone's door, and so forth. There was even a full bar in one room.

The twelfth floor of Grant North was quite different. Students had to have a key to gain access. It was all coeds and they had to be quiet 24/7. Guys were not allowed on the floor past 11 P.M. and had to be escorted at all times. There wasn't even a male restroom. A girl had to make sure the women's was empty, and then guard the door while a guy conducted business. I was up there a few times and that's how I found out that women's bathrooms are palaces compared to men's. Of course, the twelfth floor was nicknamed the virgin floor and lots of pretty women lived there. One in particular caught my eye. Her name was Bridget and she was the first woman I thought looked great in glasses. She was short and petite, with a nice body. Her black hair hung just shy of her shoulders.

I had to move slowly; girls on twelve did not like aggressive guys and most were very shy. It didn't help that I lived on five, which was notorious for its weekend antics. Bridget and I exchanged smiles on the elevator and in the cafeteria for several weeks before I chanced speaking to her. She was sweet and very smart. She had a double-major and would finish her education in just three years; pretty impressive considering my roommate at the time was in his sixth year, with just one major. She was also extremely shy; she made the other girls on twelve look like wild party animals.

Getting mail in college was big; getting packages was gigantic. Even with all of today's technology, I'm sure a package from home is a highly welcome sight. Parcels rarely made it back to rooms unopened. Most were torn into while riding up the elevator, in front of an anticipating audience of other students. What treasures could be inside?

One day I received an unmarked package. It was simply a plain small box with only my address on it. I waited alone for the elevator while I shook the light package, wondering what was inside. Nothing rattled. Bridget and a few of her floor buddies returned from lunch and waited with me. I decided right then and there that this was the time for me to make my move. I was going to ask Bridget out, probably as I got off the elevator. (That way if she declined, I didn't have an awkward ride to my floor with her.)

She smiled at me as she asked, "What's in the box?"

"No idea."

"Really?"

All the girls got excited.

"Open it."

"Yeah, open it."

A few other people from various floors arrived and inquired about the package as well. When the elevator arrived, we all got on and I started to tear open the box. Inside was that off-white packaging paper.

"What is it?" Bridget anxiously asked as she placed her hand on my shoulder and moved to get a better look. It was funny, but her touch gave me a warm twinge. I lowered the box so she could easily see inside. I sifted through the paper carefully but didn't find anything, so I just yanked it all out. All eyes were on me and my exciting package. I held the balled packaging in my hand and caught a glimpse of red. I separated the papers to take hold of a piece of balled-up red fabric.

"What is that?"

An insert fell from the wrapping. One of Bridget's friends picked it up.

"It's some sort of red scarf."

I opened the scarf to learn that it was not a scarf at all. Instead, I was standing before a woman I badly wanted to date holding a pair of red crotch-less panties.

"Eew!"

"Oh my God!"

Bridget immediately withdrew to the other side of the elevator. Her friend read the insert aloud, "As a preferred customer of Frederick's of Hollywood, it is our pleasure to present you with this free gift. Enjoy!"

Welcome to Frederick's aggressive marketing tactics to regain a customer. The elevator stopped on four. Bridget and her neighbors got off. "We'll wait for the next one, pervert!"

Bridget scowled at me as the doors closed. The elevator opened on my floor, where some of my neighbors got on.

"Nice panties, Ian. Those for your mom?"

I realized I was still holding the panties in front of me for the entire world to see. I never did get a date with Bridget—or any of the girls on twelve, for that matter. Word of my perverted ways spread quickly among them. Good thing the women on twelve were quiet and kept to themselves. The story spread no further, leaving coeds on other floors open for dating, at least for the time being...

I learned two things from my experience with Bridget:

- Never open anything in front of anyone without being absolutely certain of what's inside.
- Buy discreet items with cash or have them mailed to a friend's address. Better yet, have them addressed to the boss or a bad professor.

Ordering discreet items puts one on an endless mailing list. If a credit card is used, the company has to have the cardholder's billing address, even if the items are being mailed somewhere else. The address is sold to other companies in similar businesses; endless mailings of propaganda ensue.

My dad bought me a membership to *Writer's Digest* one year. It's a book club. Once a month I was supposed to receive a book in the mail, along with deals on other books. I never received the books, just a bill for them, probably because they didn't have my credit card information; my dad signed me up with a money order. I got bills followed by collection notices for said bills. They hounded me for years to renew my membership after it expired. I also got all kinds of mail solicitations to buy books on writing and publishing, not to mention countless book scams from unscrupulous companies looking to cash in on someone's dream of being published.

I asked my dad not to sign me up for such things in the future. He didn't. Instead, for my birthday the following year, he got me a subscription to *Playboy*. Granted, that had its perks, but it wasn't really my style. I'm not a window shopper. Do fat people just look at pictures of food? Do hunters just admire animal heads hanging on the wall? Oh sure, I often end up window shopping, but it's not by choice.

My subscription to *Playboy* put me on a lot of porn mailing lists. It was a hassle. I didn't feel comfortable having new girlfriends collect my mail when I was out of town. I couldn't open my mailbox in the lobby of my apartment building as an excuse to linger and strike up a conversation with a pretty woman getting her mail; she might see some porn material. Eventually, because I didn't reply to anything, all the junk mail stopped; but, what a hassle in the meantime.

Ironically, the first issue of *Playboy* I received featured a Playmate spread-eagled in crotch-less red panties. (I wondered if they were from Frederick's of Hollywood.) Were they mailed to her for free to regain her business? Perhaps they're what got her started posing naked. She was on her way to becoming a veterinarian when WHAM, out of the blue, free panties. Next day, she's posing naked. Free panties change everything, I know. Come to think of it, the Playmate looked familiar. I think she lived on twelve...

 **quickie**

THE TWO BIGGEST PERSONALITY TRAITS WOMEN LIKE IN MEN ARE confidence and a good sense of humor. How can a guy who doesn't have these traits get them?

Confidence is not hard to develop. Most people who lack confidence believe they don't have anything of value to offer. Wrong. Realize that everybody has value, including you, and offer it. Express ideas and opinions. Keep doing so; the confidence will build. Note that being loud and interrupting other people are not acts of confidence, they are acts of non-confidence. People use these techniques to overcompensate for a lack of confidence.

Humor is harder to develop. It takes timing, presence, delivery, wit, and quick thinking. Regurgitating funny lines from movies does not qualify as a sense of humor but it's useful in a pinch. Don't overdo it; it can become annoying and forced.

The roots of humor are relativity and logic. People have to be able to relate to the topic to find the joke funny, which is why many women don't laugh at *Star Trek* or *Three Stooges* jokes. Women typically don't watch these shows, so how can they find references to them funny? Guys who joke about these shows risk being dubbed dorks by women. Know your audience, guys.

Conversation and topics have a flow of logic to them. Interrupting or changing that flow often results in humor. My good friend Greg and I walked back to my car one afternoon after a grueling game of tennis. The bumper of my car was being held to the frame by a bungee cord. He pointed at it. "Hey, your bungee cord is pretty frayed; looks like it's gonna snap at any moment."

"Oh, thanks. I better get that taken care of; I got a big date tomorrow.

How embarrassing would it be to show up with a frayed bungee cord holding the bumper onto my car?"

Greg laughed, "Yeah, you definitely want a new bungee cord for big dates or special occasions."

Obviously, any type of bungee cord is not good. See how I interrupted logic to make the joke? The only way to get funny and to develop timing and delivery is to test out the material. Pay attention to what works and what doesn't; stay with what works. Don't be afraid not to get laughs; it happens to everyone.

Go To Your Own Class

NEVER GO OUT WITH A WOMAN WHO LIVES ON AN ALL-GIRL FLOOR IN A coed dorm. In college, it was a common rule among guys. Coeds on all-girl floors were usually the most immature girls on campus. They gossiped; they giggled and pointed at people while they whispered secrets; they went to the bathroom together in droves, like herds of animals headed for a watering hole in Africa. They were third-graders masquerading in women's bodies. The only exception to the rule was the twelfth floor. Women on twelve were simply serious about school and didn't want unwelcome distractions; nothing immature about that. In fact, a guy who managed to become a distraction to a resident of twelve quickly became a bit of an idol to the other men in the dorm.

Women on the other all-girl floors, though, needed to be avoided at all costs when it came to dating. I knew this. I agreed with it. I preached it. Yet, once I ignored it. Why? As I've already pointed out, I'm an idiot.

There was a pretty redhead I saw every now and then in the dorm, always in passing or from a distance. She was around 5'7", skinny with a nice rack and shapely butt. Her pale skin looked good on her and she had a sensuality about her I couldn't explain. Mostly she smiled a lot, which is always attractive. Although I wanted to talk to her, the opportunity wasn't presenting itself. One day I was waiting for the elevator by myself when she came into the building and waited as well. We smiled at each other.

"How ya doing?"

"Good, thanks."

"I've seen you around; what's your name?"

"Amy."

"I'm Ian, nice to meet you, officially."

"You, too."

We shook hands.

"What floor do you live on?"

"Nine."

Uh-oh; all-girls floor. *Run away, make a break for it, don't look back!* All these thoughts raced through my head, but then she said something that got to me. "And you live on five, right?"

Whoa, hold the phone. She'd been watching me. She'd been noting where I live and maybe asking around about me. She immediately realized that she had revealed too much and tried to recant, "I mean four, right? You live on four."

I grinned. Too late.

"No, five is right."

A guy in a hurry joined us. He pressed the elevator button over and over. Lots of people do this while they wait for elevators. I'm not sure why. They swear that it brings the elevator faster. Really? I can't remember the last time I was on an elevator, just riding along, whistling a tune, when all of a sudden, whoosh! The elevator just started zipping along at an alarming rate, bouncing me and everyone on it around like lottery balls.

"What's going on?"

"Someone must be pushing the button a whole bunch of times! That makes us move really fast!"

Press the elevator button one fucking time. It doesn't do anything except annoy people to press it repeatedly. It also looks foolish, dumbass.

Realizing the importance of humor when just meeting someone, I leaned in and whispered my elevator theory to Amy. She laughed. The elevator arrived and the three of us rode up together. We reached five first.

"Well, nice meeting you. I'm sure we'll see each other again soon."

"I'm sure we will, Ian."

The next night my friend Bob and I sat down to dinner at a table behind Amy and a bunch of her neighbors, just as they were finishing their meals. They giggled and pointed at me.

"Dude, stay away from her."

I don't know why I didn't heed Bob's advice. Perhaps it was because I was a senior and had missed out on the whole college dating scene. Between classes and traveling for comedy, I didn't have time to meet anyone on campus. I always thought I would meet my wife in college. It was beginning to occur to me that my chance to do so may have slipped between my fingers. This could be my last chance. College is an ideal place to date. There are a variety of personalities and classes are the only real distraction. Most students have the same amount of money…zero dollars. It's like standing in a storm of snowflakes. Look them over and find the one that matches best. If it doesn't work out, try another.

I live in Lincoln Park now, a Chicago neighborhood that teems with single young professionals. There is one huge difference between college and the real world. In college people still have a glint in their eye for life and what's ahead. They haven't been hardened by harsh realities, burned by lovers, or become untrusting skeptics of each other. They are happy. This no longer holds true for the majority of young professionals, which makes them far more difficult to meet and know.

A fresh group of coeds from Amy's floor arrived to dinner. She remained with them while the rest of her original group left. Bob and I heard one of them wish Amy good luck. That was my cue. I quickly ate, then went over to her table, carrying my drink.

"Hey Amy, how are you doing?"

I took a sip of my drink.

"Good, how are you?"

"Good, thanks. What classes did you have today?"

I took another sip of my drink. Back at our table, Bob laughed raucously. I frowned at him. He held up his drink and pretended to take a sip. He lowered it, then raised it and pretended to take another sip. I laughed.

Amy asked, "What?"

"I do standup comedy. I have a bit in my act about how when guys hit on women, they always take a sip from their drinks after they ask a question. It's like our safety blanket."

I mimicked myself asking a question then drinking. The women all laughed.

"Oh my God, that's so true. I never noticed that."

"Oh, that is too funny."

"So, you're hitting on me?"

"I guess. How do you feel about that?"

I took an exaggerated sip to punctuate the joke. They all laughed again.

"I think I like it."

We smiled at each other. I sat down and invited Bob to join us. Amy introduced everyone and we hung out for another ten minutes. There were all sorts of red flags. None of the girls, including Amy, took a class unless at least two of their friends took it. There were a few classes that some of them wanted to take badly but, because none of their friends would sign up, they didn't. Each semester they all sat down and did their schedules together, signing up for the same classes. Some of them didn't even go after the major they wanted because they didn't know anyone else taking that major. Instead, they chose the same major as most of their friends, even if they had no interest in it. What a brilliant way to choose a career path.

These coeds never went anywhere on campus alone. They always had someone else with them. They couldn't go to the library or computer lab alone. They wouldn't eat alone or even head to the shower without company. It wasn't a safety issue; they just didn't like being alone. Their relationships didn't last long. Most guys got fed up with never having any alone time with their girlfriends. The girls always insisted that their friends join them on their dates—business as usual among the "brat pack," as I later came to call them. If one of them went back home for the weekend, they all went back home. They only stayed on campus when the entire group stayed. Since NIU was a suitcase school (a school at which a lot of students go back home for the weekends), these girls weren't around much.

In short, the entire group shared one brain. They weren't individuals, they were a team, nay, more like a pack. They were utterly, completely, unequivocally immature; unwilling to think for themselves when it came to making even the smallest of choices. Really, they were afraid to live, afraid to be individuals. Mostly, I suspect they were afraid to be accountable. They spent a lot of the conversation blaming one another for choosing a class with a tough professor or for screwing up each others' relationships. It's hard to fix blame on individuals in a group, so they were all protected from accountability. That's the real safety they sought.

Also, Amy was a sophomore. It is unadvisable for upperclassmen to date underclassmen. The two tend to be in different places in their lives with different goals. Upperclassmen are looking toward leaving school, making plans for a career and life, while underclassmen are selecting a major and trying to decide if they want to rush, and if so, for which house.

Idiot that I am, I ignored all the red flags. I liked Amy and that was all there was to it. I got her number and then ended the conversation, "I'll call you. Perhaps we can do something next week?"

"Sure. I have to see what my ladies are up to first, of course."

Run away, run away! Bob and I left.

"Dude, you're not going to call her, right?"

I didn't say anything.

"Oh my God. Are you nuts? She can't even think for herself. You know what? You go out with her and you deserve exactly what you get. Don't come to me for sympathy. Nice job with the drink thing, by the way."

We joked some more about my drink bit. Incidentally, the bit was more than a smart observation turned into a funny routine; it got me into the Improv chain of comedy clubs.

I performed in two of the annual homecoming talent shows at NIU. One of them was hosted by comedian Henry Cho. Henry can't help but be funny. He is an Asian who was born and raised in Tennessee. Naturally, he has a thick Southern accent. When he speaks, it is instantly surprising; no one expects an Asian to speak with a Southern drawl. Surprise is a key element of comedy. He is also a smart observer and witty writer. It turned out Henry had his own drink bit, which was very similar to mine. He didn't have a punch line, though, as his accent alone made the bit work. I told him I had the same bit after he did it between two acts. We argued about it behind stage while some poor student, who could certainly hear us, performed a dance routine.

Once I told him my version, though, he told me I had to keep doing it, that it was very clever and funny. He liked it a lot. I stayed away from the bit until I began headlining regularly, though; otherwise, the industry would have assumed I had stolen it from Henry. Once acknowledged as a headliner, no one thought I took it from him; we just had a similar bit, which happens in the biz. Henry asked me where I worked in Chicago. I named the big clubs I worked: The Funny Firm, Laugh Factory, KJ Riddles.

"No Improv?"

The Improv? I'd been trying to get into the Improv for two years. I called them twice a week and couldn't even get the booker on the phone. They didn't have an open mic night, so I really had no way to penetrate their fortress.

"Call 'em next week."

I didn't have to call them; they called me. The following week, Neil, the booker of the Chicago Improv, called and told me Henry Cho said to take a look. He invited me in for a showcase. (A showcase is when an act is booked to perform ten minutes for free so that the club booker can decide if he wants to hire the act for a paying gig.)

During my showcase, Neil left the showroom. He missed the entire set. Another headliner from the South came to my rescue, a guy named Vic Henley. He was walking through the club lobby at the same time Neil was asking the emcee how I did. Vic spun around, "He's funny. Give him a week."

Again, timing proved critical. I got two weeks and my foot in the door of every Improv around the country, thanks to Vic and Henry.

The night after I got Amy's number at dinner, I ran into her and the brat pack at a party. Not good. I didn't want to see her again so soon. Once I get a number, I like to wait a few days before having contact with the woman again. Too much too soon tends to be detrimental, so I like to set a slower pace, which is accomplished from the start by not calling for a few days. We made eye contact, so I had to go over to her.

"Hello."

"Hi Ian. How are you?"

We talked for a little bit.

"All right, while it was nice running into you, Amy. I'm going to roam around, say hello to some people. I'll call you in a few days."

Perfect. I handled the situation without a hitch. I turned to walk away.

"Okay, well, I'll be downstairs by the keg. Don't be a stranger."

Damn it. She wanted me to meet her at the keg. A few weeks

before, a woman dropped a similar hint to me at a party. I had gotten her number, so I didn't pay attention; I'd call her later. When I did call in a few days, she was angry that I had not met her later at the party; she had been keeping an eye out for me. She asked me not to call again. According to her, if I had really liked her, I would have looked for her later at the party. I didn't want to make the same mistake with Amy, so I mingled for a while, then headed downstairs to the keg. Amy seemed glad to see me and we spoke for a while. A few of her friends dragged her away. As she left, she called back to me, "Hey, I'll be outside on the porch!"

Shit. She wanted me to find her out there. I didn't like playing the role of a puppy following her around, so I decided to put an end to it. A little later I headed out to the porch, intending to say goodbye. As soon as I got there, Amy and her friends, who were talking to a few guys, decided to head to yet another room. They left the guys behind, but Amy made another point of letting me know where she was going. I didn't pay attention. I spoke to a few friends, had another drink, then I looked for Amy, to say goodbye. Her friends pointed and giggled at me as I approached. I told her I was heading out and would talk to her soon.

The next night I went down to dinner with my roommate, Derrick. Amy and her friends were a few groups ahead of us in line. I went over and made some small talk—asked her what time she left the party, things like that. I headed back to Derrick. After dinner, he and I ended up in a packed elevator with Amy and the brat pack. They hid her behind some girls and giggled. Derrick and I got out off the elevator. He turned to me. "Dude, you are fucked."

I called Amy to see what all the fuss was about, but her roommate said she wasn't home. I heard Amy and the brat pack giggling in the background, but I decided to let sleeping dogs lie. Unfortunately, the brat pack didn't see it the same way. For the next week I had girls from all over the dorm pointing and giggling at me. The brat pack had spread some rumor about me and I didn't even know what it was. Bob was right; I went after a coed on an all-girl floor. I knew the danger, and now I was paying the price. I was getting what I deserved.

Things only escalated. I started to get crank calls. Ripped-out magazine pictures of women in lingerie were slid under my door late at night while I was sleeping. Derrick passed Amy and the brat pack on his way back from class one day. They were walking twenty yards behind me, trying to figure out how to pass me without being seen. I had no intention of spending my senior year dealing with such antics. I called Amy again. Her sister answered the phone.

"Amy is in the shower."

They sounded identical and I thought it was Amy.

"Come on, Amy, gimme a break. What the hell is going on?"

"This isn't Amy; I'm her sister, you freak."

She hung up. A little later the phone rang. It was Amy.

"Ian, it's Amy. That really was my sister. Don't call me again. You made me really uncomfortable following me around at that party."

"Following you around? The only reason—"

"No, don't even try to explain. My sister wants to talk to you."

Immediately her sister got on the phone. "Don't talk to my sister, don't look at her, don't follow her to class. Yes, we know you've been following her to class."

She hung up. Whoa, whoa, whoa! Follow her to class? I didn't go to *my* classes, let alone someone else's. If I started going to classes, they certainly would be mine. What the hell was wrong with this chick? She was nuts.

The crank calls and giggling coeds continued. I couldn't talk to a woman in my dorm, let alone get a date. I found out Amy's room number and left a note in her mailbox. I simply explained the misunderstanding and asked that she call off her brat pack, they were all being annoying. Of course, I did it in a rather edgy, curt poem in which I referred to her and her roommate as the female versions of Beavis and Butthead. I then hit the road for a week of hell gigs.

When I returned to school, I found a response in my mailbox. I threw it away without reading it, intentionally in front of a group of giggling girls from nine. I knew they'd tell Amy and I hoped my message would be received loud and clear. No such luck. The antics continued for another week. Understandably, my roommate was becoming quite annoyed with the crank calls, especially since I was on the road most of the time, so he was the one the girls were really bugging, not me.

A few days later I was invited to appear on a radio show. I was playing the Laugh Factory in Aurora, which is roughly halfway between DeKalb and Chicago. The headliner couldn't make the radio show and the feature act didn't want to do it alone. I thought it would be good experience, so I accepted.

In the sound booth I was pretty nervous. It was weird not being able to see the audience. Once the show started, though, I was fine. It was much easier than standup. There was no live crowd, no pressure if there wasn't a big laugh—the laughs were just assumed. Everything we said was funny; there was no proof otherwise, such as a quiet audience or chirping crickets. There was no pressure; we just had to keep the banter going. After the DJ finished interviewing the feature, he turned to me, "And also with us is this week's emcee, Ian Coburn. You're a student at NIU, Ian?"

"I am."

"We're on air out there. We get a lot of student listeners. What's going on at NIU these days?"

"Some girl accused me of following her to class."

"Following her to class?"

"Yeah, which is ridiculous because I don't even go to *my* classes."

The entire booth laughed on air.

"Why would you be following her?"

"Well, my major is Criminal Activity and I'm taking a stalking class."

"Oh, so it's just a class project."

"Exactly. She's a homework assignment. The entire class is following her all around campus."

"So you should get an F in the class, since she's identified you."

"Yes. The A students are completely undetected. If you steal a copy of her schedule from her room, you get an A+."

I spilled the entire story without mentioning names. A few callers phoned in to rag on Amy and the brat pack. They became the focus of our hour on the air. I don't know how many students listened to the show. I don't know if any of them belonged to the brat pack. I do know that afterwards I never got another crank call and coeds no longer giggled and pointed at me. Amy had obviously called off the brat pack and they had recanted whatever rumor they spread. Maybe they were embarrassed. Maybe they didn't want to get picked on themselves. I suspect they stopped for the same reason they did everything—they were afraid of being held accountable. They didn't want to be singled out; they preferred the comfort of a group.

I learned three things from Amy:
- Don't make people into something they're not.
- Never ignore red flags.
- Don't ask out immature people.

I liked the way Amy looked, was flattered that she had been paying attention to me before we actually met, and liked that she was a happy person. These things blinded me. Instead of seeing Amy as who she was, I chose to see her as who I wanted her to be. Lots of people do this, especially women. Many women are always working to "change" a guy. They have a vision of how they want him to be and, instead of seeing him for who he is, they try to force him to be who they want him to be. This isn't fair, just as it wasn't fair for me to see Amy as someone she wasn't.

There were tons of red flags with Amy. Because I wanted her to be as I saw her, I chose to ignore them. Bob was right; when things went sour I had no one to blame but myself. Helen Keller could have seen what was going to happen.

Immature people are not good people to ask out, let alone date. They're simply not ready to live in the adult world. Many of them never will be.

I stayed away from asking out coeds on all-girl floors from then on, as well as immature women. I also heeded any red flags. Just to be certain no one thought I was following her around campus, I never went to class again. Hey, I was a senior; how much could I miss?

Quickie

I HAVE A LOT OF WOMEN FRIENDS. MANY OF THEM COMPLAIN THAT GUYS don't approach them, whether they're at a bar, sporting event, party, or so forth. Contrary to popular opinion, when we guys are "on the prowl," we're not looking for pretty women with great bodies; we're looking for approachable women.

When a woman catches a guy's eye, he watches her for a moment before deciding whether to approach. Is she smiling? Laughing? Does she look like she's having a good time? Is she drinking? Are her arms crossed? Is she arguing or debating with anyone?

The guy is trying to determine if she's approachable, if she wants to meet someone. Women with crossed arms or who are debating a serious topic, tend to be much harder to approach. Women who aren't drinking tend to be out because their friends dragged them out, not because they want to be, at least as far as guys are concerned. Women that don't catch a guy's eye when he originally surveys the room often will catch it later with lots of smiling and laughter. Their demeanor makes them attractive.

Look around. Are the guys hitting on the smiling, laughing women, or the sourpusses? Among friends, who gets hit on the most—the smiling, laughing ones or the frowning ones with crossed arms?

A lot of my women friends don't look approachable. They're great women, but they're not sending out a welcoming vibe.

Want to meet more men? Smile. Laugh. Have fun. The guys will come.

Lingerie Party

"HEY, HEY, WE'RE THE COBURNS! PEOPLE SAY WE'RE FOOLING AROUND! But we're just causing trouble! And we're heading back into town!"

My two sisters and I sang these words to the tune of *The Monkees* theme song every year as we flew back from our annual summer trip to Canada. We were a perfect example of why people hate it when parents fly with their kids. To make matters worse, we belted it out as loud as we could the entire flight; just those few lines, over and over. Little did I know that as an adult I would actually meet the composers of the Coburn's travel song.

One night I headed into downtown Syracuse, New York. I had a few nights off between a gig at Nick's Comedy Stop in Boston (one of the best clubs in the country, an absolute blast) and some college shows in Pennsylvania. There's not much to do in downtown Syracuse; most everything closes up before five o'clock in the evening. I played a comedy club there once a year, though, called Wise Guys. The club was located in a hotel and I had befriended the staff. They gave me a huge discount on a room anytime I was there. So, whenever I was traveling near Syracuse, that's where I crashed.

The only place to hang out was the hotel bar. I headed down that night and sat at the bar, several stools away from two familiar-looking guys who were in their fifties or sixties. I kept looking over at them, trying to figure out who they were. Another guy between fifty and sixty joined them. The bartender noticed my puzzlement, and he leaned in as he handed me another beer. "They're the Monkees."

"What?"

"The Monkees."

I looked at the guys again. Oh my God; they *were* the Monkees. Once I knew, I easily saw it.

"They work the area a few times a year. They always stay here when they do."

"Really? My little sister and I used to love that show. We watched it all the time."

"You can go over and talk to 'em but don't let on you know who they are. As long as you don't talk about it, they'll talk to you. If you say anything about them being the Monkees, they'll up and leave."

I went over and started a conversation with one of the Monkees. Before long I was talking with all of them about all kinds of things. Actually, it was just three of the Monkees; one of them didn't tour anymore. I later learned from the bartender that it was Michael who didn't tour. His mom invented whiteout, so he didn't need to gig. We discussed sports, politics, dating, traveling, the entertainment industry, and family for over an hour. I never let on I knew they were the Monkees and they never brought it up; they were simply a band on the road talking to a comedian on the road.

There wasn't anyone else in the bar except for the occasional passerby—someone who came in to find out what time it was, or ask if the bar served some ridiculous drink no one ever heard of, or to grab a book of matches. An hour before closing time, I was about Monkee'd out. I started to get up and say goodbye when two gorgeous women with long hair walked into the bar. They were very slim with pronounced butts and breasts that were too big for their bodies. I imagined that they didn't eat, but just fed their breasts.

"Jesus, whaddya think they feed those things?"

"They don't look like they eat much at all to me."

"I didn't mean them, I meant their breasts."

The Monkees laughed loudly. I went on about how the girls must have just dropped each breast into a bowl of soup for dinner and allowed them to soak it all up. I coined a new phrase for such breasts that didn't fit their owner's bodies—Bounty Breasts, named after the popular absorbent paper towels. I felt pretty good and cocky as I watched the Monkees wipe tears of laughter from their eyes. I made the Monkees laugh so hard, they cried. Pretty cool. In fact, I felt so cocky I decided to meet Bounty Breasts. I excused myself, promising the Monkees I would do my best to learn the secret behind Bounty Breasts. I walked over to the women's table.

"Hi, how are you ladies doing?"

"Fine."

"Just fine, thanks."

"Mind if I join you for a round?"

"What about your friends at the bar?"

"Well, let's see. I could sit with two very pretty twenty-year-old women or three old dudes. Hmm," I scratched my chin in deep thought as I sat down, "This is a tough one."

They laughed and we shook hands. "I'm Ian."

"Nice to meet you."

"Hi."

"No names?"

"Did you come over here because of our names?"

Ouch, this was some serious hardball.

"Yes, I often go to bars and ask women their names, then leave."

They frowned at me. Okay, this wasn't going well at all. I needed to make a smooth exit. (It's amazing that no matter how bad a situation gets, a guy thinks he can always make a "smooth" exit. Yeah, right. An exit? Yes. A smooth one? Please. Who do we think we're fooling?) I was trying to figure out how I could get out of there with my balls intact when one of Bounty Breasts stared hard at the Monkees, "Who are those guys? They look so familiar."

"The Monkees."

"Who?"

"You know, the Monkees. The musical group. They had a TV show?"

"What? They are not."

"Okay, they're not."

I was back in the game. I stood up. "Well, it was nice not meeting you, but—"

"Are those really the Monkees?"

I sat back down. "Who do you want them to be?"

"What do you mean?"

"Well, I say they're the Monkees, you say 'No.' I say they're not the Monkees, you ask if they are."

"Well, are they?"

"I had such a crush on them when I was a little girl."

I looked over my shoulder; the Monkees were looking at us. They had to know what was happening.

"Yes, they're the Monkees."

"No they're not."

Clearly these skinny girls had gone so long between meals, they were confused and delirious. I started to get up again. "Whoever you two are, you're bugging the hell out of me."

One grabbed my forearm. "No wait. Are they the Monkees? Really?"

I sighed and sat back down. "Ask the bartender."

She went over to the bartender while her friend said to me, "No way they're the Monkees. What would the Monkees be doing here? And why would they be talking to you?"

"I tell you what. I'll make you a bet. If they're the Monkees, you have to—"

Her friend returned and whispered excitedly as she sat back down, "Oh my God, they *are* the Monkees!"

Damn it! I was just about to bet the other girl that if they were the Monkees, she had to sit on my lap for the rest of the night.

"Are they really?"

"Yes!"

"What were you going to bet?"

I shook my head. "Doesn't matter."

"You know them? You know the Monkees?"

"I was sitting with them. What do you think?"

"The bartender said if we let them know we know they're the Monkees, they'll leave."

I nodded and tried to sound like I was good friends with the Monkees, "That's true; they're very modest."

"Can you introduce us?"

"Maybe...actually, no."

"Pfft, that's just rude. Why won't you introduce us?"

"Well, it's kind of hard to introduce people when you don't know their names."

I had a point. Bounty Breasts didn't say anything. They just looked up over my shoulder. I turned around. The Monkees stood behind me.

"Hey, Ian, we're calling it a night. See ya later."

"Oh, okay."

I stood up and shook their hands. "Break a leg tomorrow, guys."

"Yeah, you too."

One of them leaned past me and looked at the women. "He's a really funny comedian, this guy, he is."

They waved to the women and left.

"Oh my God, the Monkees. You know the Monkees. And you didn't introduce us."

"Just for that, we're not telling you our names."

Had I known their names, I would have introduced them. I didn't point out the folly of their reasoning. Instead, I just shrugged, "I didn't come over here for your names, remember?"

They laughed.

"Are you really a comedian?"

"Oh good Lord, we're not going to do this again, are we? I'm not even going to answer that. Go ask the bartender."

"No, are you really a comedian?"

"Ask the bartender."

She got up and headed to the bartender again. She returned. "You are a comedian."

"I am? Thanks for telling me. I better write some jokes."

She punched me in the shoulder as she sat back down. We hung out until the bar closed. It turned out they were lingerie models, in town doing a photo shoot. Perfect.

"You don't work for Frederick's of Hollywood, do you?"

They didn't. I told them my Frederick's of Hollywood story, which they thought was hilarious.

"It's not funny! I loved that girl. I blame models everywhere for what happened. How are you gonna make it up to me?"

"Why should we? We don't work for Frederick's of Hollywood."

"Hey, you're the only models I ever met, so you'll have to do. Are you gonna make it up to me?"

They smiled coyly, "Maybe."

The bar closed and we left. The women wanted to call it a night.

"Not so fast; I don't believe you two are really lingerie models."

"What?"

"We are."

"Prove it."

"Prove it? What do you mean, 'prove it'?"

"I mean prove it. You made me prove they were the Monkees and I'm a comedian. Prove you're models."

"We're not going to prove anything."

"That's what I thought; because you can't. You're not models."

They were getting really annoyed.

"We are too models!"

"How are we supposed to prove it? You just had us ask the bartender. We can't do that."

I shrugged, "Not my problem. Without proof, I'm leaving here thinking you're not models."

"What does it matter?"

"Better story. This could be the night I met two sexy lingerie models and hung out with the Monkees, or it could just be the night I hung out with the Monkees."

"You're going to be sorry, we have catalogs back in our room."

"Our" room? They were sharing the same room? This was too much; I was burning up.

"Fine, let's go."

We headed off to their room. I had counted on the fact that they had photos with them. I carried headshots with me wherever I went, so I figured models had to carry portfolios or something. We wound up back in their room, where they showed me all kinds of proof. They had headshots. They had pictures of themselves in catalogs. Most importantly, though, they each had a drawer full of free lingerie given to them at the shoot that day.

"You guys don't really wear this stuff except at the shoot, do you?"

"Of course we wear them. Why wouldn't we?"

"Even the thongs? I've had tons of waitresses tell me they ride up, so they won't wear them."

"Sweetie, all women's underwear rides up anyways, so you mise well put it there to start with. I'm wearing a thong right now."

I sat down on one of the beds. "Show me."

"I'm not going to show you."

I ran my palm over the bed. "You know, I was hoping you guys just had one bed. Kind of my little fantasy to think two models were in here, sharing a bed, having pillow fights in their free lingerie..."

We all laughed.

"So, show me your thong."

"I'm not showing you."

I wouldn't have pressed it and normally I would have figured I had no chance, but she was twirling her hair in one hand and rubbing the outside of her thigh with the other. Remember, actions speak louder than words. Plus, out of nowhere she had called me "sweetie."

"What's the big deal? I can see you in a thong right here, anyways."

I grabbed a catalog and started to flip through it. She yanked it away from me. "All right, all right; you made your point."

She unzipped her jeans, then zipped them back up. She unzipped them again, then zipped them back up. She lowered and raised the zipper a few more times.

"You know you're killing me, right?"

She laughed as she unbuttoned her jeans and turned away from me. I heard the zipper go down again. She stuck her thumbs into either side of her waistband and wiggled as she slid her jeans off. She got 'em halfway down her butt and stopped. Yup, she was wearing a thong all right; a light purple one, to be precise.

"You really are wearing a thong. That's very tasteful, by the way. A lot of women's thongs stick way up out of their pants."

She pulled her pants back up. "That's because I'm a professional and I know how to wear them."

"But of course. You know, this is wild. When every guy's twelve, we totally get turned on by these magazines."

"Really?"

"Yeah, things are just starting to happen then; we don't know what's going on. Suddenly we see one of these magazines and stuff just starts happening."

"So you guys like...beat off to this?"

"Not to this, to you. I mean not now, but when we're kids, yeah. It's all we have. We're too young to do anything with girls and we can't buy *Playboy* to see what you look like naked. So we just imagine with these pictures of you."

"How do you get the catalogs?"

"Are you kidding? They come in the mail. It's awesome. All twelve-year-old boys have a sudden interest in getting the mail. And suddenly, no more lingerie catalogs make it to their moms."

I held up some of their free lingerie. "How about a fashion show?"

"What?"

"I don't think so."

"Seriously, you guys try this stuff on, I'll tell you what looks best. You do it everyday for magazines, why not a live show? I mean, this is like a huge fantasy for me, since I was twelve."

They looked at each other. I couldn't believe it; they were actually considering it! They huddled in a corner, whispering. I remained on the bed, very much appreciating that the Monkees had played it like they knew me well when they left the bar. The girls broke huddle and walked over to the bed. "All right, but no touching. And no nudity."

"And you have to stay on the bed. If you leave the bed at all, show's over and you leave the room. Got it?"

I was so excited. I couldn't believe it; I simply couldn't believe it! I tried to nod as slowly as I could, to look calm and cool, like this happened all the time to me and was no big deal. I nodded so quickly my neck hurt and I had to rub it while the models headed into the bathroom with some lingerie. They came out looking totally hot. My first thought was *man, the Monkees are totally awesome!* Then, I focused entirely on the girls. They put on all kinds of sexy outfits and struck a variety of poses. I was dying. I took my pants off while they made a change, surprising them upon their return. I shrugged, "I figure it's only fair. Plus, things were starting to hurt with my jeans on."

They smiled and continued with the show. They were so skinny, yet sexy. Their ribs didn't show or anything like that. Frankly, I don't know how they kept from toppling over with those Bounty Breasts, they looked so top heavy. No matter how much I tried and pleaded, they wouldn't get naked. They used the same rebuttal every time and so much blood had gone directly from my brain to my penis, I couldn't think of a response that would change their minds.

"We're lingerie models, not nude models."

They said it every time I suggested they get naked. I was sorry when they grabbed the last outfits. They nearly killed me when they came out of the bathroom wearing them. One came out topless, hiding her nipples with her hands. The other turned away from me and dropped her top to the floor. She shoved one hand backwards down the back of her panties and slid one side of the waistband down with her other hand. She then reached over and slid the other side of the waistband down with the same hand. She stood there with her panties just below her ass, her one hand covering her butt crack, palm toward me. She looked over her shoulder at me, "This is because you were so good keeping your word and not getting off the bed."

"That's it. I can't stand it anymore."

I slid my underwear down and started to jerk off.

"Oh my God!"

"You guys showed me how you pose for those catalogs. Now I'm showing you what boys do with those catalogs."

They struck different poses as they watched me. They commented on my technique and said they were learning a lot about how guys like to be touched. It is a strange phenomena, but when people near orgasm, they are at their most honest. I had intended to tell the girls the truth about the Monkees. I uncontrollably blurted it out through my clenched teeth. "I just met the Monkees tonight at the bar."

They didn't seem to mind. They just smiled and responded, "That's okay; we didn't tell you our names."

"What are your names?"

They shook their heads. I uttered something about them being beautiful and thanked them profusely, then came. They went into the bathroom and returned with their clothes on. Both yawned and stretched.

"Oh, I'm so tired."

"Me, too."

I wasn't done, yet, though. They looked at me. I had wiped up and resumed business.

"Oh my God, you're still...up."

"Yeah...help me."

They shook their heads again.

"Just take off your clothes again."

They did, this time both removing their bras while facing away from me. They turned around and fondled their breasts with cupped

75

hands until I had another orgasm. I wiped up and still had an erection but they had had enough.

"It took you nearly thirty minutes that time. We have to go to bed."

They threw me out. I tried to give each a kiss before leaving but only got their cheeks. As the one closed the door behind me, she looked me square in the eyes. "If you had gotten off the bed when we were covering ourselves naked, we would've fucked you."

She shut the door and locked it. They laughed. D'oh! Of course! I remembered what the one had said: "This is because you were so good keeping your word and not getting off the bed."

That was my cue to get off the bed. How could I have missed it? My first and probably only shot at a threesome and I blew it! I was extremely pissed at myself. I had forgotten that actions speak louder than words because I was nervous about them halting the show. Stupid, stupid, stupid! All in all, not a bad night, though; I only wish I knew where I could send a thank you card to the Monkees.

I learned four things from the lingerie models:
- It's not "who you know", it's "who people think you know" that matters.
- Remember lessons learned.
- Not knowing a name can be very erotic.
- Discuss fantasies openly.

People treat an individual differently than they normally would, if they think that person knows someone they deem important. The lingerie models knew who the Monkees were. They saw me sitting and talking with them. I had a connection to the Monkees. They wanted a connection to the Monkees. By being with me, they got that connection. It isn't logical but it's human. We've all done it. I live in Chicago and have seen people fall all over themselves when they meet someone who's a production assistant for *The Oprah Winfrey Show*. They ask the person all kinds of questions, none of which can be answered due to the contract Oprah supposedly has all her employees sign, which bars them from discussing anything related to her or the show. That only seems to excite people more. It's a small connection; they want that connection. It's human.

Remember lessons learned. I could've had a threesome with two lingerie models had I remembered that actions speak louder than words. Once again...D'OH!

Fooling around with a woman without knowing her name can be extremely erotic. I've done it a few times, although I've never had sex with someone whose name I did not know. That would not work for me; I'd want to know her name. Although the night I met the lingerie models, I could have cared less. I would have slept with them without knowing their names.

Talk about fantasies; for that matter, talk about sex. It amazes me how many people sleep together but don't discuss sex or their fantasies with each other. They may discuss them with friends, but not each other. This is a huge indicator that, in all likelihood, they are dating the wrong person. How can people sleep together but not discuss sex? It's beyond me. If I can sleep with someone, I can certainly talk about sex with her. Yes, it can be awkward, but that passes quickly. Once I was out with a lady and her friends. The conversation turned to sex and one of the friends noted that she had never had sex in any position but on her back. She was nearly forty! She never had an orgasm and didn't discuss sex with any of her partners because it was too embarrassing.

"It's too awkward to discuss it with the guy."

Too awkward? What is more awkward than lying naked underneath a naked guy? If she could do that, she could certainly discuss changing position. If she changed position, she might have that elusive orgasm. Different positions provide easier access to key areas, as well as new angles from which to approach those areas.

I know a few guys with some very simple fantasies, like wanting to bang a cheerleader or schoolgirl. These desires are easy to satisfy, yet they do nothing about them. It seems that far more people bury their fantasies than act to realize them. Discussing fantasies fans the sexual flames. It turns the heat up and often leads to a sexual situation that would not have otherwise occurred. It opens the door to comfort and open discussion. A partner should reveal fantasies, as well. Fulfilling a fantasy for someone is extremely satisfying. I am pretty well adjusted when it comes to sex because I've fulfilled most of my sexual fantasies. This allows me to move on and explore new things, to reach a higher level of intimacy and not be distracted. A lot of guys I know are distracted by other types of women while they are dating someone.

"I've never been with a waitress."

"I've never had a blonde."

"I've never dated anyone with big tits."

When they were single and they met someone who could fulfill one of these fantasies, they never brought it up. It went unfulfilled, and in a way that non-action hurts their current relationship. Want a blonde but you're dating a brunette? Tell her.

"I don't want anyone but you, even though I've had this quirky desire to know what it's like to be with a blonde. I don't know why. Isn't that silly?"

She may offer to wear a wig or dye her hair. If she doesn't, suggest it. Tell her the urge is overpowering. What is her fantasy? She has one, I guarantee it. Oblige her. I picked up a gymnast very simply one night at a party. We were talking and she mentioned she used to be a gymnast.

"Really? I've always had this fantasy of sleeping with a gymnast."

Mentioning the fantasy turned a non-sexual conversation into a sexual one. Eventually, we wound up spending the night together. Had I not brought up the fantasy, it never would have happened. Another time I met a woman who went to a Catholic school and she still had her uniform. I told her how all guys had a fantasy about girls in those uniforms. We went out a few times and she wore the uniform the first time we had sex.

It is impossible to fulfill all fantasies because men simply have too many of them. Fulfill enough, though, and it seems like they are all fulfilled. Few things are more annoying than lingering fantasies, which is why I work to fulfill them. Trust me, when I do it is immensely gratifying. Till this day I can't help but smile when I see a lingerie catalog.

 **QUICKIE**

NEVER ASSUME. PEOPLE MAKE LOTS OF ASSUMPTIONS WHEN IT COMES TO dating. *She wouldn't be interested in me. He'd hate my cat. She's with that guy she's talking to.*

A few months ago I was at a party with some friends. One of them, Matt, met a woman he liked. They spoke for over an hour. When we left, I asked Matt how it went.

"Did you get her number?"

"I didn't try. She came in with a guy."

I knew the hostess of the party, who was good friends with the girl. I followed up with her the next day for Matt. It turned out the guy the girl had come to the party with was just her ride. There was absolutely nothing going on between them. My friend had assumed that they were dating simply because they came to the party together. Huge mistake. The girl was interested in Matt.

Do not assume anything. Ask. It's not hard. If my friend had asked, perhaps today he'd be dating the woman he met that night. Instead, he is hanging out with me. Pretty sucky tradeoff.

seize The moment

I DIDN'T DATE IN HIGH SCHOOL. I DIDN'T HAVE THE MONEY OF MY PEERS. I didn't have access to a car. I was working hard to get a scholarship to pay for college. I had five jobs. And in my spare time, I was always practicing trumpet, trying hard to be a professional musician. Mostly, I was completely clueless when it came to girls.

A lot of girls liked me in high school, many of whom were very pretty and friendly. I didn't realize it until years later, when reading their signatures in my yearbook as I strolled down memory lane. I was an idiot. Girls that I liked had dropped all kinds of clues in their signatures that they liked me, too.

"You are the coolest guy. I look forward to seeing you everyday."

"You are the best guy. If anyone says otherwise, I'll beat them up."

I completely missed these hints. Back then, I was voted sweetest guy in my class, which is like having girls say "most like a brother." I got it in my head that women didn't like sweet guys, when the truth is women do like sweet guys. It's just that sweet guys need to make a move at some point to find that out. They need to read the signals, know what they want, and go after it, especially in high school. (Contrary to the plots of most of today's WB and Fox television shows, there aren't many confident teenage girls relentlessly chasing chaste boys for incredible sexual encounters. These shows reflect the writers' fantasies, not reality.)

Ironically, at the senior breakfast—where they give out the class awards—the presenters ran over their allotted time. In an effort to get back on schedule, they decided to skip one of the award presentations...sweetest guy. *Sure, why not? He's the sweetest guy, he won't mind being skipped.* I decided that day never to be voted sweetest guy again (I haven't been).

My senior year I fell for a girl named Marcie in my psychology class. She had long black hair and a great smile. Her eyes were brown with long lashes and she had this very sexy way of not opening them all the way. She had a great body with big, supple breasts. It was her laugh, though, that got to me the most. Till this day I have not heard a similar laugh. I loved hearing it and made Marcie laugh every chance I got.

Marcie was a jock; she played volleyball, softball, and basketball. She dated a jerk. He was a full-of-himself wrestler who I didn't know, but even his wrestler buddies seemed not to like him. Teams tend to be closely knit, so for his teammates to dislike him meant that he must have been a pretty big ass. A few years later I found out just how big an ass. He had beaten Marcie while they dated in high school and college. She blamed the bruises and injuries on her sports' games and practices. No one was the wiser.

I went out with Marcie a few times a couple years later when we were both home from college. She was still dating the wrestler for most of that time, so nothing happened but we always had a lot of fun. When we were twenty-three and both living back at home, we ran into each other on the street and made our first real date.

I had the place to myself one weekday and Marcie and I decided to make tacos for lunch. As usual, we had a lot of fun. We went to the grocery store and joked around while we bought the ingredients. Then we went back to my place and made the tacos. We threw food at each other, laughed, all that stuff. It was a blast.

When I drove Marcie home, she told me she had just broken up with her latest boyfriend. Excellent. We made tentative plans for the weekend. I leaned in to give her a kiss on the cheek. She closed her eyes and went for my mouth. I couldn't change direction easily and we'd had such a good time, I knew we'd see each other again very soon. There'd be plenty of time for kissing then. So, I planted a soft kiss on her cheek. But I didn't see Marcie that weekend. I left her a few messages, we played a little phone tag, she got back together with that boyfriend she mentioned, and I didn't see her again...until five years later at our high school reunion.

High school reunions are fascinating events. Most alum have

moved on with their lives and changed; some have not. Marcie hadn't. She was surrounded by the same group of friends she hung out with in high school. They giggled, gossiped, went to the bathroom together, and were basically still very high schoolish. I had changed, though; a lot. Marcie and I stepped aside to talk. Almost immediately, one of her friends rushed over to us. She grabbed Marcie's arm and started to pull her away toward the restroom, gushing, "Oh my God, Marcie, you have to hear what I just heard. You'll die."

Back in high school, I would've sighed, watched the two head to the bathroom together, and waited for them to come out. They would have hurried past me, Marcie informing me that she would talk to me later, something big had just come up. Bullshit? Probably. At the most, it was a way to escape me; at the least, it was rude. But this wasn't high school. I no longer tried to figure out what was going on inside a woman's mind. I stepped between Marcie and her friend. "You know what? She'll be along in a second; we're talking here."

Her friend seemed surprised. Neither one knew how to react. Marcie's friend headed to the bathroom and I turned back to Marcie. "You know, if I had known I wasn't going to see you again after we got together the last time, I would have kissed you. I didn't because I figured you were just getting over that guy. I've always liked you."

"Oh my God, call me. You have to call me."

She gave me her number. I wasn't really interested in her anymore. She was still in high school, I had moved on. I only dated grownups. I was pleased that I saw Marcie for who she was and didn't try to make her something she wasn't—one of the lessons I had learned from Amy.

I spent the rest of the night getting my biceps squeezed by various women. I had been very skinny in high school and they were subtly trying to learn if I had bulked up. (I hadn't.) I got a kick out of them checking, though. I called Marcie twice. I never heard from her. Not surprising and actually anticipated.

I learned four things from Marcie:
- Some people never mature.
- Seize the day; tomorrow may never come.
- Closure rocks.
- Don't get pushed around or ignored.

Some people simply never mature. We've all met people who

83

behave like they're still in high school or younger. I try to stay away from such people; they offer nothing but heartache and trouble. Immature people have nothing to offer themselves, let alone anyone else.

When opportunity knocks, jump on it. I had a chance to kiss Marcie and maybe even make out. That probably would have led to more dates and maybe even a relationship. Instead, I assumed (remember, never assume) that I would have another chance to kiss Marcie. By not kissing her, I probably even jilted her a little, making her feel self-conscious and awkward, maybe even undesirable. Those feelings probably went away when I called, although Marcie may have thought I was never going to make a move and didn't want to waste any more time with me. After all, she had been out with me a few times while she had a boyfriend and I didn't make a move. When she didn't have a boyfriend and she opened herself up for some action, I passed over the opportunity. Seize the moment; there may not be another one. It may take seizing to guarantee you ever get one in the first place.

I have to speak my mind. If something bugs me, or I'm uncertain about why things turned out the way they did, I have to say something. Women call that closure. Closure is quite satisfying and keeps me well-balanced; I don't have all these annoying "what ifs" roaming around my head.

People shouldn't let themselves be pushed around. That leads to disrespect. Women won't date or sleep with guys they don't respect. Men will sleep with women they don't respect but they won't date them. People don't have to behave like asses to keep from being pushed around. They just need to make a small stance, a statement or action that says, "Hey, I'm here, I have value, and I won't be overlooked."

 **Quickie**

THINKING OF MARRIAGE SOMEWHERE DOWN THE ROAD? DISCUSS MONEY, sex, and children with that special person.

When traveling on the road, I stayed in a lot of condos with married, separated, and divorced acts. I even had one guy try to hire me to kill his wife. He was so vehement about it, I was never sure if he was kidding or serious. I never saw anything on the news about her dying, so I figured she was safe. They all gave me this same advice. Who am I to ignore it?

"Before you get married, make sure you discuss sex, children, and money. Anything else you can work around, but if you aren't both on the same page with those things, the marriage will fall apart."

Most of them had not discussed these matters. They just assumed that the other person had the same preconceptions they had, often with disastrous results.

When it comes to money, talk about how much should be saved each month, if it should be kept all together in one account, and so forth. Cover the basics.

Most husbands assume sex will remain the same in marriage, both in frequency and in actions performed. A lot of wives intend to make changes in the bedroom after marriage. If couples don't discuss sex before marriage, they may be in for a real shock.

Children are the biggest point of contention. Surprisingly, it's not the number desired or whether each couple even wants kids. Rather, it's how the kids should be raised. I think probably most couples do talk about kids' names they like, how many kids they want—whether they even want kids at all—before getting married. But they overlook discussing how the kids should be raised.

If each parent tries to raise a child differently, the child will become confused in testing boundaries. Parents will be pitted against each other. What is a reasonable bedtime? For what ages? What about allowances? Spanking, timeouts, or both? If one parent thinks their five-year-old, Nancy, should stay up until she falls asleep, while the other believes Nancy should be in bed by seven, there are going to be a lot of arguments with Nancy caught in the middle, telling one parent, "Mommy (or Daddy) said I could."

Discuss these three topics before marriage or wind up on a crummy afternoon court television show; or worse, a show where a nanny comes onboard to raise the kids and restore order. How embarrassing.

Also, save one sex act for marriage. Married people tell me they wish they had saved one sex act for their spouse, something they've never done for anyone else. When I first started to hear this advice, I had not performed much oral sex on women. I decided to save that act for my would-be wife, although if I don't meet her soon, I'll probably acquiesce. (How long can a guy wait? Worse, what if I never get married?)

Lots of married couples tell me they wish their spouse was the only person they ever slept with. I find that hard to believe. Are they just jealous that I can still play the field, so they're trying to spoil it for me? I guess I'll learn the truth when I tie the knot.

REJECTED!

I POINTED OUT EARLIER IN A QUICKIE THAT REJECTION IS AN UNAVOIDABLE part of success. I cannot emphasis enough that I have had many more failures with women than successes. Getting back in the saddle relentlessly led me to the right women at the right times. Still not convinced? Think I lead some sort of charmed life to have such stories to share? There's no secret. I pay attention, I use what I've learned, I know what I want, I go after it...and I usually fail. I pick myself up, dust off, and don't shy away the next time I find myself wanting to meet a particular woman. Still don't believe me? Don't believe I've been rejected in ways far more embarrassing than most men can stomach? Fine. Here are some of my most embarrassing rejections, offered as proof.

Last summer I was at a bar named Stanley's in the Lincoln Park area of Chicago. A few of my good friends and I were out specifically to meet women. Stanley's is an ideal place because they have good food and an eclectic crowd; some patrons are there to watch whatever games are on, others for the eats, others to mingle, and so forth. Stanley's also doesn't get mobbed; it gets crowded, but not mobbed, which we preferred.

I met a pretty woman, Darla, who was out with four of her girlfriends, as well as a few guys. Darla and I talked for a while. Things seemed to be going well, so I signaled for my friend Steve to come over and join us. Steve and I talked with all five girls while their guy friends were off hitting on other women. My friend Steve, a really good guy, has cerebral palsy. It's hard for him to be heard in a bar, let alone understood, especially by someone unaccustomed to his speech. Typically, he needs to break off a piece of a large group to form a small one in which he can participate in the conversation.

Steve successfully maneuvered two of the girls into a smaller group and the three of them got their own conversation going. The two other women went to see if their other friends had arrived, leaving just Darla and myself. We spoke for another half-hour. Again, the conversation went very well. She excused herself to use the restroom, for which I was grateful because I needed to do the same. She told me to meet her in the same spot in a few minutes. I pushed through the semi-thick crowd toward the men's room.

When I returned from the restroom, I noticed Darla's entire group had vacated the area. My friend Steve was talking to some new gal a few yards away. I waited for a while before realizing that Darla wasn't returning. I decided to look for her. I made two laps around the bar. Nothing. There was no sign of either her or her friends. I had been ditched. I went back to my friends, who were sitting at a table ("home" or "base" as men call it) to regroup.

"Where's that girl you were talking to? She was something else."

Yes, Darla was just that. At the time, I didn't realize just how much something else she was; she really must have thought that every guy she met just instantly became enamored with her. I told them what happened and withstood a light ribbing. A few minutes later Steve returned and we decided to head on to new territory. We went to the bar next door, Sedgwick's, another good place. Sedgwick's is deservingly renowned in Chicago for its quesadillas. Before we entered, I joked, "Bet that girl and her friends are in here."

We walked in. And who did we see, standing at the bar, just getting a batch of fresh drinks? Yup. Darla's friends pointed at me and laughed. She looked like she had seen a ghost. One guy said something to the rest of the group and they all booked, leaving their untouched drinks behind. A couple of them, including Darla, literally jogged to the entrance and out of the bar.

"Dude, what they hell did you say to her?"

That was just it, I hadn't said anything. We had a nice conversation with lots of laughing, she touched me a bunch of times, and I spent a lot more time listening than talking. (I've been known to talk too much from time to time. Surprising, isn't it?) The bartender stared after them, shrugged, and offered us their drinks, for which they had already paid. We found a table and drank up.

"You guys want another round?"

"No, we're not buying any more drinks tonight. We'll just keep going wherever Ian's girlfriend goes and he can keep scaring her and her friends into leaving their drinks behind."

We did hit a few more bars in the area, but we didn't run into Darla again. For a good month I endured the ridicule of my friends as they pointed out the various women they wanted me to scare away so that they could get free stuff. One afternoon we pulled up to a new Porsche being driven by a woman.

"Hey, Ian, quick, go talk to that woman; maybe she'll run away in such a hurry she'll leave her car behind with the keys in it."

This past fall I was out again with Steve, watching some college playoff football during a pub crawl. I wound up meeting a solitary woman in her mid-thirties at the bar. She seemed very interested at first, but in the end she thought it was more pleasurable to complain about her cheating boyfriend in Georgia than to listen to me. She invited me to head to the bar next door, where she was going to meet some of her friends. Steve went home while I decided to tag along with the woman. I found myself at a table of a half dozen men with an additional four or five women, all a good ten years younger than the woman who had invited me. Incidentally, she didn't stick around; she introduced me, got an important call—a bootie call—and left. I couldn't have been in a more awkward situation.

I talked with the two women closest to me for a few minutes. All of the guys decided they were going to head out to another bar. The two women I was speaking with excused themselves to go to the restroom. While they were gone, the other women in the group said goodbye to me and left. I didn't want to stay; the entire episode was very uncomfortable. Besides, although the women who went to the restroom were pretty, they were about as interesting as a strand of hair stuck to a piece of old candy, lying at the bottom of a grandmother's purse.

I didn't want to be rude, so I decided to wait at the table, alone, until they returned before leaving, in order to say a proper goodbye. I checked my watch a few times; they were taking an awfully long time in the restroom. I could see the women's room door from where I sat. I noticed other women entering and leaving while there were still no signs of the women from my table. Their jackets were still hanging from the back of their seats, so I knew they hadn't left.

After a while, I noticed the restroom door would open every now and then, just a crack, and someone would peek out at me. Then the door would close. It took me a while, but I finally realized what was going on: They were checking to see if I was still at the table! They were not coming out of that restroom until I left. One of the few things I can't stomach is being treated rudely. Who did these women think they were? Some amazing goddesses with whom men became instantly infatuated? Please. Here I was, sitting there simply to be polite, and they were being as rude as possible.

I wanted to leave but I was bored and was just going to hit another bar for a lonely drink, so I figured *why not have it here?* I decided to fuck with them. I ordered a beer and slowly drank it to the very last drop. I stood up, put on my coat like I was leaving, then suddenly decided to order another drink. I took off my coat and sat back down, catching the disappointed faces of the two idiots still hiding in the restroom. I drank the second beer slowly as well. The two girls kept peeking out the door, more and more frequently. They were extremely pissed. I finished my beer and then made a few cell phone calls. Finally, after nearly an hour, I got up and left. They remained in the bathroom the entire time.

I hit a happy hour at a popular bar named Duffy's five years ago, where I met a very pretty blonde with swollen breasts that were trying their best to bust out of her shirt. They were so taut it looked like they were being levitated. I suspected they were fake, which is usually a huge turnoff to me, but it had been a long time between women and I was very thirsty. She was in her early thirties and quite pretty.

We hung out for nearly two hours; it was very touchy-feely. She excused herself a few times to make a phone call. She didn't have a cell and neither did I at the time, so she had to keep roaming around to find one she could borrow. Guys were all too happy to let Miss Big Breasts use their cells, no questions asked. She returned from making her last call and invited me to join her and some friends downtown at a very fancy restaurant, the name of which I can no longer remember. I didn't really want to go all the way downtown, but she gave me a kiss on the cheek and I was sold.

I paid the rather pricy cab fare and we headed into the restaurant's bar area, whereupon she promptly introduced me to the first person who greeted us...her boyfriend. I was pissed; this chick was just stroking her ego at my expense. I hung out with the group for a while and chatted. The bar was separate from the dining area—one of those very fancy places where people go for dinner after going to the theater, often not arriving until after eleven.

The restaurant served food in the bar area. My hosts insisted that I eat, which I didn't want to do because it was extremely expensive and I was seething—Miss Big Breasts was groping her boyfriend a mere five feet from me. I ordered a few appetizers and some drinks; it was eight dollars just for a crappy beer. I spent a lot more than that, though; no crappy beer was going to help sooth my ego. I racked up two hundred dollars on their tab and left. I've never done anything like that before or since, but I was really perturbed. Also, I didn't have a credit card with me and was toting only forty dollars in cash. I figured, let doctor-to-be boyfriend pay for it. If he didn't have the money, the girl could return one of her breasts to get some cash.

The road can be a very lonely place. It's hard to keep in touch with home. Comedians are off during the day, but their friends are busy working. At night, their friends are off, but the comedians are working. There wasn't an Internet for emailing back when I was touring. Days would go by without speaking to friends or family. Those days can easily turn into weeks and then months. Loneliness can drive a person to do irrational things, things he wouldn't do normally.

I played a small town in Oklahoma one night, where I made out with a coed in the parking lot. She lived a few towns over and invited me to visit her when I got a chance. (In that area of Oklahoma people have to drive forty or fifty miles to find something to do, like see a comedy show.) The feature act (I was headlining) distracted the coed's friend—who wanted to start the sixty-mile drive back home as soon as possible—while I made out with the coed. She couldn't come back to my room that night because she had to drive her friend home. I was leaving for Texas in the morning, the location of the next one-nighter on the tour.

The Coed invited me to stay with her for a few days in Clinton, Oklahoma, where she lived. My immediate thought was *bad idea.*

But I had been touring small towns in Texas, Oklahoma, and Kansas for nearly two months. Most of the crowds were overweight guys; fun people, but they weren't exactly what I needed to stop the loneliness digging hard at me. I agreed and got The Coed's number. I also left her my number, which was my home phone in Chicago. She could reach my machine there any time, and I checked my messages daily. I specifically told her, "In case you change your mind, which I would understand, just give me a call and let me know, before I drive all the way out to Clinton."

The following week I had Monday and Tuesday night off. My original plan was to go camping for a few days. My Sunday gig in Texas was near a state forest where camping was free. Instead I drove 240 miles out of my way to see The Coed in Clinton. Man, I was lonely; no way would I normally do such a thing.

I called her the morning I left to make sure she was still okay with me coming. She said she couldn't wait to see me. I followed the directions to her place and rang the doorbell. No answer. I found a phone a few blocks away and called her; got her machine. I drove back to her place and waited for a while. I didn't know where to track her down and I didn't want to pay for a motel for the night, so I found a diner and ate; it was not as fulfilling as the big meal she had promised to make us. At 5 P.M. she still hadn't returned home, so I decided to see all there was to see in Clinton…at 5:05 P.M. I returned to her place, done with my tour.

I went for a walk to kill some more time. At seven I rang her bell again. She was still not home. I was worried about her. Did something happen? She had been expecting me. She wouldn't blow off someone who drove 240 miles to see her, would she? I drove to the outskirts of town, where I found a motel. I got a room and settled in for the night. I left her a message checking to see if she was okay and leaving her my number at the motel. In the morning I packed up and prepared to leave. My phone rang just before I checked out. I wish I had missed the call. It was The Coed, who was very apologetic. Her sister had had an emergency and she had to go help her, an hour's drive away. She invited me over.

"Should I check out of my room or keep it for tonight, too?"

"Oh, checkout, absolutely. You're crashing here."

Okay I checked out. We hung out for a while in her awesome

place. (People who live in big cities are about to become exceedingly jealous. Those with weak stomachs and high rents should skip the rest of this paragraph.) She had a large two-bedroom place with one-and-a-half baths. The dining room was big; the living room even bigger. The kitchen was also large, with tons of counter space. She had a dishwasher. She had a washer and dryer. The place came fully furnished.

She paid $310 a month.

That's right, $310 a month. At the time, I was paying $500 for a studio in Chicago that didn't have a washer, dryer, or dishwasher. Hell, it barely had a bathroom. The kitchen was so small, I couldn't have both a knife and fork in it at the same time; there wasn't enough room. I had to leave one of them in the main room and go back and forth to switch them as needed while I ate.

Around noon she announced she had to go to work. *Huh?* I thought she had the day off. She would be back at five. I thought it very odd that she was willing to let me, practically a stranger, hang out at her place for five hours while she went to work. Bizarre, but I wasn't about to point that out. She headed off to work while I watched television and a few movies. She called a few times to make sure everything was fine. I went out later in the day to see some of the sights she had told me about; not only had she let me stay at her place alone, but she had also given me a key. I could have copied that key and robbed her or worse. Again, bizarre.

She came home from work with a friend who announced that she would be staying overnight as well. I was a little disappointed but I thought it reasonable that The Coed would have second thoughts about being alone with me and invite a friend. Also, people probably pointed out the folly of her actions to her while she was at work.

Things unraveled from that point. She couldn't make up her mind if she wanted me to stay. She said her parents were mad I was there and were going to drive the one hundred miles from their place to hers, and make me leave. The friend was having a crisis and they needed to be alone. In between each of these sudden developments, she kissed me. Talk about getting mixed signals, she was all over the place. My brain told me to cut my losses and leave, but he wasn't in charge at that point. I shut him up and went with the two girls to rent a movie. We returned back to the apartment, where The Coed announced that I should immediately leave.

There was a problem. I had poor vision at the time. I am nearsighted in one eye, farsighted in the other. This wreaks havoc on my night vision, as my depth perception is a jumble. Objects a mile away appear to be ten feet in front of me while objects ten feet in front of me appear to be a mile away. I hadn't bothered with contacts or glasses yet. By that road tour, I was making myself do all my driving during daylight hours; it was now well into the night.

I told her my problem, which she undoubtedly did not believe, and asked if they could drive with me back to the motel. Once I saw the way at night, I could bring them back home without any trouble. They decided instead to let me follow them in her car, which I was not a fan of, for fear of losing them. We found our way back to the motel. The Coed left her friend in the car and came up to the room with me, where we made out and groped for around twenty minutes. Then she left. I extended an invitation to her to return later that night, should she change her mind. She said she'd think about it.

After they left, I suddenly became very annoyed. My free camping trip had turned into a 480-mile out-of-the-way bust. It cost me eighty dollars to stay in a crappy motel for two nights. Plus, I had paid for the movie they were going home to watch! Having lost all my senses, I drove back to her place and rang her bell. I could see them inside, watching the movie. They knew it was me and refused to answer the door. I was really pissed, but I wisely decided to just leave and not end up on an episode of *COPS*.

The next day I drove back to Texas, mulling over what had transpired. Why was I behaving so strangely? Normally, I never would have gone so far out of my way to visit a woman. I certainly would have left at the first sign of a red flag, like her NOT BEING HOME! It finally occurred to me that I had been on the road for four months straight, mostly touring the Southwest. My only company out here had been a few rattlesnakes and mosquitoes. All my accommodations had been hotel rooms; no condos, so I didn't have much time to associate with the other acts. I hadn't called my friends or family during the tour, mostly because I was driving hundreds of miles each day from show to show. I was extremely lonely. And that loneliness had pushed me to do weird things.

When I was twenty-eight, shortly after my last comedy club show as a touring comedian, I went out to dinner with a new friend named John. We headed to a nice restaurant with a good-sized bar on a Saturday night, around nine. We sat at the bar while we waited for a table. There were a number of women waiting for their own tables. Two in particular caught my eye. Before I had a chance to approach them, our table was ready.

I was pleased when the two women were seated near us, although they were a little too far away to start a conversation. I waited for a common-denominator to arise. It did. The women's dessert arrived, which they shared. John and I were still trying to figure out what we wanted for dessert. I called over to the women to find out what they were having, because it looked so good; of course, it was hard to hear them, so I had to walk over to find out what they had said. All four of us went to a bar and eventually back to my place. It was the most people I've ever had in my studio apartment—John and the two sisters from Romania, both very pretty brunettes with long hair.

By the time we got to my place, it was three in the morning. We shared a bottle of wine. Things were going very well and I decided it was time to make a move. I leaned into the older sister, who was sitting next to me on the couch—John and the younger sister sat on the floor—and attempted to kiss her. She pulled away, "Vhat ere yu doing?"

What am I doing? That was a new one.

"Ah, nothing."

I pulled away. We sat around and chatted for another hour before the sisters left. I went out with the older sister once after that, but she still didn't know what I was doing. At that point I decided neither did I, so I called it quits.

Another time John and I went to a picnic at his church, where I hit it off with a pretty 23-year-old woman. My ego got quite a boost, as almost every guy at the picnic was trying to win her interest. She chose me. When the picnic was over, a group of us headed to Guthrie's. Guthrie's is a bar that's added a neat twist to the bar scene—it is full of board games. Instead of just hanging out on another weekend night, drinking, people can drink while they play their favorite board games from when they were kids. Guthrie's has dozens of games like

Sorry, Monopoly, Yahtzee, Boggle, and *Pictionary.* It's a novel idea that's lots of fun.

At Guthrie's, the pretty 23-year-old sat next to me. She complained about being cold, so I gave her my sweatshirt to wear, which she eagerly took. Someone went to choose a game and returned with *Men are from Mars, Women are from Venus.* (The game is based on the book. The guys form one team, the women the other. They ask each other trivia and "what if" questions.) I was delighted that as someone read the rules, the girl in my sweatshirt laid her head on my shoulder. Things were going very well...then we started the game. My questions sucked. They were the worst possible questions I could have been asked.

"Have you ever had a threesome?"

"Have you ever had sex on the first date?"

"Would you offer a woman at your place tea, coffee, or yourself?"

John laughed loudly at every one of my questions and clapped his hands. He knew the answers to these questions far too well and could not control himself. He then commented on the questions, "Well, since Ian doesn't have tea or coffee back at his place, I would say 'him.'"

The other guys all got soft questions.

"How many dates before you buy a girl flowers?"

"Would you let a girl drive on a date?"

Give me a fucking break. By the end of the game, the 23-year-old was no longer resting her head on my shoulder; instead, she was sitting at the opposite end of the table, glaring at me. My balled up sweatshirt rested in my lap, where she had thrown it when she got up to change seats. Oh well, at least I won *Sorry.*

Boston is a great city, one of my favorites. I love everything about it, except for the prices and trying to find your way around. Everything is expensive and it is impossible to get directions to anywhere. No one knows how to get to a place; they just somehow magically arrive there, even to their jobs.

A typical Boston street contains 472 curves, is a little over six feet wide, is one way during certain hours of the day, then the opposite way during the other hours. Drivers can make left turns onto some streets during certain hours but not during others. Every time I'm in

Boston, I give up and just drive in the wrong direction, making illegal turns all over the maze of roads. The cops see my Illinois plates and just wave; they know it's impossible to drive in their city. Supposedly, the reason the streets in Boston are so crazy is because many of them were built over the old, windy canals the city formerly used for transportation. I impressed a Bostonian coed with this knowledge one night as I hung out in a bar after a show at Nick's Comedy Stop. We got to talking, she didn't have class the next day, we started to kiss, and we decided to head back to my hotel.

We sat in my room and talked for a few minutes before I excused myself to use the bathroom. When I came out, she was nowhere to be found. I checked the hallway and walked around, calling her name. No luck. I returned to my room, where I sat down on my bed and decided to wait for her to return. *She probably just went to get ice*, I told myself. Why didn't I see her by the ice machine, then? *My floor was probably out of ice and she had to go to another floor to get it.* I sat on the bed for nearly an hour, making up other stupid rationalizations. Finally, I decided to call it a night. I put on my zit cream and went to bed. (I never put zit cream on until I was sure I was going to be alone for the night. I didn't want to be caught with that stuff on my face—a definite mood killer—and I didn't want to waste it by having to wipe it off before it did its work, should someone suddenly show up at my door.)

The coed really threw me a curve ball. There is an immense satisfaction for a guy when a woman comes back to his place. He's done his best to prove himself worthy of her and she's chosen him. Often times it is success at last for the guy after numerous failures. This coed killed that feeling of satisfaction for me not only that night, but for the next few nights I was fortunate enough to have a woman come home with me. I kept being afraid to leave them alone for fear they might book, too.

I understood that she possibly realized what was about to happen and decided she couldn't go through with it. I'd had that happen before; but, it was the fact that she didn't say goodbye that hurt me. I was completely blindsided and left feeling very insignificant. My ego rebounded quickly, though; the next night I met the Monkees in Syracuse and was the lone guest at a lingerie show.

I learned six things from this collage of rejections:

- Some people need to get over themselves.
- Some people need to stroke their egos, no matter what the cost to others.
- Never play revealing games with good friends present when trying to meet a woman.
- Some people are simply rude and thoughtless.
- Chain women to the hotel bed before going to the bathroom.
- Family and friends are strong deterrents of loneliness.

Darla—who ran from bar to bar to avoid me—along with the two women who hid in the restroom to avoid me, need to get over themselves. They were literally enthralled with themselves and thought they were the bombs. A simple "Nice meeting you" or "Have a good night" would have gotten their points across and I would have replied in kind. Instead, they just thought they were too special to have to take the time to be polite and practice some simple common courtesies. They were rude and not worth anyone's time.

Miss Big Breasts, the woman with the nice but fake tits, could care less about anyone but herself. Her ego needed a boost and in her relentless pursuit to give it one, she gave no thought to my ego as she purposefully walked all over it.

Don't play revealing games with good friends present when trying to meet women; they know far too much, which they're usually delighted to share with the group.

Of course, I'm just kidding about using chains to keep women from leaving. Rope is far more practical and lighter to transport. Also, it doesn't set off the metal detectors at airports. In all honesty, after some further thought, I could see why the Bostonian left my room without so much as a hint. If she had changed her mind about being there, she may have felt uneasy, not knowing how I'd react to that change. She may have left to avoid a possible altercation, which I could certainly understand. There are a lot of safety issues to consider these days.

Family and friends are strong deterrents of loneliness. Communicating with them regularly and honestly is important to a healthy mind. They offer comfort, support, and familiarity.

I've had many more failures than these, but these seven are the most memorable ones. Get out and fail; each failure is one step closer to success and makes that success all the more satisfying.

 **QUICKIE**

"EVERY WOMAN FUCKS."

This is by far the best advice I've ever been given about women. It opened my eyes in a kind of "Dah!" fashion. It may sound crass, but it's true.

The advice came from comedian Rod Paulette. We worked together in Dayton, Ohio, for a week at a club called Wiley's. He made the profound statement when we were back at the condo after a show, in response to me whining about some girl who I couldn't figure out. I was nineteen at the time.

"Every woman fucks. You just have to figure out what it is that gets her to do it and then decide if you want to do that."

Rod was talking about more than sex. He was getting me to ask myself if I really liked this girl enough to agonize over her. Did I want to date her badly enough to spend time devising how to do it?

Every woman fucks. It really is that simple. Most of the time, though, I don't want to jump through all the hoops or maneuver around all the barriers a woman has set up, to date or fuck. I just don't care enough. When I do care enough, I know I really am interested... or very horny. It's always one or the other.

If a man likes a woman, he should ask himself if he's willing to go through the process she requires to date or sleep with her. The same advice applies to women, with only a slight modification.

"Every man fucks; you just to have to name the time and place."

Women can Fight

THE ADVICE IN THE LAST TWO QUICKIES DIDN'T COME FROM ME; IT CAME from other comedians. That is one of the great things about being a standup, especially when you start at the young age of eighteen. The other acts are willing to offer all kinds of advice and have been on the circuit longer. It's like having big brothers or uncles around all the time who will talk about stuff uncles usually don't talk about. I don't have a brother, so I really enjoyed the camaraderie and am very grateful for it.

Comedians also have great stories. My favorites were the ones about acts that no longer worked the road. Comedians who I would probably never get to meet, like Robin Williams, and Tim Allen. These guys were before my time, but not before the time of a lot of comedians with whom I worked. Many of them knew acts like Jerry Seinfeld or Roseanne Barr before they became famous.

Comedian Rocky LaPorte told me my all-time favorite story about a famous act. Rocky is not only one of the best comedians ever, he is one of the best guys on the circuit, and I'm not just writing that because he gave me permission to tell this story. He is very easy to get along with, offers all kinds of advice, and is friendly. He truly wants to see each and every comedian reach ultimate success. That's just not the case with a lot of other comedians. I worked with Rocky in South Bend, Indiana, at the Funny Bone. It was January and there was a big blizzard. The show was cancelled for the night and we were snowed in, so we swapped some stories, mostly about the other Funny Bone locations we had worked.

Rocky worked the Funny Bone in Columbus, Ohio, with Brett Butler, back when he was a feature himself (I was the feature the week he and I worked together). Most Funny Bones are located in outdoor malls, and the one in Columbus was no exception. Also in the mall, near the Bone, was a movie theater, as well as a few bars. The centerpiece of the mall was an elaborate fountain, which both the Bone and the theater faced.

One night after the crowd had cleared out from the show, Rocky wandered out of the club. A boy about 11-years-old, stood outside the theater with his friend. He was dialing the payphone next to the theater when some huge drunk guy walked up to him and tried to grab the phone. The boy managed to make his call. Rocky didn't pay much attention until a few minutes later, when the boy walked up to him. "Hey mister, we're waiting for my mom to come pick us up and this guy is bugging us. We can't walk away because we have to stay where my mom is meeting us."

"Okay, well, go wait for your mom and I'll stay out here and watch. If he causes any trouble, I'll come over."

The boy headed back to the spot where he was supposed to meet his mother while Rocky sized up the drunk guy. Now, Rocky is not a small man. He has some size and he's tough. He was not only a trucker before he was a comedian, he was a trucker who got shot twice. Most people get shot once, they quit trucking. It took two shots to make Rocky quit. That's tough.

Rocky really hoped this guy wasn't going to do anything. The guy was huge and he preferred not to face him; he knew he didn't stand a chance. That had to have been a really big, tough guy for Rocky to be wary of him. But Rocky wasn't too concerned, figuring the kid had to be exaggerating. After all, what big bruiser would pick on a couple kids?

All of the sudden the guy grabbed the kid and hauled him over to the fountain. He shoved the kid into the water and held him under by putting his knee on his chest. Rocky rubbed his eyes and looked again from his initial disbelief. He ran over and grabbed the guy from behind. He pulled him off the kid and shoved his face into the water. "Let's see how you like it."

That lasted all of two seconds. The big guy released the kid and took hold of Rocky. They struggled for a moment before the guy began to easily manhandle Rocky.

"I thought I was a goner," Rocky recalled. "This guy carried me around on his back like he was giving a five-year-old a piggyback ride. I was using all my strength to avoid being pulled off his back by him. I hung in there; I wasn't about to let him hurt some kid."

Then Rocky heard this horrible shriek, like a banshee's wail. Much to his surprise, Brett Butler had joined the fight. She kept punching the guy in the jaw and tearing at his face with her nails until Rocky was able to get off his back. Once he was down, the two of them repeatedly punched and kicked the guy, until he finally fell to the ground. They managed to hold him down until the cops arrived. Not an ideal threesome but a threesome just the same. They later found out that the guy wasn't drunk; he was jacked up on PCP.

"Man, that chick can fight!"

Of course. Brett was the headliner. The headliner always takes care of things.

I learned one thing from this story:

• Do not fuck with Brett Butler.

I have never seen a woman fight, outside a girlish brawl. I certainly have never seen one take on a guy, let alone a huge one. It's totally naïve, but it never even occurred to me that one would try it. I've seen plenty of women pick fights for their boyfriends, usually by antagonizing another guy's girl. When the two guys came to blows, the two girls just stepped aside and watched. So women can fight. I had a new found respect for the "weaker" sex.

By the way, the first thing Rocky did when he and Brett got back to the condo was to put the toilet seat down.

 **QUICKIE**

Flirting is key to successful dating and picking up women. Some guys are naturals, some aren't. How can a guy who's not good at flirting get good?

I used to suck at flirting. Now, I like to spend almost the entire first date flirting. I find it leads to more second dates. In fact, the best two relationships I've had started with excessive flirting.

How did I get good? I watched other guys flirt. I said things that popped into my head that I thought were too risqué to say. I pushed the envelope. These are the ways to get good at flirting.

Guys can practice flirting with other guys. What?! Relax, pay attention. When I'm out with other guys, we rip on each other all the time; it's how guys bond. This ripping is not all that different from flirting. Consider a tennis match I recently played against a friend. He hit a ball into the net softly several times in a row. I ribbed him, "Hey, if you're gonna play like that, at least trade those shorts in for a skirt."

After he had a few miss hits—gifts to me on points he otherwise would have won—I ribbed him again, "Slut; I'll drop you off later on your corner."

One day I was playing hockey when the opposing team scored a soft goal through our goalie's legs. Our best defenseman turned to the goalie and said, "Close your legs, you whore."

This is not that different from the day I approached a woman who played on four different volleyball teams and asked, "You're just a volleyball slut, aren't you?"

Practice with the guys then tweak it a little for the ladies. Good flirting will be the result.

Damn Blizzard

MY LAST NEW YEAR'S EVE GIG WAS IN SIOUX FALLS, SOUTH DAKOTA. I loved playing South Dakota and became a big draw there, even selling out all the standing room at my shows. South Dakotans make some of the best crowds and are very grateful to entertainers for traveling, typically, a long way to perform for them. I was special to them because I wrote a lot of material about South Dakota, which I could only perform there. They loved that and showed their appreciation by coming out in droves.

The gig was in a nice hotel where the comedians also stayed. There were three stages, each in a different room, and we all performed on each stage for two different shows. The idea was very simple and like a marathon for the comics. Four comedians were on the bill, each expected to perform twenty to thirty minutes of material depending upon their spot in the show. The later an act went on in the show, the more time he did. The times of the shows on each stage were staggered. The first comic went on the first stage then headed to the second stage to perform again. When he finished there, he headed for the third stage, just as the second act walked in to perform on the second stage after completing his set on the first stage. After all four comedians hit all three stages, the three rooms were cleared and the second show seated. The acts then repeated the marathon. It sounds hairy but it was actually a lot of fun, although I wouldn't want to do it every night. It also paid great.

At the end of the first show, I set up shop in the lobby to sell t-shirts I had made up, and my glow'n-the-dark condoms. A beautiful young woman approached me. She was twenty and all dolled up, wearing a short skirt with black stockings and high heels. She was probably 5'5" but looked a few inches taller in the heels. She wore a lot of makeup, typically a turnoff for me, but she wore it very tastefully and I liked it. Her hair was long and dark brown.

"Can I have one for free?"

"Why should I give you one for free?"

"I never have to buy anything."

"Oh yeah? Why is that?"

"I don't know. Guys just always buy me stuff. Guys I don't even know."

"Well, there's a lot of guys here you don't know; I'm sure one of them will buy you a shirt."

She pouted, "You're mean."

Her friends and fiancé joined her. They all bought shirts and I signed them. That wasn't enough for her. She pulled the top of her low-cut shirt down with both hands, revealing the tops of very full and ripe breasts.

"Sign here, too."

Who was I to argue? Her fiancé was obviously annoyed but I didn't care. Anyone stupid enough to date this girl got exactly what he deserved. I wrote *More than a mouthful* and signed my name. She read it and laughed.

"Come out with us, we have VIP tickets to the hottest club in town."

"I can't, I have a second show. Not that I want to miss out on going to the hottest club in Sioux Falls."

She handed her fiancé her camera and turned around. *Oh my God*; she had a great ass. Guys favor either breasts or butts; I'm a butt man.

"Take our picture, honey."

She planted her bountiful, firm butt smack into my lap.

"You like that, don't you?"

She wiggled her butt while her fiancé took some snapshots.

"How about that? Like that?"

What kind of moron would put up with this? Her fiancé was a total pushover. She got off me. I dropped a few shirts onto my lap to cover my erection.

"Come out when your show is over."

"I won't know where you are."

"What's your room number?"

I told her.

"All right, I'm bored, let's go. Remember, my name is Tracy. Don't forget."

She walked toward the exit, her entourage following. I figured I wouldn't hear from her. I did the second show and crashed for the night. At two in the morning my phone rang. It was Tracy.

"My fiancé's passed out. I want to come over and fuck you."

I wanted her bad. I would've ridden her from behind while holding onto her breasts all night. God, I wanted to see that ass bare and have it relentlessly smack against my stomach. Ah, but this was just another cruel joke from God, sent purely to torture me. A huge blizzard was heading toward Sioux Falls. I had to leave in a few hours if I wanted to miss it. I knew if Tracy came over it would go much longer than a few hours. I would not be able to go once and leave; I would want to go over and over. I would want to get nice and sweaty with her, then jump into the shower together and have her blow me. I couldn't do that and get enough sleep for the long drive home.

How cruel of God to use the elements to stop me. South Dakota does not plow the roads. Instead, they close them, even the Interstates…both of them. If I slept with Tracy, I would be trapped in South Dakota for three or four days. After taking it to town with another guy's fianceé, it is best to immediately get as far away as possible, not sit trapped in a hotel room. Tracy pleaded with me on the phone but I resisted.

"All right, but it would have been un-be-liev-able. I mean un-be-liev-able, like you could never even imagine."

I hung up and shook my fist at God. I left for Chicago a few hours later and was very glad I did. I literally raced the storm. I could see it in my rearview mirror, maybe only half an hour behind me most of the way. A few cars raced out of it and caught up to me. They were shrouded in snow. An hour after I arrived back in Chicago, it began to snow. We got twenty inches. I listened to the news; South Dakota was shutdown for days.

I kept in touch with Tracy. Shockingly, her fiancé dumped her a few weeks later. (I couldn't imagine why.) We kept in touch for several months and she decided to visit. She wanted me to show her all around Chicago, every sight and hot nightclub. I had no idea what the hot clubs were in Chicago or where to take her. She wanted to go out with a group and have fun.

When the day of her arrival came close, Tracy called to fill me in on her plans. She was going to stay with an ex-boyfriend in a far north suburb of Chicago. She and he would come into the city one night. She was only going to be in town for three days. I made preparations. I planned to bang this chick all night, in every position and on every piece of furniture, from kitchen table to...well, the only other furniture I had was a bed and couch. All of our conversations had centered on sex and we badly wanted each other. I went out and bought whipped cream and lotion, two items I never buy. My preparations consisted of making those two purchases and vacuuming.

I invited several friends to join us, one of whom was a girl I had been previously greatly interested in. Her name was Laura and she was very cute, with hair that hung halfway down to her shoulders, big brown eyes, and a nice butt. We had fooled around a few times but she refused to allow anything else to happen, let alone get serious. I would have dated her had there been the opportunity.

We decided it was best to meet at a popular bar with a dance floor, as opposed to a dance club. Laura, Steve, and a few other people showed up first. Laura wore a small amount of makeup and jean overalls. A little later Tracy and her ex walked in. We immediately nicknamed them Ken and Barbie. Tracy was decked out to kill. She wore a white top and a short, white skirt with white heels. She didn't wear pantyhose or stockings and the skirt just barely covered her butt. Her ex was tall and well-built. He had dark hair and made Brad Pitt look like a dog.

I made introductions. We hung out for a while and drank, then decided to head upstairs. A few of my friends were very anxious to walk upstairs behind Tracy, as they would get a great show, considering the skirt she was wearing. They could barely contain their excitement and were drooling. When we reached the stairs, Tracy turned to me, "Walk behind me, please; I'm wearing a really small thong and I don't want anyone to see it."

I obliged, much to the disappointment of my friends. Upstairs we shot pool, where she asked me again to stand behind her as she took her shots; otherwise, she would've shown her red thong off to the entire club every few minutes. She pulled me up tight against her every time she shot. And every time, her practically bare ass popped out from under her skirt and her red thong pressed against my rising erection. No one could see any of this except for me. There wasn't a guy in the place that didn't want Tracy. As for Laura, hardly anyone noticed her; but, she noticed me.

After I danced a few times with Tracy, rubbing up against each other wantonly, Laura cut in. As we danced, Laura started to kiss me. Next thing I knew, my hands were fondling her ass underneath her overalls while we made out. I slipped my hands between her panties and thighs. It took every ounce of self control I had not to take things further as we danced. We went back to the table and sat down, where Tracy was sitting in her ex's lap. Laura sat in my lap. Tracy looked at me questionably. I shrugged. I had no idea why Laura was behaving this way but I liked it. I hadn't realized my feelings for her were so strong and I was looking forward to taking her home with me.

Ken and Barbie left for his place as Laura and I headed for mine. On the walk back to my place, we stopped several times to make out and grope. We could barely control ourselves. Upon reaching my apartment, Laura suddenly clammed up. She didn't want anything to do with me. She crashed on the sofa and wouldn't even let me give her a goodnight kiss. In the morning we walked back to her car, still parked at the club, holding hands. I kissed her goodbye and told her I would call. I phoned her several times over the next two weeks but didn't hear back from her. As for Tracy, we kept in touch for a few more months. I explained to her that I had liked Laura for a while. She was completely understanding.

"I'm glad I could help. You know, what would've happened with us would have been great, but it wouldn't have been what you could have with her. That's more than just chemistry; that's real."

She was right. Unfortunately, I didn't hear from Laura for nearly a month. I was very distraught about the whole thing; it took me weeks to get over it. I had known Laura for years and she made it appear as though we were going to start dating, not only with her actions but also her words. Laura had played me like a fiddle. She wasn't interested in me; she was only interested in Tracy not having me. How could she do that? We were supposed to be good friends. I never got to date or sleep with Laura. I never got to have incredible sex with

Tracy. (After a few months, Tracy and I stopped calling each other. Laura and I still keep in touch.) Oh, what a cruel, cruel God!

I learned six things from Tracy and Laura:

- Women are not the emotionally caring creatures they are made out to be.
- Women are catty and jealous.
- Sluttiness is a frame of mind, not an appearance.
- Honesty to one's self is an important trait to look for in a woman.
- Once a ship has sailed, let it sail if a new ship is in port.
- Sex doesn't stand a chance against love.

Laura could have cared less about my feelings that night. She was extremely selfish for no purpose. She didn't want to sleep with me or date, so what did she care what happened between Tracy and me? She didn't. Laura's only interest was to show up the decked-out girl she deemed to be a slut. Laura was jealous of all the attention Tracy was getting from guys and simply wanted to outdo her. She made that night a competition between her and Tracy, not caring if she badly hurt a friend during the contest. Her only resolve was to win at all costs.

Many people would call Tracy a slut. Many would call Laura a nice girl. Why? Because of how they dress and the attention they get? That is one of society's biggest crocks.

Tracy is not a slut. She is honest about what she wants and goes after it. She dresses the way she feels and goes after the attention she craves. She openly talks about sex and is direct. She doesn't hide anything from anybody; she openly made passes at me in front of her fiancé. She takes responsibility for her actions. True, I would not want to date Tracy, but I respect her. Tracy is honest to herself about who she is and that is a highly desirable trait in a woman. A guy knows what he is getting with a woman like Tracy.

Although Laura is not a slut, she behaved like one that night. She allowed a guy, me, to grope and kiss her when she had no such desires herself. She even had the gall to blame that night on me.

"I learned I have to be careful with you. You can't handle it."

Handle what? Dishonesty? Games? Being played? I knew not to put my heart on my sleeve with Tracy; I got no such indication from Laura.

Laura had her chance with me long before Tracy came along and she didn't take it. There was no reason for her to suddenly like me and I should have seen that. I should have stuck with Tracy, even though I cared a lot more for Laura. I didn't love her but I had feelings along those lines, as opposed to just sexual ones for Tracy, albeit very strong sexual ones. Sex is no match for love.

Every now and then I still get bummed thinking how I blew it with Tracy. Which reminds me, I really should throw out that can of unused whipped cream that's still in my fridge.

Quickie

IF GOD WERE A MAN NOTHING WOULD EVER CHANGE. THERE WOULD BE ONLY one season—summer—and no one would ever die. Think about it. When are men most comfortable? Wearing a twenty-year-old-ripped fraternity sweatshirt while sitting in a ragged recliner they bought back in college. Women are the ones always changing things. They get bored.

"We need new furniture, ours is so out of date."

"We need to make new friends, ours are passé."

Death and seasons are God's way of redecorating and coping with boredom. That's why I always crack a smile when I read the headlines on women's magazines by the checkout counter.

Changes Every Woman Needs to Make to Keep Her Man

How to Change So He'll Stay

How to Change Him

These articles exist merely to push the products advertised in the magazines. Buy a new perfume, get some new lingerie, blah, blah, blah. It's really sell, sell, sell.

What does a woman really need to do to keep her man? Nothing. If he's chosen her, she's in for good. Women lose more men because they change themselves or try to change their men. Most male conversations about ending a six-month or longer relationship begin with "She changed." Oftentimes this really means that she kept trying to change the guy—something she didn't try to do when they first started to date—so the guy sees it as "She's changed."

Don't believe me? Peruse the headlines in men's magazines.

Is She Trying to Change You?

How to Keep Your Relationship the Same Forever

Has She Changed? How to Dump Her and Date Her Hot Best Friend

Relationships slowly change people without help. Don't force it, ladies. Be the old sweatshirt, the old chair. We like the old perfume just fine. Yes, new lingerie is nice but that old nudity standby? Much better.

swoon

I PLAY A LOT OF SPORTS. THERE ARE A FEW PRIVATELY-OWNED SPORT LEAGUES for adults in Chicago. They find different venues to host seven-week seasons followed by two weeks of playoffs for all kinds of sports, including basketball, floor hockey, softball, tennis, even kickball.

Chicago Sport and Social Club is one such league. The organization is geared more toward the social aspects of sports, and focuses much of its time on organizing events such as ski trips and European group vacations. Players is another league. They tend to have the highest level of competition but don't offer refs for all their sports, which can result in heated arguments during games. Another good league is Sports Monster, which runs leagues in various cities throughout the U.S. Sports Monster provides refs for all their sports and thus tends to attract better athletes, allowing for better competition. I've met a lot of women with similar interests in their leagues, some of which I've dated.

Volleyball is one of the most popular sports, especially for women. It is non-contact, the ball doesn't hurt, and it offers many different skill levels. In the summertime Chicago's beaches are overrun with volleyball leagues on weeknights. Although I prefer to play competitive volleyball, for years I formed one social team every summer. I had both male and female friends who wanted to meet someone and get out socially. So I put a team of players together who I thought would hit it off, either with each other or with players on other teams.

A lot of the women I recruited were very pretty but of no interest to me. I knew other guys would like them. I never set anyone up—I'm not a chick for crying out loud. I just put people on the same team and if something happened, so be it. A few years ago I stopped putting the social team together because the women were always a hassle. They weren't serious about volleyball and it showed. They tended to be either stupid or inconsiderate, I'm not sure which, perhaps a combination of the two. They meant well and were nice people, but they just weren't used to having to think about others, so having them on the team just wasn't working.

The problem was, these women were so pretty they were used to getting their every whim. Guys put up with their behavior because they hoped to sleep with them. Women put up with it because these girls always attracted guys to the group. The last season I formed a social team was the one that broke the camel's back. One of the girls called me a few hours before a game one cloudy night, "Hi Ian. I'm not going to make it to volleyball tonight."

"Oh, okay. Thanks for calling. Is everything okay, I hope? Are you sick or something?"

"Oh, I'm fine. It's just that it's dreary outside and I don't like to go out when it's dreary. It makes me feel dreary and I don't like feeling dreary."

Was she fuckin' kidding me? The team's counting on her to show and she thought this was a legitimate reason to miss?

"Okay...well, thanks for letting me know. I'll get a sub."

"Oh, don't get a sub. It might clear up and get sunny; then I'll come."

How stupid of me.

"Look, if you want to miss that's fine, but I have to fill the slot or we'll be short. I can't wait to see if you might show."

There was no response. She was probably in shock. She did things like this all the time and no one ever questioned her. Who did I think I was? How dare I expect some common courtesy!

"Okay, well, don't get a sub then. I'll be there."

Bullshit. She just said that in case it cleared up. I got a sub, counting on the fact that Flaky Girl wouldn't show. (She didn't.) One of the other women missed the following week's match. When a player missed without letting me know, I automatically feared something tragic had happened. I left her a message to call me and let me know if she was okay. She did not return my call. The next week she showed up for the game. "How'd we do last week, Ian?"

"Actually, we didn't have enough people to play and had to forfeit. We just hit around with the other team."

"Oh, bummer."

"Were you sick or something? You didn't return my call."

"No, I wasn't sick. I was on my way here when I walked by another team and they asked me if I could play. So I played with them."

I didn't know what to say. I should have buried her in the sand and left her there. One of the other guys on my team overheard and interjected, "Oh, that's okay; that was nice of you to sub for them."

I came down on both of them, "No...no it wasn't. You're on a team who's counting on you to show up and play. If you can't make it, that's fine, but let me know ahead of time."

The other guy defended her. Typical. These women walk over a lot of men because of some very nicely packaged T&A. Men swoon in their presence. See why I had no interest in them? Imagine what a nightmare it would be to date one of them. I didn't swoon over such women. I met tons of them after comedy shows and quickly learned that most of them had little to offer. In the end, putting up with their crap just wasn't worth the payoff. Such women can wreak havoc on a guy and set off a domino effect that can screw a lot of people. I know. My older sister, Mary, is one of these women and I've experienced firsthand what can happen when she digs her claws into an unsuspecting guy.

Mary is one of the sweetest people on the planet. She has a very good heart and is always willing to believe the best about people. Unfortunately, she isn't honest with herself about who she is and has low self-esteem, making her horrible dating material. At the same time, according to other guys (I'm her brother so I don't see it), she is very pretty. I've seen this deadly combination damage lives repeatedly. I could recount countless stories such as the following.

In her late twenties Mary got a whim to become a truck driver. She wanted to drive eighteen wheelers cross-country. While the vocation was surprising, the call of the open road wasn't. My father had the traveling bug; until he married my mother, he had not stayed in the same place or kept a job for more than a year. I enjoyed the traveling aspect of comedy; getting paid to see all of the U.S. and Canada was a great perk of the business. My mom traveled across Europe in her early twenties.

Mary's arrival at a trucking school in Iowa created instant chaos. The other women truckers tended to be big and enjoyed hobbies such as arm wrestling. Mary was 5'6", slender and blonde, whose primary hobby at the time was belly dancing. She brought her belly dancing outfit with her and practiced outside. The men fell over themselves wooing Mary. The other women were jealous of the attention she received. Fights and arguments broke out everywhere. The instructors were accused of giving Mary better grades than she deserved because of her looks. One instructor took it upon himself to provide Mary with previous Iowa State trucking exams, which she studied to prepare for the licensing exam. It was against Iowa law for instructors to show previous exams to students.

The day my sister took the state exam she brought her study guides with her because she didn't know about the law. The tester confiscated them and reported the school. Their training program was temporarily suspended and they had to send their students home. The funny thing is my sister still got her license that day; even the tester was affected by her beauty.

None of these things were my sister's fault and she could hardly be held accountable. She did, however, notice that she was getting special treatment and she knew why. She could have stopped it by making it clear that she was not interested in anyone at the school, that she was there only to become a trucker. She liked the attention, though, so she let things continue. She led some of the guys on by being ambiguous in regard to her feelings about them.

Mary's first trucking job was in Texas. She was hired as an assistant to a more experienced driver to haul cattle to various parts of the state. She lasted a month before she returned to my mom's in Chicago. While she was in Texas, she met another trucker, Gary, on the job. Gary was a nice guy, but not too attractive. He was 5'5", nearly 300 lbs, and had horrible acne scars. How do I know? He was so smitten with my sister, he talked his co-driver into traveling 300 miles out of their way to visit her in Indiana at one of my comedy shows. I liked Gary. I could see he had a good heart. I could also see that he was completely enthralled with Mary. He hadn't seen her in months and they had never had a date, but that didn't stop him from bringing her flowers and other gifts. I warned him.

"Dude, stay away from my sister. I'm telling you right now, she's my sister and I love her to death, but she's trouble for guys. She doesn't have her life together or a clue as to who she is, and that makes her no good for dating. Once she gets that stuff figured out, she'll be a catch, but until then she'll bring you nothing but trouble."

"Thanks for the warning but I know what I'm doing."

Yeah, right. Gary was a few days older than me, making him twenty-two. He had never had a woman like my sister give him the time of day. He was in way over his head. His partner, thirty-something, saw it, too, and tried to warn him as well. Gary hounded my sister for the next six months. He called her six times a day. He sent her flowers. He mailed her long letters. She showed him little interest but she did keep in touch. She knew she had a big fish on the line and that he could come in handy one day. She wasn't malicious, she just wanted to leave herself options.

My mom got fed up with my sister living at home. She didn't have a job and when I wasn't on the road, I lived at home, too. (It made little sense for me to rent my own place when I was gone an average of two months at a time.) My sister would do stupid things like steal all of my socks, which led to some terrible fights.

One night I was packing for a long trip. I couldn't find any of my socks and I had just bought several new pairs that afternoon. I confronted Mary. She denied knowing about the socks, so I searched her belongings, constantly shoving her aside as she intervened. Sure enough, I found all my new socks. I took the socks and started to leave when she jumped me. My mom came into the room to see what all the commotion was. I tossed Mary onto her bed and told my mom what was going on, while showing her the socks. Just then my sister kicked me as hard as she could in the back. My mom had it. She threw Mary out of the house. I still feel guilty about it, even though it was all Mary's fault. She's my sister, though, and I will always feel bad about that night, that's simply how things work.

Mary had nowhere to go. Before she left, she called Gary. I don't know what she said but he quit his job and moved to Chicago the next day. Mary and Gary moved into a dive motel. I visited her there a few times; it was pretty scary. The desk clerk sat behind thick bullet proof glass. I had to leave an ID with him to go up to her room. It wasn't long before Gary had two jobs to Mary's none. She had him wrapped around her finger because he could not believe his luck that they were together.

One of Gary's jobs was driving local deliveries in eighteen wheelers. One day he called home to check up on Mary. She insisted that he come home immediately. He left in such a hurry, he left his truck's trailer unlocked. He returned later to find that all of his merchandise had been stolen. The trucking company for which Gary worked lost their insurance provider. They had already lost several previous insurers due to silly accidents and mistakes. There was only one high-risk provider remaining to which they could go for insurance. The rates and deductible were high and the company was warned if they had another claim within ninety days, their policy would be terminated.

Two months after my sister moved in with Gary, we got word from Mom's family that her mother was suffering from Alzheimer's. The disease was rapidly progressing. Grandpa had died two years before and Grandma was alone, three hours away from the closest family member. Mom talked to her siblings and then to Mary. Mary agreed to move in with Grandma. She would make sure she was okay and start to prepare the house for sale. My mom and her siblings would join her in a few months, once they were able to organize their schedules. They would move Grandma into a retirement home and sell the house.

Mary prepared to leave for Canada, where my grandma lived. My mom's entire family is Canadian. She met my father in D.C. while working for the Canadian Embassy. When his company transferred him to Chicago, Mom quit the embassy and married him. It rocks because we kids are all Canadian citizens, as well as U.S. citizens. There are huge advantages to being Canadian, like the ability to move to Australia relatively easily. Also I get big discounts on hockey equipment and ice skates.

Gary was not happy Mary was moving to Canada. Who could blame him? He had dropped everything to be with her, gave her the best home he could, and adored her. Mary had no more use for him, though; living with my grandma in a house was much better than living with Gary in a sleazy motel. My sister hadn't intended to be cruel to Gary; rather, just like the girls in my volleyball league, she wasn't used to thinking about other people. She didn't have to because most of the time people put her first. Her lack of consideration made it easy for her to be dishonest with Gary. She told him she didn't want to go to Canada; that the family was forcing her.

At seven on a Monday morning Mom, Mary, and I left for the train station. Mary had spent the night at our place and would spend the day on the train. Mom's brother would pick her up in Toronto and drive the three hours to Owen Sound, Grandma's hometown, the next day. That Monday morning it was pouring rain. It was the kind of pouring where a person can't see more than ten feet in front of him. As we drove out of our parking lot and down the street, I thought I saw a truck cab following us. I lost it in the downpour, though, and figured I was imagining things. A few minutes later I heard a boom behind us and looked back. I thought I saw the same cab slamming into a tree but again lost sight of it.

"Did you hear that?"

"Just thunder."

My mom was probably right, it was just thunder. We got to the train station, where we put Mary on the train. We waited until it pulled out of the station at nine before heading back home. We wiped our hands of my sister and congratulated each other. How naïve of us. My mom dropped me back home and went to work. At ten the phone rang. It was Gary, "Someone's gonna pay for this, someone's gonna pay! Did you see what happened to my truck? This is your fucking fault!"

He hung up before I could say anything. I walked over to the police station, a mere block from where we lived, to file a complaint. It was then that I found out I had not been imagining things in the rain. Apparently, Gary had decided he was going to save my sister from her evil family. He followed my mom's black Jetta—a popular car at the time—in his truck cab. In the downpour, Gary lost us. He inadvertently mistook the next Jetta he saw for my mom's. He passed the Jetta, then cut it off. The Jetta ran into him just before he plowed into a tree. Gary was stuck in his cab, helpless to jump out and save my sister. The poor family in the Jetta had no idea what the hell was going on as Gary yelled for Mary from his cab. When the family got out of their mangled car, he realized his mistake.

Do not harm a tree in Oak Park. Trees in Oak Park are sacred because more than half of them were wiped out by Dutch elm disease in the 70s. Oak Park is very serious about its trees. The tree Gary hit was an old one valued at $500,000!

Gary was fired. The truck company he worked for lost their insurance and went out of business, displacing a dozen workers. The Jetta was totaled. Thank God no one was injured outside a few bruises and scrapes. Mom and I were grateful we were not involved in the accident and thought the entire ridiculous affair was over. Wow, we really were naïve. Twenty minutes after I got home from the police station, my mom called. She screamed through tears, "He got her off the train! He got her off the train!"

Gary had called the police in Battle Creek, Michigan. He told them he was in a terrible car accident. When the train pulled into the station, the police scoured each car looking for Mary. They told her what happened and she got off the train. Luckily Mary made the mistake of calling Mom. My car was in the shop but I implored her to let me take her car, pick up Mary, and drive my sister's sorry ass to Toronto. She was hesitant, "I don't know."

"You know Gary's heading up to get her. He's probably bugging everyone he knows right now, looking for a car."

My mom decided to lend me her car and I zipped the few hours to Battle Creek to get my sister. (Mary wasn't good with math. It didn't occur to her that she could swap her ticket to Toronto for a cheaper ticket to get back to Chicago.) I beat Gary to her. She was very surprised. "What are you doing here?"

"Get your bag, get in the car, or the rest of the family will be coming here for your funeral."

She could see I meant business. We drove most of the way to Toronto in silence, although I did assure her that Gary had not been injured and lectured her about her poor treatment of him. I also explained that she did not live in a vacuum, that there were serious consequences to her actions and lies. I drove the twelve hours straight, dropped Mary off at two in the morning, and returned home, for a total of twenty-four hours of straight driving. I was supposed to fill in for my dad at his security job the day after I left to take Mary to Canada. Instead, I was driving back to Chicago. Dad ended up working a sixteen-hour shift and was sick for the next week. My mom's boyfriend had to cut a trip short, so that he could drive my mom to and from work until I returned with her car.

The mission was accomplished. We got Mary safely to my grandma's. We also had the added bonus of not getting killed by her boyfriend en route. Yeah for us!

I learned three things from my sister the day I drove her to Toronto:

- The definition of a trixie.
- Don not fall for a trixie.
- Don't let a woman lead you on.

My sister is a trixie. A trixie is a woman who meets several criteria: The most important person in her life is herself, often unbeknownst to her. She gets caught up in the latest fashion fads. Her appearance is tremendously important. She pursues money and the good life. Her biggest goal is to have lots of money without working. She has low self-esteem. She is manipulative. Notice that trixies don't always have lots of money. Notice they don't always have the most fashionable clothes. They simply pursue these things, sometimes successfully, sometimes unsuccessfully.

Mary doesn't have lots of money, but she does have dozens of how-to books on meeting rich men and becoming a millionaire. She can't afford the latest fashions but she does have the latest magazines depicting these fashions. She is extremely absorbed with her looks. She spends hours every day doing her makeup and hair. She won't go out if she has a zit, often canceling plans. It is ridiculous.

Notice that my sister was not affected in the least by what happened the day she left for Grandma's, as is often the case with trixies. Gary was affected, the trucking company and its employees were affected, the family in the other Jetta was affected, my mom was affected, I was affected, my uncle was affected (he had to get up at two in the morning to let my sister into his house), my mom's boyfriend was affected, and my dad was affected. Fall for a trixie and this is what the cards hold. She often gets her way without lifting a finger. There are rarely consequences in her life, so she is very unfamiliar with them. She simply does not understand the correlation between action and reaction because she is often protected from the latter by other people, or they ignore her behavior because of her looks.

Trixies need to understand that they are doomed to a life of grief. If they meet the rich men of their dreams, the men often could care less about them. They are trophy wives. Their husbands almost always cheat on them and pay them little attention. When they lose their looks, they are often kicked to the curb for a younger trixie. Typically, only two types of men waste time with trixies: losers and guys looking only to get laid.

Losers don't get good-looking women—typically because of low self-esteem—so when one shows them even the smallest amount of interest, they fall all over themselves in an effort to keep that attention. Losers can end up with trixies because the trixies need them to fulfill a purpose. Such a relationship rarely lasts; once the trixie gets what she wants, it ends.

Trixies are easy to fuck, then kick to the curb. Their antics are completely undesirable, so it's easy for guys to remain emotionally detached from them. At the same time, they tend to be hot, which affects men's hormones. In other words, we want to be with their bodies, not with them. Once we've had the body, we're done with the trixie. Yup, trixies make perfect targets for men just looking to scratch an itch. Interested in a trixie? Stop being interested, forget about her. Can't do it? *Sigh.* There are two ways to hook-up with her.

Be a sap. Bug her endlessly for months. She'll need something eventually and break down. It could be something as simple as a ride. Use the opportunity to make a move for repayment.

Don't want to take months? Treat her like crap. What? That's right, like crap. Trixies are used to being treated like princesses. Treat them badly and they will feel a need to prove they are worthy of princess treatment. They'll argue and moan about the poor treatment but they'll keep coming back for more. Push the envelope further and further. Make her prove her worth. Challenge her and make it sexual.

"I've been watching guys buy you drinks all night. I don't get it; you're not that hot. I bet you're a bad kisser, too."

"I am not a bad kisser."

"Prove it."

"No! I'm not going to kiss you."

"Yeah, because you're a bad kisser."

"I am not."

"Then prove it… Okay, you're not a bad kisser, but your butt doesn't look that firm."

"My butt is firm!"

Smack her on the ass, "Okay, your ass is firm. But I bet it loses its round shape when your pants come off."

Get the idea? Push, push, then push some more. Most trixies can be landed in a night. We've all witnessed conversations like this one, been shocked when the girl lets the guy go further and further, and then watched as she leaves the bar with him only a few minutes after they met. *How did he do that? Why did she let him practically grope her in public?* She's a trixie, that's why it worked. It also helps to be very attractive, dress fashionably, or have something shiny, in order to catch a trixie's eye. Remember, looks are very important to her, she likes fashion, and she wants to land a guy with lots of money.

I used to have a friend who cracked me up every time we went out to the bars. He dressed in the latest fashion and owned a cool car. He'd push a trixie—the dialogue above is clipped from one of his actual conversations—into leaving the bar to see his car. The guy had no money, he just looked like he did. His apartment was a dump but it was of little consequence. He usually fucked the trixie in the car, then drove away when she got out. I stopped hanging out with him because he became too big a jerk, and the women I liked to meet were completely put off by him. He chased one after another away.

Where do trixies come from? All different walks of life. They can be poor, rich, from the big city, from the country, it doesn't matter. What does matter is the way they were raised. Most trixies come to believe at some point in their lives that the only thing they have of value are their looks. They are taught that these looks are so good, they deserve to be treated better than other people. They work to keep these looks pristine, which is why they become engrossed in makeup and fashion. A lot of this special attention comes from their fathers. How do trixies come to the misconception that all they have to offer are good looks? Many times it starts early in life. Ever see people fall all over a cute baby with praise?

"You are so cute."

"You are just the sweetest little thing."

"You are so pretty. Pretty like a princess."

Told that repeatedly the first couple years of her life, it's no wonder a girl becomes a trixie. Boy babies can be made into male trixies (more commonly called preppies), in the same way, but it's rarer, because boy babies typically receive more balanced praise.

"You are so cute."

"You are so strong."

"You are so fast."

"You are so smart."

Most girls who are late bloomers don't become trixies because they didn't receive such praise earlier in life. Instead, they received praise for being smart, having talent, and so forth. They know they have value beyond their looks.

My older sister was praised continually as a child for her luxurious hair and her silky skin; by teachers, friends, and family alike. She works hard to maintain these features for erroneous fear she doesn't have any worth without them. Give babies and children balanced praise to avoid making them trixies or preppies.

One final word on trixies for those who want to pick them up: Make sure the woman targeted is really a trixie. If she isn't, insulting her will not get her to drop her panties; it will, however, get her to throw one hellacious right cross.

QUICKIE

GUYS SHOULD ALWAYS PROVIDE THEIR OWN CONDOMS EARLY IN A RELATIONship and for one-night stands. Why?

I have a friend whose girlfriend was convinced he was going to break up with her. She knew he was a class act all the way and decided to take advantage of it. Four months into dating, she poked a hole in a condom and slept with him. She got pregnant and he married her. Now they are in a bad marriage with a kid. When the child turned five, she confessed her crime to him, straining the marriage even more.

Several comedians I worked with hooked up with women in small towns. These women were desperate to get out of these towns. They poked holes in their condoms and got pregnant, thinking the comedians would marry them and take them out of their small towns. All the women got was the headache of having to go to court to get child support…oh yeah, they also had to raise a child they didn't really want.

Having a child for any reason other than love between two people is sick and cruel, particularly to the child, who is completely innocent, and has done nothing to deserve such awful treatment. It is both unfair and stupid to bring children into a loveless relationship, or into one in which they won't have a father figure.

Bring the condoms, wrapped and protected. Don't let them out of sight. Don't let women open them. It's the only way to make sure the condoms aren't sabotaged. Better safe than sorry, guys. Bring the condoms or don't have the sex. Period.

Rubber Band, Please

My BODY PRODUCES MORE THAN THREE TIMES THE AMOUNT OF TESTOSTERONE as that of the average male. This has fantastic perks in bed, but it also makes it harder to get there sometimes, what with its other perks, namely pimples and a widow's peak.

Being thirty-three and still getting pimples is ridiculous. It's embarrassing buying zit cream at my age. I don't even do it anymore. Instead, I hang outside convenience stores and approach teenagers, "Hey, kids, I'll buy you a bottle of Jacks and a *Playboy* if you go inside and get me some Oxy."

I learned about my testosterone level when I went to a few hair clinics to check on my widow's peak. I was not happy with hair loss at age twenty-five. Thankfully, Propecia is working well and my peak has remained the same for years.

I visited a hair clinic in The Loop (downtown Chicago) one afternoon. I was the only scheduled appointment that day, although clients did come in to buy hair-restoring products from time to time. The girl at the clinic was hot, especially in her lab coat. I don't know what it is about uniforms on women that makes men want to take those uniforms off, but we do. I found myself extremely attracted to this woman and I couldn't figure out for the life of me why. I didn't know her. We had never spoken. She was Asian. I rarely am attracted to Asian women, which is odd since most men seem to adore them. They tend to be petite, have perfect skin, and they typically have pleasant dispositions (I think that's the problem).

My lack of attraction to Asians is not a physical thing, it's a cultural one. Culturally speaking, they tend to be quiet and somewhat submissive to their male counterparts. I like my women vocal and somewhat edgy. I like them to challenge my ideas and statements when they disagree. Over the years I've met few Asian women who did either, and that eventually resulted in a lack of physical interest on my part.

At any rate, this Asian assistant to the doctor and I were the only people in the clinic. We were sitting in a regular doctor's office—me in a chair and she on a stool with wheels—next to one of those leather black beds with the rolling tissue paper sheets. We kept eyeing each other while she went over my chart and gathered up the various antidotes to balding the doctor had prescribed on my last visit. She was in her early twenties, slender with a good body, and had a very pretty china-doll face with long, coal-colored hair. She smiled at me over and over and said "Hi" three times when I caught her looking at me. Each time she said "Hi" I replied suavely with the perfect response.

"Hi."

God, I was smooth. I watched her bag up all the products and thought about how badly I wanted to bag her. She stood up and handed me the bag. Our hands touched and I ran my fingers over the back of her hand and fingers. She smiled at me. I swallowed hard, unable to believe what I was about to say. I was going to take a huge risk; if I offended her, I would be cut off from the clinic and doomed to baldness.

"Ever want someone so badly and you don't know why? Know what I mean?"

She swallowed and nodded. I took her hand and gently led her to the leather bed. "Ever wanted to jump up on this and…you know…"

She became very serious as she nodded. She looked at me with this want in her eyes that I had never before seen. I sat on the bed and pulled her to me. I leaned in to kiss her, then pulled away and looked at her, making sure we were on the same page. She still had that look in her eyes. I kissed her. Within seconds we were completely naked. I was so glad I had learned to always carry condoms. I lay down on the bed in a half-lying, half-sitting position and she rode me. I loved the sound and tearing of the tissue paper. The whole thing took like twenty seconds. We kissed for a few seconds when the bell up front rang. She jumped up and shoved herself into her clothes, then hurried out of the room. I heard voices and a door close. She returned, "Someone just wanting to buy some stuff."

I nodded. I was ready to go again. This time she got on her hands and knees and I stood on the footrest of the bed. I was able to raise it and do her from behind. I think I doubled my time to forty seconds. The bell up front rang again.

"Ooh," she whined, "No one ever comes at this time and now suddenly everyone is here!"

She got dressed again—this time more slowly—and headed to the front office. I was out of condoms, so I got dressed, too. I waited in the lobby area, holding my bag full of cures while she finished selling some more products to a patient. He left and I asked her out.

"No, sorry; my parents would not like me to be with a…you know."

I nodded, "All right, but I have a feeling I'm gonna use this stuff up real fast."

She grinned. I returned two weeks later to find that she no longer worked there. I blew $100 on products I didn't need, to keep the doctor from getting suspicious as to why I would travel to The Loop for no apparent reason.

While their customer service was great, the hair-restoring products the Asian girl's office sold sucked. I found a new place, where I found myself attracted to an African-American. She, too, was attracted to me and we flirted constantly. I had no idea why these women at the hair clinics liked me. It probably had nothing to do with me and more to do with the fact that I had by far more hair than anyone else they saw all day. To them, I was Bon Jovi.

Her name was Aretha. She was average-figured with Bounty Breasts and a pronounced butt. She had a strong sarcasm and feistiness to her that I liked. We went out on a date to dinner and then to an elegant pool hall. We had planned to play pool for a few hours, but instead only played one game before hurrying back to her studio apartment. We sat on her sofa, me trying to figure out my move. She didn't want to wait. She lay on her back and pulled up her sweater; there was no bra underneath. Her big breasts had nice, big nipples.

"Do you like my breasts? Are they firm?"

"Yeah, they're beautiful."

"You can't tell by just looking."

She grabbed my hand and placed it on her breast. It was quite mushy. She stood up and led me over to the bed, which was against a large, front window that nearly spanned the entire wall.

"You just want to fuck me."

She took off her clothes and I followed suit. She opened an end table drawer by the bed. She took out a box of magnum condoms, and handed them to me. "Here."

I took one condom out. Now, I don't know if the stereotype is true or not, but the thing was huge. I barely started to unroll it when it just fell open on its own, it was so big. I bent down to my pants and started to pull out my own condoms.

"Uh-ah. We use mine or nothing happens. I don't trust anyone else's condoms."

Reasonable. Given my own similar attitude, I couldn't quibble with that. I put the condom on. I should have slid into a Christmas stocking, it would have been smaller.

"Jesus...do you have a rubber band?"

She looked at me with disappointment. Now, I am by no means small. Women either complain that I am too big, or beam declaring that I am just right. A lot of them whine about sore jaws when blowing me and some can't manage to give me head at all, as their mouths are too small. But I was no match for the monster that belonged in this rubber. I lay on the bed and she rode me. The damn condom was so baggy I could barely feel anything. The incident was very unsettling and I came in less than a minute. Stupidly, I thought if I didn't feel anything, maybe she couldn't either. I kept letting her ride.

"Are you done?"

I nodded, embarrassed.

"Then what the hell are you doing?"

I shrugged, "I don't know. I thought maybe you wouldn't notice."

She frowned at me. We paused for a few minutes, then I was ready to go again. I put on another garbage bag and we got back to it, this time with me on top. It lasted a little longer, but not much.

"This is crazy," I said as I got up and grabbed my own condom.

I still had an erection and put it on. Ah, a good fit; this was more like it. I got on top of her, ready to finally give her a thrill, when a huge shadow appeared outside the closed curtains of the front window. A fist pounded on the same window, followed by a voice that boomed,

"Aretha! Aretha, I know you're in there! You better answer this door, girl!"

Aretha freaked out. She jumped up and turned off the lights, "Oh my God, hide! Hide!"

"What? What's going on?"

"Aretha, I saw that light go off!"

"If he finds you here, he'll kill you."

She had to be kidding, right? She got back onto the bed and pulled me under the covers with her. We lay there for several minutes while Paul Bunyan continued to yell, "Where are you, girl? I saw you turn those lights off!"

He pounded on the window some more. Then it got quiet. Then the doorbell rang twenty times. This went on—him pounding on the window for a minute, then incessantly ringing her doorbell for a minute—for a good fifteen minutes. Aretha and I whispered under the covers.

"Who is it?"

"He's my ex-boyfriend. His wife is out of town this weekend and he wanted to get together."

"His wife? You dated a married guy?"

"You haven't dated a married woman?"

"Am I on the Lifetime Network? No, I haven't dated a married woman. Why would I?"

"Aretha, you better open this goddamn door, girl!"

"He's huge; if he finds you here, he'll kill you. He gets pissed when I go out with other guys."

Well, that made sense. Can't blame a married man for being pissed when his mistress was unfaithful.

"Did he fit into your condoms?"

"Yeah…"

"Yeah, I don't want to meet him."

Based on the condoms, his penis was roughly the size of one of my thighs. I did not want to meet the man who fit into those condoms. We lay quietly until we heard his truck start and screech away. Aretha pulled the covers off us, "You ready?"

"Yeah."

I was shaking like a leaf. Try as I might, I had no chance of getting it up again. Aretha was not happy.

"You know, this is sad."

"Thanks, Aretha, that helps a lot."

I got dressed and left. Aretha and I tried to date, but she was too hung up on me being white. She tried to turn that around on me.

"You'd never bring your chocolate girlfriend home to meet your mom. I'd just always be your thing on the side."

Huh. She complained about being a thing on the side, yet she was perfectly comfortable dating a married guy, which would make her... yeah, a thing on the side. Hello?!

I learned three things from Aretha and the other assistant:

• Sometimes just swallow hard and ask.
• Minorities can get hung up on mixed relationships.
• Size matters.

The Asian assistant gave me so many signs, I could no longer resist my own strong desire to have her. I had no lines, no smooth moves, and most likely no chance. All I could do was swallow hard and ask, hoping for the best. The best happened twice...in a combined one minute, but it still happened.

Both the girls at the hair clinics had a problem handling mixed relationships. Generally, the angle on interracial dating is that Caucasians have a problem with it, not minorities. The truth is, minorities can have problems with mixed dating, as well. That had never occurred to me.

Size matters. One can be too big, too small, too skinny, or too thick. Fortunately, there seems to be a wide range that each woman can handle. Most guys fit into that range. In cases where a guy doesn't, there are always rubber bands.

 **quickie**

GOD'S CRUELEST JOKE ON MAN IS THE VAGINA. I HAVE NO IDEA WHAT GOES on with this thing. There are all these flaps and folds and just when things start getting good, parts of it decide to play a game of hide and seek.

"Olly olly oxen, home free, home free! Come out, come out, wherever you are! I said come out, come out wherever—where the fuck are you, damn it?"

Ironically, my lack of knowledge has done my sex life good. When I'm with a woman, I take the time to probe around and find what works well for her. What does she like? What makes her sigh and quiver in delight? What makes her grimace and push me away?

There are all kinds of books full of tips about spots and places guaranteed to make a woman get so excited she will buy the guy a car, and then send all of her friends to experience him because he is so good he needs to be shared.

Bullshit. Each woman is different. Touching the guaranteed spot on one woman may make her cry out, while touching it on another may make her kick her date in the face. The best way to find out where a woman's spots are is to probe around gently. When the right spots are found, try different motions, movements, and speeds to give the most pleasure possible.

Both lovers and women friends alike have complained to me that most guys just jump in and do whatever they think works without bothering to try different things. Men, try different and new approaches. It's surprising; using different approaches often results in me finding motions and spots a woman didn't even know she liked before I came along. It's far more desirable to be remembered for that, than to be remembered as the guy who needed a rubber band to make a rubber fit.

Of course, it is important to have some basic knowledge. She doesn't want to feel like aliens are probing her body. Don't be afraid to buy an anatomy book with some diagrams. It can provide a good starting point.

ПIKKI COX-GOldthwait?

NIKKI COX IS VERY PRETTY. SHE WAS HOT IN *UNHAPPILY EVER AFTER*, A second-rate sitcom she starred in years ago, where she was the designated eye candy. The show was basically a less popular *Married...with Children*. I had a huge crush on Nikki. When I was hitting puberty, I had huge crushes on Heather Thomas and Heather Locklear. All the comedians I worked with were older and when they were kids, they had huge crushes on Marsha Brady. Sorry, not nearly as attractive as "the Heathers" and thus not nearly as frustrating.

My mom did not allow me to have any posters of models as a teen. Once my older sister bought me one and my mom shredded it while I was at school. (By the way, that's a pretty cool older sister.) I could do nothing about my crushes on the Heathers. When I liked Nikki, I was no longer a kid; I was an adult with options. By now it should be clear that I am not the kind of person to sit idly by and do nothing if I want something. What I'm willing to do depends upon the degree of wanting. If I'm walking into a bar and a woman who just knocks me out of my socks (very rare) passes me on her way out, I'll talk to her and give her my number. I've never heard from any of these women, with the exception of one, which makes this Hail Mary effort all the more worthwhile. I wanted to be a musician. I tried my best; but I couldn't hack it. I wanted to be a comedian; I tried my best and was very successful. There is something inside me that just won't let me not try. It can actually be very annoying at times.

It was annoying with Nikki. It bothered me that I couldn't talk to this girl, that I could only see her on TV. I was able to control myself, though, as what else could I do? I wasn't going to turn into some weirdo fan or stalk her. I wanted to meet Nikki but I couldn't. I settled for promising myself that I would approach her if I ever had the chance.

My friend Steve threw a party one night while I still lived back home in Oak Park. I drove into Lincoln Park for the fiesta and had quite a night. Immediately upon entering the bash, I noticed that almost all the guys were gathered around the sofa—and with good reason. Two very pretty young blondes were sitting on it, both with hair just shy of their shoulders. I went over. My first thought was *why weren't any of these guys sitting down?* There was enough room on the couch for one more person. I noticed that one of the girls seemed to be doing all of the talking, while the other one was quieter. I flirted immediately with the chattier girl. She was talking about music and how she thought she had a good voice.

"Darling, how are you? So good to see you again."

She looked at me, "What?"

"Oh my goodness, don't you remember me? We cut an album together."

I plopped down beside her, "I keep telling you if you're going to make it in this biz, you're going to have to remember people and get over your shyness."

"Oh, I was just kidding. Of course I remember you. We did that album in Miami, right?"

"Pfft, please, like I remember. I was wasted the entire time. Oh, that Bono can par-tee."

"Yes, I seem to remember doing some partying with him myself."

We both laughed pretentiously. She played right along. Her friend (actually, younger sister) joined in intermittently. We spoke about only our phony music careers for twenty minutes, with the exception of revealing how we knew Steve. She worked with him. The other guys all stood around and watched, laughing at our antics. Abruptly, the older sister checked her watch. She turned to her sister, "Darling, we really should get going."

The posse of guys stirred, each quickly trying to figure out how to get digits (the phone number). The older sister looked at them, "Nice meeting all of you," she commented as she searched her purse. Then she looked at me, "YOU can call me."

She pulled out a business card and jotted down her number. She handed it to me. We stood and I gave each girl an exaggerated kiss on each cheek, "Simply marvelous to see you both again. We must do lunch. Have your people call mine. I'm Ian, by the way."

The younger sister introduced herself. The other simply referred me, "My name's on the card."

The girls left. A couple guys tried to get me to give the one sister's number to them. Before I had a chance to reply, a woman who had been watching the events unfold came over to the sofa and sat beside me. We hung out and talked for a while, having a real conversation. We even played a very unserious game of chess. When I decided it was time to leave, she offered to walk me to my car, parked a few blocks away. Pay attention; a woman doesn't offer to walk a guy to his car at a party unless she's interested in getting at least a kiss. We walked to my car engaged in pleasant conversation. I drove her back to the party, where we parked out front and made out for a while. She went back into the party and I drove home.

The following week, I moved into my own studio apartment on the border of the Lincoln Park/Lake View neighborhoods of Chicago. These two areas are full of young professionals and businesses that hold their interests, such as bars, coffee houses, and bookstores. I had no furniture outside a bed and TV—which I've been told is not furniture, so I guess all I had was a bed. The sisters from the party invited me over to their place to watch the Bulls latest playoff game. (This was back when the Bulls were clobbering everyone in the league.) They made it clear that I was to be the only guest at their barbeque.

The sisters were quite a pair, especially the older one. She was chatty and lively, which appealed to me more than the quietness of the younger one. They had a pet hedgehog and blow-up furniture. That's right, blow-up furniture. They had a blow-up sofa, a blow-up armchair, and a blow-up ottoman. It was all quite comfortable and very inexpensive. The sisters swore by them.

After eating, watching the Bulls pummel Utah (it was the game in Chicago in which the Bulls obliterated a usually strong Jazz), and playing with Sonic the hedgehog, we were pretty tired. The girls closed their eyes and nestled up to me on the couch, one on either shoulder. I kept looking at one and then the other. I had already had a few threesomes by then and really wanted to have one with them. The opportunity and signals were there; but, they were good friends with my buddy Steve, and I just couldn't bring myself to make a move. I nestled with them as long as they let me and all three of us actually fell asleep. A few hours later I woke up, woke them up, and then left.

I kept in touch with the older sister. We planned a date but she had to cancel due to work. I hit the road for two months and both sisters moved to Miami while I was gone. Too bad. I had hoped to have another crack with the older one. A year later I told Steve about the incident.

"Ah, Ian, I hardly knew them. I just worked with one of them and they came to my party, that's it. And if I did know them well, I wouldn't have begrudged you hooking up with them."

Damn it, damn it, damn it, damn it! I could have had a fabulous sister sex sandwich. How often does a guy have a chance at that? Try never! For whatever reason, I had thought they were very close friends with Steve. I didn't want it to get back to him that I had tried to not only screw them both, but to screw them both together, whether I failed or succeeded.

I was more aggressive with the other woman I had met at Steve's party. She lived way out in the burbs and we made a date for me to drive to her place. I didn't have contacts then, either, so again my poor night vision was a concern. I told her that and made it a stipulation of our date that she let me crash at her place, so I could drive home in the morning daylight. She agreed. She was a pretty redhead with a nice figure, divorced. I don't know why, but men think that divorced women more readily have sex than other women. Is it true? I can't say for sure but I can say that every divorced woman I've gone out with has given me a lot of action on the first date.

The night of the date, I slept in bed with Steve's friend in the burbs. When things started to progress along, she walked me over to her guest room. I told her I didn't like being in bed alone in a strange place. She played along, "If you get lonely, come back to my room."

She tucked me in with a kiss and left. I counted to ten and went back to her room, where I climbed back into bed beside her.

"What are you doing back here? Lonely?"

"That and it was too cold in that other bed. We already got this one warmed up."

It got a lot warmer. The next day, on my way back home from the burbs, I passed a store advertising a sale on, of all things, blow-up furniture. I stopped in and picked myself up a wine-colored sofa and ottoman. I got home, blew 'em up, and tried 'em out; comfortable. Great, my apartment was now furnished. I checked it off my list.

Two days later I headed out West for a long tour. One of my gigs on that tour was with Bobcat Goldthwait. Bobcat and I were playing Punch Line in San Francisco on a Friday and Saturday night. I was pleased to learn I was working with Bobcat because he played the voice of the puppet used in *Unhappily Ever After*. He might know how I could reach Nikki Cox. (Like I said, the something inside that makes me try won't quit.)

I instantly liked Bobcat. He was very friendly and asked me a lot of questions about my career. He also thought I was extremely funny and naturally talented. What's not to like? He was quite personable and we talked about everyday things. I did not ask him about Nikki... yet. Bobcat's twelve-year-old daughter had come to the show with him. They got along great and she was a good kid. I kept her company in the green room while Bobcat did his set. She was very excited because she had just redecorated her bedroom. She told me all about her stuffed animal collection or something and a bunch of other things I don't quite remember. Then she said something that kicked me in the nuts.

"And, best of all, I have blow-up furniture. I have a blow-up couch and a blow-up ottoman."

I stared at her. I had the same furniture as a twelve-year-old. Suddenly, blow-up furniture didn't seem so cool.

"What color are they?"

"Maroon."

Fucking unbelievable. Bobcat finished his set and returned to the green room. We all hung out and joked about how I had the same furniture as a twelve-year-old. Suddenly, who should walk into the room? Nikki Cox. I couldn't believe it. Here she was, in-person, pretty and laid back, wearing sweats and a t-shirt. She wore her hair in a ponytail. This was my chance. I simply could not believe it. After introductions, she gave Bobcat a somewhat long kiss. Yeah, she was his girlfriend. She flew up from L.A. to visit him and his daughter for the weekend. Oh what a cruel, cruel God!

Here's your dream girl, Ian, placed right in front of you. Oh, but you can't have her. Even trying could ruin your comedy career;

Bobcat could destroy your name in the biz. A HA HA HA HA HA! A HA HA HA HA HA! That Bitch was screwing me again!

Nikki turned out to be very cool. We hung out in the green room while Bobcat performed his next set, then again during both his sets the next night. I liked her. She was friendly and charismatic, not the least bit full of herself or pretentious. I never tried to make a move, but that annoying thing inside me was quieted just the same. I did invite her to join me on my blow-up sofa for a glass of wine if ever she was in Chicago. She laughed, unimpressed. Go figure. How could a blow-up couch not impress a woman, especially one of her stature?

I learned four things from this chapter of my life:

- Flirting works much better than substance when first meeting a woman.
- Good T&A can make anything seem like a good idea.
- Don't worry about friends; they'll understand if you hook up with their friends.
- To have a greater appreciation for the women I meet everyday.

Steve's party is where I learned that flirting is the best way to break the ice with a woman and get digits. Flirting leads to one-night stands better than substance, and more first dates wind up in bed when flirting is the theme. Why? Flirting makes people laugh and feel at ease; it reduces both the man's and woman's inhibitions. The second woman at Steve's party had conversations of substance with me with hardly any flirting. Ah, yes; but she only came over after she watched me flirt with the sisters. It was the flirting that got her attention.

Good T&A can make anything seem like a good idea. I still can't believe I bought blow-up furniture! When I got home from that trip, I traded my blow-up furniture in for a futon.

Friends understand if their friends hook up. There's no reason to worry about it or to change behavior in anticipation of a friend's reaction. If a friend does get upset, he may not be a true friend.

Meeting Nikki Cox was a great experience and not at all what I expected. After speaking with her for a short time, I realized I wasn't interested in her. I didn't see Nikki as someone I could sleep with or date; rather, I saw her as someone with whom I could be good friends. When I had a question about dating, Nikki would be the friend I'd call. When I needed to get the attention of a woman I liked, Nikki would be the friend I'd ask for advice. Nikki could be someone I liked, respected, and laughed with, but not someone I'd be interested in beyond that.

Meeting Nikki wasn't beneficial because it gave me a chance to hit on her; it was beneficial because it gave me a chance to realize I didn't want to hit on her. I met my dream girl and realized she wasn't for me. I had met other women I was far more attracted to than Nikki. They were prettier to me, they were more fun, there was chemistry; there was none of that with Nikki. Having met Nikki Cox makes me appreciate all the women I know much more than I would have, had I not met her. It opened my eyes to the fact that I meet beautiful women all the time, many far prettier than popular actresses and models.

Most of the women I meet that are prettier than actresses I'm not interested in for any reason, friendship or otherwise. There is something else about a woman that draws me in, not just how she looks. It's the real essence of who she is, what she wants, how she looks, and what she offers. If those things line up well with me, I'm attracted to the woman. I am grateful to Nikki for helping me realize this and wish her and Bobcat all the happiness in their engagement. Appreciate the women out there everyday, guys. They are the real dream girls.

 **quickie**

Do not ask a woman if she has a boyfriend when meeting her. This is a huge mistake many men make. If she has one, she'll reveal it. Or, she may not want to reveal it, so why be concerned?

The reason most men ask is because they don't want to waste time talking to someone who's already taken. Asking a woman if she has a boyfriend announces interest and is a huge turnoff to the woman, regardless of her dating status. She might even lie and say she does, just to get rid of the guy.

Men who ask women if they have a boyfriend come off as trolling. The woman's guard goes up and she shuts down. Don't think it's disguised by waiting fifteen, thirty, or even sixty minutes before asking, either; it's not.

How many stories have I told in which I fooled around with women who had boyfriends or fiancés? If I asked them up front, those hookups never would have happened. A woman is not going to say, "Yeah, I have a boyfriend, but shove your hand up my shirt anyway."

A lot of women don't break up with one guy until they meet another guy. You don't get to be that other guy by asking if they're dating someone, then moving on right away when it turns out they are.

A woman friend of mine explained something to me one day.

"A lot of women feel like they need to be in a relationship, so they get into a relationship with the best guy around at the time, not necessarily the best guy for them. It would be better if they just stayed alone, but women feel all this pressure to be dating someone, so many date just to date."

If a woman offers up that she has a boyfriend, chat a little more, then tactfully end the conversation.

Unless a woman I'm interested in makes some kind of statement of loyalty about her boyfriend, like "I really like him a lot," or "My boyfriend is wonderful," I don't worry about it when she mentions him. Who knows why they're together? They could be completely wrong for each other and she may know it. Maybe that's even why she's out talking to other guys.

Do not ask about the boyfriend. Now, asking if she has a girlfriend... that's a whole other matter and completely acceptable.

Chivalry Ain't Dead

I WAS CLUELESS ABOUT GETTING LAID IN COLLEGE. (I WAS BETTER IN COLLEGE than I was in high school. I was no longer the sweetest guy and I asked out a lot more women in college than I did in high school, most of whom shot me down. I let that get to me but I shouldn't have.) I had not yet learned that a guy needed to be the aggressor and make a move. It was too bad because college was a buffet of women and men exploring their likes and dislikes when it came to dating and sex. Actually, students didn't really date in college, they hooked up. They went out with a group to a bar, drank, and went home with someone. They went out with a group to a party, drank, and went home with someone. Drinking was a big factor in hooking up. A lot of guys asked out women who turned them down, only to meet them at a party sometime down the road and fuck their brains out. I was completely out of that circle.

My problem was I was treating women like they were delicate flowers. This naïve behavior came from my mom, who taught me and my sisters that girls did not like sex. I can't blame her. A single mother raising three children hardly needs the added headache of her teenage children sleeping around, maybe making babies. I was especially naïve during my freshman and sophomore years. I went out with a cute junior with a good body three or four times my first year. Twice she brought me back to her room. We sat and talked both times, she walked me out, I got a goodnight kiss, and then I went back to my dorm. After the second time I was in her room, she stopped returning my calls. She gave up on me making a move.

There were two really cute girls I liked in my freshman English class, Dana and Jennifer (the only two real names I've used in this

149

book). I was especially interested in Dana, who had very pretty eyes. Both girls seemed to enjoy the stories I wrote for class. Jennifer invited me back to her room after class one day. We sat and talked for ten minutes, then she told me she had to get going. I headed back to my dorm, wondering why Jennifer had invited me back to her room when she had to go somewhere so soon. I had not even tried to kiss her because it didn't seem like something people did during daylight hours. (Yeah, I was that stupid.)

I wanted to ask Dana out badly but I never worked up the nerve. The semester ended and I didn't even have her number. I told myself it was no big deal, that I'd see her again around campus. Jennifer, too. I never saw Dana or Jennifer again, which bugs me even to this day.

Every dorm floor had a mysterious resident, usually a guy. He was rarely on campus and rumors spread about him, like that he was a federal agent living with students to catch them with drugs. There was no way he could be a student; he never went to class, he'd have been academically dismissed long ago. In my junior and senior years, I was that guy. I was performing comedy across the Midwest most of the time. I mailed in important papers and missed midterms. I was rarely on campus, making appearances only occasionally. Somehow, I still managed to graduate with a 3.0 GPA. I had changed a lot since my first two years of school and was more aggressive with women, but I was still treating them too nicely.

One of my dorm neighbors in my senior year was a pretty transfer student from a community college. Her name was Linda and she was a sophomore. She was short, slim and petite. She had a welcoming charm that made her quite attractive. I liked Linda, but I decided not to ask her out. Instead I would just go to a party with her one night and see what happened.

Now, it was extremely unadvisable to date or hook up with anyone who lived on the same floor. If things didn't work out—which they wouldn't—there were lots of opportunities to run into each other, which could result in heated arguments. In Linda's case it was a moot point. She was not the best student, and she made it clear that she would not be returning to school after the first semester. Given that she wouldn't be around long and that I was gone most of the time, I figured our chances of running into each other would be slim. My thinking was far from unique. Whenever a hot woman moved onto the floor, it was hoped that she would be a bad student or would be moving soon, so that we guys could hit on her.

One night I headed out with Linda, her roommate, and her roommate's boyfriend. We went to a party, where we ran into five guys who lived on the seventh floor of our dorm. The guys had seen Linda around the dorm and moved in immediately. She hadn't even had a chance to have a sip of her beer, yet. She made it clear that she was completely disinterested. The guys turned to walk away, except one, who did something very interesting. He stayed behind and asked Linda a few questions.

"Who's your English teacher?"

"Ms. Boyd."

"What day do you have class?"

"Tuesdays and Thursdays."

"What time?"

She sighed, "One to two-thirty. Why?"

"Thanks."

He walked away.

"I hate it when guys just come up to you like that. I'm not here to meet anyone; I just want to be out."

Two hours later Linda was quite drunk. Her roommate, designated to remain sober that night to look out for the girls' safety, was also drunk. I took it upon myself to look out for Linda. The guys from the seventh floor returned. The tallest one, about six inches taller than me, approached Linda, "Hey, you're in my English class."

"I am? You don't look familiar."

"Ms. Boyd's class, Tuesday and Thursday afternoon, right?"

Oh, come on, please, there was no way that was going to work.

"Yeah, I'm in that class!"

She put her arm around his shoulders and looked at me, "This guy's in my English class, Ian. He's my English buddy."

I was very annoyed. I watched as the guys talked to a now very willing Linda. They pushed me out of the conversation and tightened a circle around her. (I had not yet learned how to deal with cock-blocking.) I pounded back beer after beer in frustration. Later, three of the guys huddled together and whispered. They then rejoined the circle, one of them taking the lead, "Hey, I just heard the police are on their way."

Linda was concerned, "The police?!"

"Yeah, the police. We better get going; you don't want to get arrested, do you, Linda?"

"No, I don't! I better warn my roommate."

"Oh, don't worry; we'll make sure you get back to the dorm okay."

"That's so sweet."

She gave the tallest guy a kiss on the cheek. She found her roommate and said, "Goodbye. These guys are going to make sure I get home okay."

"All right, bye."

They hugged and Linda rejoined the grinning guys to leave. I followed. One of the guys pushed me back, "Dude, don't worry, we'll make sure she gets home okay."

"I'm sure you will; I just don't want to be arrested, either."

They didn't know I was a senior.

"We don't want you coming."

The tallest guy signaled for him to relax; he must have figured the five of them could deal with me later. We walked across campus back to the dorm. The guys spoke about the various things they planned to do to Linda and of the various positions in which they planned to do them. One of them couldn't wait and turned to her, "I bet I can guess how much you weigh just by picking you up."

"No you can't."

"Let me try."

He picked her up and squeezed her tight to his body. He slid his hands down to her ass and let her slide all the way down his body to the ground. He looked at his friends and mouthed without speaking, "Wow." The other guys weren't about to be left out of the fun. They each took a few turns copping feels in the guise of guessing her weight by picking her up. I should not have allowed this to continue but there were five of them and only one of me. We resumed our walk to the dorm as I crafted a plan.

These guys are drunk, I thought, *and drunk guys can't fight, so I got that going for me. The only problem is I'm drunk, too. I better practice.* As we walked back to the dorm, I fell slightly behind the group. I shadow-boxed the air and threw some kicks. I got more and more intense as I realized more and more that the odds were vastly against me in a fight. I became aware that I was uttering things, rather loudly, "You want some of this? I'll kick your ass…you're going down…way down…down to downtown."

The guys kept looking back at me and laughing while they pointed. This served only to further infuriate me; they were really risking the taste of my wrath. I kicked and punched harder, occasionally adding in the famous *Karate Kid* crane technique. By the time we got back to the dorm, I was drenched in sweat. We waited for the elevator, which is where the guys made their error. They should have kept me from getting on with them.

Linda and I lived on five; the guys lived on seven. There was no way I was getting off the elevator without her. Also, the guys didn't know which room was mine. Linda lived in the room closest to the elevator; my room was the very next one. My roommate was in for the night, studying, so I could call to him for help, not to mention anyone else that might be on the floor. The doors opened and I took Linda's hand, "Come on, Linda, let's go."

The guys intervened, "Hey, watch out for this guy, Linda. He's trying to take advantage of you."

"Yeah, you better come with us."

They tried to push me away. I stood my ground. "Ain't happening, guys."

Linda thought about it and got off the elevator with me. As the doors closed, she spun around and shoved her arm through them, causing them to reopen. She pointed to the tallest guy, "YOU can come with me."

He grinned and got off the elevator, leaving his very disappointed comrades behind. The doors closed and Linda took him to her room. I don't know if I was more pissed or concerned. Linda opened her door and flipped on the light. She then fell to the hall floor in a drunken stupor, giggling, "I have to pee! I have to pee!"

Some of her friends came out of their rooms to see what was going on. They dragged Linda down the hall to the restroom. The tall guy walked into her room and waited. I thought this was a good time to talk to him, so I also went into her room. I had no business doing it; Linda had invited him there and it had nothing to do with me. I walked up to him and suddenly became a member of the Mafia, talking with a thick Brooklyn accent, "Hey, you better be good. She's a nice girl and

I like her a lot. I really care about her. She's in no condition to have a guy over; she should just be going to bed. You better be good."

"Oh, I'll be good...I'll be real good."

Uh-oh...now he had done it. I imagined myself reaching up to his face and lightly smacking him twice on the cheek, being the mobster I was. The thing about being drunk is that sometimes what a person thinks and what he does become one and the same. As I imagined lightly smacking him on the cheek, I saw my hand reaching out. I smacked him twice on the cheek as I uttered his final warning, "You better be a good. Don't fuck with me. Capiche?"

He just stood there and stared at me. I waited until I was sure he understood I meant business then left. I went into my room and slammed the door behind me. I whipped my keys against one of my posters, tearing a big hole, and yelled, "Women suck!"

My roommate lay on his bed, holding his gut and laughing.

"What?"

He could barely speak, "Don't...don't fuck with me? Are you kidding me?"

"You heard that?"

"I...I...I was walking..."

"What?!"

"Dude, you know I have your back and I would have jumped in there, but that guy was big. I was walking by Linda's room and saw you in there, so I stopped to see what was going on. You smacked that guy so hard, his head fucking turned both times."

"What?"

"It like snapped quickly both times you smacked him."

I couldn't believe it. The guy wasn't huge, but he was bigger than me and had a six-inch advantage. I saw him waiting for the elevator in the hall ten minutes later. My handprint was very visible on his cheek. The next day, a very hung over Linda thanked me for getting her home safely.

"It's good to see that chivalry ain't dead."

Two days later she started to date another guy on the floor. They liked to make out with her door open, so I got to see them going at it quite frequently as I got off the elevator. Ah, what a bonus to my chivalry.

I learned five things from Linda and the coeds in my English class:
- Make a move.
- Opportunity may only knock once; be ready.
- Women aren't always honest with themselves about what they want.
- Women don't want to be accountable.
- The nice guy doesn't get the girl.

When going on dates with girls in college, I waited for a sign from them to make a move that they had already given me: They invited me back to their rooms. When a woman invites a man back to her place or accepts his invite to his, that's her move. They are not likely to do anything else. It is up to the man to take things from there. A woman's willingness to be alone with a man in his place or hers is not an indication of a desire to have sex. It is, however, often an indication of a desire to take things further. What move should a guy make to find out how much further? A good one is to try to remove some of her clothes. She'll stop the guy if he goes further than she wants.

That's what I should have done with the coeds back in their rooms; kissed for a while and then tried to remove their tops. If that worked and I wanted to go further, I should have then tried to remove their bras or pants. Once the process of removing clothes begins, an interested woman will often make her own moves, but usually not until the guy has initiated the process.

Somebody once said, "Tomorrow is another day," and it became a famous quote. Bullshit. Tomorrow is not another day. Tomorrow is today's backup plan. I should have asked out Dana and Jennifer when I was in English class with them, but I waited for tomorrow. Tomorrow never came. Why didn't I ask out Dana and Jennifer? Remember that all-important rejection I mentioned? I hadn't had enough rejection at the time and was afraid of getting some. I hadn't yet learned that rejection is part of the dating process and that I would survive unscarred if I got some.

Linda was not honest with herself about what she wanted. She said she went to the party just to be out, that she didn't want to meet a guy. Later, she invited one back to her room, after letting a group of guys grope her and press their bodies against hers. Lots of women aren't honest with themselves. I have tons of women friends who utter the most ridiculous untruths.

"I don't like guys who showboat."

That friend dates only guys who showboat.

"I hate lines."

That friend gets picked up every time we go out by the lamest lines I've ever heard. Both women deny these facts when I point them out. Why? Remember? Yeah, because women want to be right.

If women aren't honest with themselves about what they really want, how can men know what women want from what they say? Oftentimes we can't, which is why we must pay attention to their actions. If their actions match what they say, they are being honest; if there's no match, go along with the actions. Their actions speak the truth.

Women like to avoid accountability. Linda didn't want to meet guys, the alcohol made her do it. She therefore was not accountable. (She actually claimed this and most of our floor agreed with her, much to my surprise.) Women want to avoid accountability so much they've coined a now popular phrase, which allows them to avoid accountability under the guise of change: "It's a woman's prerogative to change her mind."

Desire to avoid accountability is one reason why some women will knowingly date a jerk. When things don't work out, they simply blame the jerk. Everyone knows he's a jerk, so no one holds the woman accountable.

There is a real danger with women taking this attitude toward accountability. They put themselves in harm's way. Linda could have really been hurt the night of the party, had I not been present. She was easily on her way to being date-raped or worse. Certainly, Linda's drinking did not give the seventh floor guys the right to hurt her, but, being drunk did not give her the right to hurt herself, either, which is what she almost did.

Drunk drivers used to be able to hold alcohol accountable for their accidents years ago. They went right on drinking and having more accidents, even though they chose to drink and drive. A woman drinking herself into a stupor, then going somewhere alone with strangers is extremely dangerous. This woman does not have a right to be hurt by those strangers, but she needs to realize that she is behaving very much like a drunk driver. Both have greatly reduced their odds of arriving home safely. Don't avoid accountability, ladies, by drinking until inhibitions are gone. It's unsafe and a turnoff. The only guys who want to be with a drunken woman are desperate losers who have no intentions of dating her. Accountability is part of life. Accept it and be safe.

The nice guy does not get the girl. I took care of Linda, I got her home safely, I had no intention of taking advantage of her in her drunken state, and I always treated her nicely. I didn't get her; another guy on the floor, who hooked up with her one night at a party when she was drunk, did. Being the nice guy doesn't get the girl. Being a jerk is not something of which I'm capable. There is a happy medium between the two. The day Linda started to date the other guy on my floor was the day I realized it...and the day I set out to be that in-between guy.

QUICKIE

HOW IMPORTANT IS THE BLOWJOB TO A GUY? VERY. NEXT TO SEX, IT IS THE biggest thrill a woman can give a man. It not only feels great but it creates an instant feeling of gratitude toward the woman. Guys feel a stronger emotional connection to women who give us head than to women who don't.

We know many women don't like to give head. We appreciate them doing it and that appreciation takes the form of emotion. The emotion is augmented when a woman lets us ejaculate onto her breasts. It is augmented even more when she swallows.

The dilemma for both men and women is guaranteeing a good blowjob. I learned the trick to a great blowjob in Iowa, from the woman who gave me by far the best one I've ever had. The good news is that it's less work to give great head than to give bad head.

The trick is to get the guy extremely excited before actually sucking. Karla did that by using her hand only a little. What worked well was her focus on the area of my stomach and below. She started high and slowly moved down, kissing and licking as she went.

As I got more and more excited, she started to nibble. I began to beg her to put my penis in her mouth. Nope. Instead, she teased me by slowly working her way back to my stomach. She used her hand a little more and moved down slowly again. I begged her some more to put it in her mouth. She gave it soft kisses, which drove me even crazier. It wasn't until I cried out like I was in pain that she finally sucked away.

She had gotten me so excited it was over in a few seconds. It was possibly the best feeling I've ever had, certainly the best from a blowjob. (It's hard to compare to sex because condoms change the feel.)

Don't go to town right away. I've had many women do that and it doesn't work nearly as well. Make the guy cry out for it. It's a lot less work and yet far more satisfying for the guy. Who would have thought? Less work is better. Men have been telling women that for years...not in reference to blowjobs, just in general.

By the way, if the guy can handle it, I also learned from Karla that a penis is extremely sensitive after orgasm, especially with semen on it. She rubbed the semen in with her hand and I went nuts. She spoke softly, "Just relax...relax...let me do this until you absolutely can't stand it any longer...relax...doesn't that feel good?"

If a guy can stand it, this feels great.

Spread 'Em

JOAN CUSACK WANTS TO SET ME UP ON A BLIND DATE. SHE READ ONE OF MY scripts, liked it a lot (actually, the comments she allowed me to quote helped get me my manager), we've talked a few times, and she thinks I would hit it off well with one of her young artist friends. A lot of guys shy away from blind dates. They don't want to waste their time with a woman they haven't seen. And women say men are shallow. I've only been on one blind date. While there wasn't any chemistry, we had a nice night out and pleasant conversation. I gave Joan the green light to go ahead and see if her friend is game. Actually, she even offered to pay for the date. I told her that wasn't necessary; I didn't think that would go over too well with her friend. That would make a good U.S. Cellular commercial, wouldn't it? Joan Cusack standing on a bench, trying to get a signal with a competitor's cell; her friend answers.

"Hey, it's Joan. Guess what? I finally got you a date. Yeah, I'm paying this guy to go out with you! Hello? Hello?"

Did her friend not hear her or did she hang up? Be sure friends are hanging up; use U.S. Cellular. Great commercial.

Why haven't I had many blind dates? My friends never set me up. They figure I meet people easily and don't need the help. This is too bad, because no one makes a reference like a friend. Women feel like they know a guy when he's the friend of a friend. They trust their friends for better or for worse. In fact, sometimes women trust their friends too much. I was at Club Med in Cancun a few years ago, where I met a stunning blonde from Vancouver. She was strikingly beautiful and had a perfect body. She did not have an ounce of fat or cellulite, not a wrinkle in her skin. I later learned that she used to be a figure skater, which explained her exceptionally toned body. I spoke with her and her friend one afternoon. Her friend talked about a guy she was crazy about, but with whom she broke up.

"Why did you do that?"

"Well, Ian, my friends didn't like him. They said he was all wrong for me."

"So what? Your friends weren't dating him. Did he mistreat you or anything?"

"Oh no, he was really great. But my friends look out for me, so I trust them."

It turned out none of her friends were dating anyone at the time, except for the figure skater, who was engaged. The figure skater agreed with me that the friends were just jealous of the time the other girl was spending away from them with her boyfriend. So they gave her bad dating advice to cause a breakup.

I have met women through friends without being set up, like the girls at Steve's party. Actually, I've done well with women Steve knows. Women think he is a very sweet guy and since I'm his friend, I must be a sweet guy, too. At the same time, I am aggressive. I've gotten some good action several nights Steve introduced me to friends, as well as a few dates.

I've also done very well with the friends of a female friend of mine. She has some very pretty friends and I've gotten digits and dates from mere five-minute introductions to several of them. Some of her friends turned out to be quite weird, but I had great times with some of the others. Once she was working at a retail scrapbook store and brought the owner and coworkers out to a bar. The owner, Shelly, was very pretty and had a real elegance about her that made her quite sexy. It didn't hurt that she had a good, taut, full-figure and a sweet ass to boot. I am very drawn to strong, independent women, and Shelly certainly was one. She owned her own store and a house. (Pay attention, guys.) In the brief ten minutes I spoke to her, Shelly mentioned how busy she was and that she rarely got out, what with running her own business. I knew instantly that she was looking to let her hair down. I got her number and left.

We had several dates, all of them great. Shelly was very smart and interesting. She had well thought out opinions and good conversation skills. One of the best dates we had started when I picked her up at her store at closing time. She sent her staff home, locked up, and we found ourselves half-naked in the store. It was very fulfilling for both of us. She enjoyed losing control in her own store—having a guy lift her onto a counter and take off her top and bra—while I enjoyed taking charge in her store, where she was always in control. We never had sex but we came as close as two people can get without doing it. Unfortunately, Shelly got very busy with her store and we faded away, which was too bad. I was really looking forward to having sex with her. I could have given her some really good sex that she badly needed and she could have given me some really good tenderness, which I badly needed. We were good for each other.

I have had phone dates. Huh? Phone dates. That's what I call it when I ask out a woman who I have only met over the phone. Who would I meet over the phone? I went out with a couple newspaper reporters who interviewed me over the phone. We flirted during the interview, conducted for their local paper about my upcoming comedy appearance in town, and I asked them out. I went out a few times with sales reps who handled my glow'n-the-dark condoms account.

One night I called a girl to play in a beach volleyball tournament. A friend of hers—who I had met on the beach and asked to play—referred me to her. I called her up and we got to talking about more than the tournament. Her name was Julie and she was upset because some guy hadn't called her. They had been on a few dates and he said he would call, but he hadn't. We flirted big time for thirty minutes. She told me she was wearing only a little red nightie. Abruptly, she invited me over.

"I don't want to be alone; I'll just get more and more pissed about this guy not calling. You should come over."

There was no way I was going over to her place. She lived out in the burbs. I wasn't going to drive all the way out there only to learn when I arrived that she had changed her mind, and then drive back home. I told her that.

"Then I'm coming to your place. What are the directions?"

I told her and added a stipulation, "If you come over, you have to wear the red nightie. We'll have a pajama party."

She agreed. I didn't think she'd show and got on the phone with my friend John. An hour later, much to my surprise, my doorbell rang.

I blurted into the phone, "Gotta go, John; this girl just got here for a pajama party."

"What? What girl? Who?"

"I don't know, I just talked to her tonight for the first time."

I hung up, buzzed her in, searched frantically for a pair of pajamas (I don't wear pajamas), and threw them on, finishing just as she reached my door. *I hope she's pretty,* I thought. She was. She was actually a pretty farm girl from Indiana. She had big brown eyes, some freckles, and this soft, sweet smile with deep dimples.

"Come on in."

She stayed in the doorway, "I just want to tell you that I told my sister and a friend I was coming here. They know the address and everything."

"Damn it, now I have to kill them, too; that's kind of a hassle."

She laughed and came inside, "You're not really going to make me put on my nightie, are you?"

"Of course I am; I'm wearing pajamas, aren't I?"

"I'm not going to put it on."

Actions speak louder than words. She drove to my place. She knew about the pajama stipulation. Most importantly, she brought the nightie with her. If she really didn't want to wear it, she would have left it at home. She didn't want to be held accountable. If I acted like a jerk, it would relieve her of accountability in her mind. See how it all comes together?

"Okay, well, seems like a long way to drive for nothing. Have a good trip back home."

"Ah! You're not serious. You'd make me drive all the way back home?"

"Yup."

"I guess I better put it on, then."

See? In her mind, she was putting on the nightie because I was making her, not because she wanted to. She wasn't being honest with herself about what she wanted. She wasn't being accountable. In college, I would have screwed the whole thing up. I wouldn't have made her put on the nightie, I would have changed out of my PJ's back into my clothes, and we would've talked until she became bored with my lack of action and left. But this wasn't college…school was out.

She changed in the bathroom. She came out wearing this little red nightie. We danced to a song and then off came the nightie. It turned out she was a virgin, so we didn't have sex, but we did get naked and she blew me a few times.

Julie and I dated for a year. I was the first guy she slept with, and she was the only virgin with whom I've slept. I have no idea what the appeal of a virgin is to some guys. Don't get me wrong, sex with her was good—very good at times—but there was a lot of instruction on my part at first. Instruction is awkward and has to be handled very delicately; it is very easy to offend someone in bed. Thankfully, I have good people skills. I dated Julie until shortly after the day she nearly got me arrested, the day I realized we just weren't quite right for each other.

I was waiting for Julie at my place one spring afternoon. I checked my watch. She was late. I turned on the TV and started to get into some news show about an old woman who cut up her old husband into little pieces. The phone rang.

"Hello?"

"They're trying to take my parking spot!"

The phone went dead. I quickly called Julie back and got her voicemail. As I was leaving a message, she called me back. She was frantic, "These thugs are trying to take my parking spot!"

"Where are you?"

She yelled to the thugs, "Leave me alone!" then she spoke to me, "I'm on Clark Street, just on the other side of you."

A car horn honked and she yelled at someone again. This sounded serious. I threw on my jeans jacket and grabbed my six-inch hunting knife (just in case these thugs wouldn't be deterred by me slapping them on the cheeks along with a firmly stated "Capiche?"). I slipped the knife inside my jacket pocket, and ran outside holding the knife against my body, as the pocket was too shallow to contain it. Before I saw her, I heard Julie threaten the thugs. "My boyfriend's coming and when he gets here, you're in a lot of trouble."

I stopped and looked down at myself. Was she dating another guy, too? I weighed 130 lbs. at the time. I wasn't going to give anyone trouble, which is why I had the knife. I had no intention of using it, I just thought it wise to have it in case they started to throw punches. Flashing a knife would hopefully get them to back off. I ran around the corner and couldn't believe my eyes. It was a freaking *Seinfeld* episode. Julie was halfway backed into a parking spot where an old man between eighty and a hundred was halfway pulled in. A little old lady (at least eighty-five) was standing in the middle of the spot. I looked around for the "thugs" but couldn't find them. I walked over to Julie's car. She called back to them, "Here he is! Now you're in trouble!"

"Sweetie, where are the thugs?"

"What do you mean where are the thugs? That's them."

"Those two? Can I use your phone?"

"What for?"

"I'm gonna need to get some friends out here if I'm gonna take them on; they look pretty tough."

Was she fuckin' kidding me? She was fighting with two old people about a parking spot. Apparently, the old lady had been standing in the spot to save it for her husband and this pissed off Julie.

"Honey, let 'em have the spot. Look at them; every time they park could be their last time. Let's not ruin that for them."

She glared at me, "You can't save spots. We're not leaving."

A cop pulled up behind the old couple's car and sounded his siren. Scratch that—a cop who knew the old couple pulled up behind their car and sounded his siren. He stuck his head out the window and spoke to the old lady, "What's going on, Eleanor?"

"Oh, Bobby, how are you? How are the kids?"

"Good, how are the grandkids?"

"Good, good; they're all good."

"What's the problem?"

I spoke to Julie while Eleanor explained the situation to Officer Bobby.

"That's it, it's over. They know the cop, let's go."

"We're not leaving."

"Julie, they know the cop. He's gonna make us move."

"No he won't. He'll make them move because I'm right and they're wrong."

"This isn't about right or wrong. It's about who knows the cop and that's not us."

She just didn't get it. The cop yelled to her, "You need to move, miss!"

She yelled back to him, "They can't hold a spot! I'm not moving and you can't make me!"

Lovely. I was dating the only person on the planet stupider and more stubborn than me.

"I told you to move, now move!"

She shook her head. The cop got out of his car. I walked up to him. Time to use those people skills.

"Hey, how are ya?"

"Is that your girlfriend?"

"Yeah, lucky me. You wanna date her? Take her off my hands?"

He laughed, "No, I don't think so."

"Give me a second to talk some sense into her."

"You got one minute. After that, I'm fucking writing her up and if she still doesn't move, I'm taking her in."

"Got it. Thanks."

I got into Julie's car and talked her down. She wasn't happy but she agreed to move, just as the cop walked up to my door, "You moving or what?"

"Yeah, we're going. Thanks."

Having just been watching the show about the old lady killing her husband, I didn't hold anything past old people. Julie mumbled, "We shouldn't be moving."

"Sweetie, it's not worth it. She'll come back here and slash your tires or something."

As Julie started to pull out, Officer Bobby returned to my door and stopped us, "Turn off the car."

I looked at him, "Everything okay?"

"Turn off the car."

Julie obeyed without actually saying anything.

"Step out of the car."

I obeyed. He walked me back to his car. I had no idea what was going on. Like most cops, he spoke very loudly, "Did I hear you say you were gonna come back here and slash that sweet old lady's tires?"

I sighed, relieved, "No, I said she might come and slash ours."

Unfortunately, unlike me, Officer Bobby had not just been watching a TV show about crazy, bloodcurdling old ladies.

"You expect me to believe that? Huh? That you said this sweet little old lady was going to slash your tires? You said she was going to slash your tires? Bullshit. You said you were going to slash hers, didn't you? Didn't you?"

I suddenly remembered the six-inch knife. Four of its inches were sticking out of my jacket pocket. Do the math. Cop thinks he hears me say I'm going to slash his little old lady friend's tires. Then, cop finds a six-inch knife on me. Yeah, I was totally fucked if he found that knife. I had to handle this very delicately.

"That's not what he said!"

Oh, good. Julie was out of the car and talking again. Perhaps she could get me the chair.

"Get back in the car, miss!"

"But that's not what he said!"

"Get in the car, Julie!"

"Don't tell me what to do, Ian!"

"I said get in the car, miss!"

"I'm not—"

"Get in the goddamn car, Julie!"

She glared at me but she got back into the car. Officer Bobby grilled me for the next few minutes, trying to get me to incriminate myself. I refused to say anything.

"All right. I'm gonna let you go, but I better not see any slashed tires on this car."

I turned to walk back to Julie's car when she jumped out again, holding a pen and pad of paper. "What's your badge number?"

Yup, I was going to get the chair. He turned to me. "Spread 'em."

I spread-eagled over his car, holding the knife inside my jacket against my body with my elbow. If he frisked me, I was dead. Officer Bobby prepared to frisk me when he noticed a crowd had gathered. He paused to disperse them. I moved to drop my knife onto the street and kick it under his squad car. I looked to see if anyone was watching. All clear. I started to pull the knife out when the cop returned to frisk me. I dropped it back into the pocket.

"All right."

I shook my head. "I gotta break up with this girl."

He looked at me. "Actually, the worst thing I could do is make you get back in that car with her. Go."

I went back to the car and got inside. Julie got in and looked at me, "What's his badge number?"

"Drive."

"We're not leaving until I get his badge—"

"Drive woman, drive!"

She jumped and started the car. We drove away. I broke up with Julie a few weeks later.

I learned four things from Julie and the girls in Cancun:
- Some women value their friends' opinions over their own.
- The bigger the risk, the bigger the potential payoff.
- Tense situations reveal the true nature of a person.
- Women will argue about being right even when right and wrong are no longer the issue.

Women and men take their friends' advice very differently. Men will listen to a friend's advice, consider it along with their own, and form their own conclusions. Women will often follow a friend's advice without considering their own views. I was at a club one night with some friends. A guy and girl near us were having a great time. They smiled a lot and were very touchy-feely. After an hour or so, the girl's friend joined them. She introduced her to the guy. The girl's friend shook the guy's hand and was very pleasant. She then gave her friend a hug. As she hugged her, she spoke into her ear right next to me, "You know I love you, but he's all wrong for you."

The girl looked disappointed but completely trusted her friend's advice. She was a cold fish to the guy from that point. After another hour, the guy left, very confused and annoyed. The girls then complained to each other about how they couldn't seem to meet the right guy. The girl's friend was very pleased after the guy left; she had her friend back to herself.

Every guy falls victim to a woman's friends' advice. Perhaps he meets a girl in a bar one night. They hit it off and talk for a while. There is lots of smiling and touching. She goes to the bathroom with her friends and won't even talk to him after she returns. It's like a completely different woman came out of the bathroom than went in. Her friends dissed him in the bathroom and she blindly followed their advice, despite the fact that she was having a good time.

What women fail to realize is that many times the advice they're getting is coming from their friends who are not meeting guys. These girls are jealous and simply don't want a friend to meet a guy if they are not meeting one. This makes no sense to guys. Why would a woman let her friends pass judgment on a guy when her friends haven't met the guy? She speaks to the guy for an hour and likes him. She hears his opinions and learns about him. Yet her friends, who haven't spoken to the guy at all, have an opinion on him? How? They have never even met him.

This practice unmasks one of the greatest misconceptions about the sexes. Men are not vainer than women; rather, women are vainer than men. No guy would ever pass judgment on a woman his buddy has met without speaking to her. He will comment on her looks, but that's it. Ladies would fair far better in dating if they acknowledged their vanity. Yes, your friend's opinion may be important, but it should never carry more weight than your own opinion.

I took a big risk letting Julie invite herself over. She could have been a psycho or drugged me, who knows. Worse, she could have been unattractive; heaven forbid. (If she was, we would have sat and had a nice conversation, which is not a bad way to spend an evening.) Julie was attractive, though, and she didn't drug me. The bigger the risk, the bigger the reward; or, the bigger the letdown. I've experienced both. The big rewards make the letdowns worth it.

Julie behaved very irrationally in a tense situation. She was stubborn, didn't listen, and failed to make some basic observations. It's good to know how someone responds to tension because in life and relationships there can be lots of tense moments. It is ideal for couples to react to tension in a similar manner. This reduces stress and resolves the issue at hand more quickly.

Women concern themselves with being right much more than men. This is exemplified best by the number of times it is joked about in sitcoms. *The Cosby Show, Home Improvement, Family Ties,* and various other sitcoms all include at least one scene in which the father gives advice to the son about women. The premise is always the same. The son is in a rough spot with his girlfriend over an argument they had. The son is right. Everybody knows the son is right. The father always gives the son the same advice: "She's right son. She's right."

"Dad, she's not right. She's totally wrong. She's—"

"Son, do you like the girl?"

"Yes."

"Do you want to see her again?"

"Yes."

"Then she's right. All you need to know about women is that they are always right."

Men more willingly concede than women that right and wrong are not always the issue. Sometimes it's simply easier to concede than to continue to argue about what has become a moot point. Julie kept arguing about her right to a parking space when it was no longer the issue. A cop says move, you move. Obeying authority was the issue. She couldn't concede that the argument about right and wrong was over and that she had lost. Winning an argument isn't the most important thing; peace is. Men seem to grasp that more easily than women.

 **QUICKIE**

First dates can be tough. Fortunately, I'm no longer in a place where that's the case. I don't get nervous, I find plenty to talk about, and I'm not hesitant to make a move, if I so desire.

While I am relaxed on first dates, that's not always the case for my dates. One practice I've found that helps relax them is to go somewhere before the date. It's like a pre-date and it creates a less stressful atmosphere.

The pre-date takes place at a quiet, laid-back bar for a drink before heading out for the real date. This tends to relax the woman a lot. Sometimes the pre-date goes so well, we never get to the real date. We stay at the quiet bar all night or wind up back at one of our places.

I do less pre-dates these days because I'm mostly interested in a relationship that can go somewhere. I've noticed that, while a lot of pre-dates result in a lot of action, they do not result in a lot of future dates. I suspect that the women feel like they behaved slutty for a first date and are embarrassed to get together again.

A lot of guys have enough trouble just deciding where to take a date, let alone being on the date itself. Again, pay attention to the woman. What are her interests? What kind of food does she like? Use that knowledge to help decide.

Guthrie's—the bar with board games I mentioned earlier—is my favorite first date place. Such places are great for first dates. Dating is a game anyway, so might as well start by playing actual games.

People reveal a lot about themselves when they play games. Do they cheat? Are they sticklers for the rules? Are they sore losers? Can the guy handle losing to a girl? Does the girl feel she needs to lose to the guy?

Peoples' behavior in games often reflects their behavior in life. For example, if a woman only plays the games she wants to play and refuses to play any that I want to play, that's a pretty good indication that she is not very compromising.

Couples can get a vibe on how their personalities match up. Are they both sticklers? Is one a stickler, the other a cheater? That's trouble on the horizon.

Mostly, the games are fun and can serve to fill gaps in the conversation.

The Bitter Friend

COMEDIENNE RITA RUDNER HAD A CHEAP AGENT IN THE NINETIES. I AM very grateful to that agent. In my early twenties I played a club called Knuckleheads in Gulfport, Mississippi. I was the feature, and a comic named Tripp Winfield headlined. The club was located on the first floor of a large casino; there was a theater on the third floor. Rita played the theater the weekend we appeared at Knuckleheads. Her agent wanted an opening act for her shows and the theater manager approached me to do it. I initially agreed; opening for Rita in front of a thousand people would have been fun.

"Yeah, I'll do it."

"Good, I'll let Ms. Rudner know."

"What's the money?"

"One hundred dollars."

"One hundred dollars a show? I need more than that."

"No, one hundred dollars total."

"Twenty-five dollars a show?! Yeah, I retract my offer."

Tripp couldn't open for Rita because he was still onstage when her show started. He wouldn't have done it for that money either. No doubt Rita had no idea what a piddly amount of money her agent was offering. So, although he wasn't happy about it, the theater manager hired our very green emcee to open for Rita.

On Saturday night Knuckleheads did four shows. (The casino thought we were in Vegas, not Gulfport.) It was ridiculous. Instead of performing for two large crowds, we performed for four small ones. After my second show set, bored with my own act, I grabbed a fresh beer and went out to the casino to play some blackjack. I never got to a table. As I came out of the club, two women sat down at a bar table near the entrance. One was homely. The other was my quintessential woman. Every guy has a quintessential woman, one who exemplifies perfection in his eyes. Most of the time the guy doesn't even know he has one until he sees her. And meeting her is almost always out of the question because she is divine beyond approach.

Veronica was my quintessential woman. She was twenty-six and stood around 5'6". She had black hair that hung an inch off her shoulders and framed her face beautifully. A black shirt and pair of black jeans were painted onto her perfect body. I mean perfect. She had wonderful, full, medium-sized breasts and a phenomenal ass. It was the perfect tight bubble-butt. Neither her ass nor her breasts had heard of gravity. Her luscious legs narrowed and swelled in all the right places and her hips cried out for a pair of hands to squeeze them. Everything had the perfect amount of curves in the perfect places to curve. Even her cheek bones were high and sexy.

And then there were her eyes. I am a huge sucker for eyes; it is my one weakness. A woman can have everything else and I can resist. A woman can have beautiful eyes and I want to buy her a house. Veronica's eyes were unforgettable. They were green with long eyelashes. More than that, they were warm, inviting; coupled with her welcoming, perfect smile—complete with deep dimples—she was irresistible.

I sat at another table and watched Veronica and her friend for a few minutes. Not a guy walked by them without looking back at Veronica at least four times. I was afraid someone would approach her, but no one did. She was so beautiful, they were too intimidated. They probably assumed a woman like that had to have a boyfriend. (Remember, never assume.) Thirty minutes passed before I knew it. The staff cleared Knuckleheads for the next show. I found myself whispering to God, "Please, God, please; let her come to the show. Make her come to the show, I don't care how, just get her in there."

To my delight, Veronica and her friend went into Knuckleheads. I hurried into the club myself. I asked the doorwoman to seat them right up front. She did. I had several places in my act where I talked to a woman in the crowd. I always spread the talking around; hitting a different woman each time a bit required me to talk to one. This show I selected Veronica every single time. The rest of the audience wasn't even there; I only saw her. I found out everything about her I could while onstage: Her name, where she was from (New York), her job (she was a civilian who worked for the military), her goals (she wanted to go back to school), even the name of her imaginary friend growing up (Daryl). I was helplessly hooked. I even loved her voice.

After the show, I shot over to her table like a sailor on leave for the first time in six months. We sat and talked for a while. I was careful to include her friend in the conversation; I could have easily forgotten her, which would have been extremely rude and certainly would have been noticed by both women. Veronica informed me they were going up to the top floor of the casino to dance.

"Would you like to join us?"

Would I? Damn fourth show!

"I have another show to do, but after my set I'll come right up."

"Okay."

I walked them out; I wanted to be near her as long as possible. I couldn't explain it, it was insane. A woman never got hold of me like this. I rushed through my last set and hurried upstairs. The emcee followed me, "Dude, I gotta go, too. She was so incredibly hot, Jesus Christ."

"Aren't you forgetting something?"

"What?"

"Rita..."

"Oh shit; damn it! Mother fucker!"

He sprinted away to open for Rita, leaving Veronica all to me. Thanks again Rita's cheap agent; thanks again. I headed into the large, crowded dance club and held my breath. It had been nearly two hours since Veronica invited me to hit the club with them. I feared they might have left, or worse, that I would find Veronica in another guy's arms. I don't think I could have handled that and I almost left just from thinking about the possibility. I gave the room a complete sweep. Nothing. I went through it again. There was no sign of Veronica or her friend. Had it been any other woman, I would have called it a night and gone back to my hotel room.

I wanted to see Veronica again so badly, though, that I went through the club for a third time. There was still no sign of her. Again, I found myself whispering to God under my breath, "Please, God, please let her be here. I want to see her again so bad."

I walked through the club one last time, checking carefully. My heart jumped. Veronica was sitting at the bar, talking to some guy. Her friend sat next to her, facing away from them.

"Thank you, God, thank you."

I walked over to them. Veronica leapt out of her seat, "Hey Sweetie, how are you?"

Much to my delighted surprise, she gave me a peck on the lips and a big, warm hug. She whispered into my ear, "Play along."

She turned to the guy she had been talking to, "Craig, this is my boyfriend, Ian. Ian, this is Craig."

We shook hands. He looked devastated; I would have been too.

"Come on, let's dance."

I spent the next hour dancing with Veronica. Her friend joined us occasionally, then went back to the bar and sat down, watching us. Craig hung out for a while, then gave up and left. I was afraid that with him gone, Veronica would want to stop dancing. Nope. Her favorite position was to turn away and pull me up to her. She placed my hands on her hips and then slid hers over them. She rubbed and rolled her delicious ass against me.

"Someone's happy."

"Yeah, sorry about that. Can't help it."

"Don't be sorry. I'm flattered."

"Yeah?"

"Yeah. Let's go back to the bar and have a drink."

Veronica, her friend, and I went downstairs to the tables, where it was quieter, so we could talk while we drank. Again, Veronica's friend faded from the picture. I had a great conversation with Veronica. She was fascinating and very intelligent. She pointed out a lot of things I hadn't thought about as we spoke on various subjects.

The time came to say goodnight. I didn't want it to end. I had found out in our conversation that Veronica and her friend drove separately to the show. Neither needed to drive the other home. The situation was ideal. God was smiling on me for a change. Veronica stood up and extended her hand, "It was very nice meeting you, Ian. Thanks again for posing as my boyfriend."

"No problem. Can I talk to you for a second?"

I feared the dreaded, "No, there's no need for that. Have a good night" line.

"Yeah, sure."

I gently took her hand and led her several yards away. She looked at me, "What is it?"

"This." I placed one hand on her hip, one on her cheek; I leaned in and kissed her. She kissed me back. We kissed a few times and gazed into each other's eyes. I wanted to say something that would drive her wild and make me as irresistible to her as she was to me. "Look, Veronica, I don't have any lines, no smooth moves, nothing. I just would really like for you to come back to my room with me."

D'oh! What a horrible pitch. The most important wind-up to date and that's all I could manage? She smiled. "I'd like that, too."

Oh my God, I couldn't believe it. No games. No "I'm not sure" followed by her biting her lip. No dilemmas. Better yet, the hotel was just down the beach from the casino, so there'd be little time for her to change her mind. Finally, God was on my side. We squeezed hands. Abruptly, Veronica's friend interrupted us. She wore an ugly scowl and snarled at Veronica, "I need to talk to you, I need to talk to you!"

"I'll be back in a sec."

They walked twenty feet away. I don't know what they said but hands flew in a flurry of gestures and there were a few shouts. The friend wiped a tear from her cheek and folded her arms. Veronica sighed and returned to me, "I'm really, really sorry. I can't tell you how sorry I am. I have to go."

What?!

"My friend has a lot of issues; she's really messed up. She's threatening to commit suicide."

Suicide? Pfft, please. I'll kill her right here. This will only take a second; I'll be right back.

"Seems a little dramatic, doesn't it?"

"I know, but you don't know her."

"She's just bummed because she didn't meet anyone."

"I know…dating is tough for her. It's hard for her to meet guys."

"Well, she never smiles and her arms are almost always crossed. She's very unapproachable."

We spoke for a little longer and agreed to meet the next day, my last one in Mississippi, for lunch at a nearby bar. I knew she wouldn't show but hope is the last to die, and I was clinging to it like a smoker to his last cigarette before quitting. She said goodnight, turned to walk away, and I spun her back around. I couldn't let her leave. We kissed some more. Her friend cackled from her place of misery, "Roni... Roni! We have to go Roni! I'm going to do it, I mean it!"

Veronica sighed and the two left. I was incredibly pissed. I went back to the hotel sporting a boner the whole way. I got up to my room, still furious. I checked my watch; it was a little after three. I pounded on Tripp's door, next to my own. He woke up and opened the door, half-blinded by the hall light, "What?"

"That woman we were all gaga over at the show was going to come back here with me. Can you believe it? With me!"

"Dude, that's awesome. I was pulling for you."

Tripp was married and one of the few comedians faithful to his wife. He looked around, "Where is she?"

"Her friend threatened to commit suicide. Can you believe that? What kind of bullshit is that? I would have killed that bitch for free."

"'For free'? You're not even making sense."

"Of course I'm not making sense! I came this close to being with the most beautiful, wonderful woman I ever met and her bitter friend fucked it up. I can't even think straight."

"Clearly. Why are you bugging me at three in the morning?"

"Because if I'm going to be miserable, someone's going to be miserable with me. I hope you can't fall back to sleep, you asshole!"

Tripp doubled-over with laughter.

"You wanna come in and cool off some? I got some beers."

"No, thank you; I have to go jerk off. Goodnight."

I went into my room and slammed the door behind me. I could hear Tripp laughing in the hallway. Veronica really missed out. She got me so charged up, I could have gone all night. Somehow I think I missed out, too. I was crushed. God was in good form fucking with me that night. What happened at the bar the next day? Thanks for remembering, because I want to relive that again. I waited at the nearly empty bar. Veronica did not show. After an hour, hope finally died and I got up to leave. Who should come in? Yup. Veronica's friend. She gave me a note from Veronica: *I just couldn't do it to a friend. Sorry, hope you understand. I had a wonderful time meeting you.*

"Do what to a friend?" I foolishly asked.

She erupted like a volcano, "I like you! Can't you see that? I noticed you before we even met you. I wanted to go to the show because I saw your picture on the board outside the club. She only thought you were kind of cute but wasn't really interested until after meeting you."

I stared at her in disbelief. I had tried to be friendly with this girl the other night and given up. She hardly spoke two words to me, never smiled, was bitter, and anytime I asked her how she was doing, she retorted, "Do you really care?"

What a bonehead I was. How could I not see that she liked me, what with all the clear signals she had given me? She liked me? I didn't even think this woman liked herself, let alone anybody else.

"So, want to have lunch?"

"I already ate, as far as you know. Nice meeting you."

"Well, maybe—"

"No, maybe-nothing. I'm sorry, but me and your friend really liked each other a lot. I rarely invite women back to my room and I can't begin to tell you how badly I wanted her to come back with me, even if nothing happened, even if we just talked all night."

"You just like her because she's hot."

"No, I like her because she is friendly and fun and interesting and smiles a lot. You know, all the things you don't do. And you had no right to mess it up for us."

I left. That night at the show I kept staring at the club entrance, hoping Veronica would walk through the doors. I even stuck around for an hour after the show ended, clinging to a last bit of desperation. I never saw her again.

I learned two things from Veronica:

- The quintessential woman is very approachable.
- There are ways to defeat the bitter friend.

Most guys never meet their quintessential woman. They see her, maybe more than once, but are far too terrified to speak to her. They place her so high up on a pedestal, the moment they see her, she becomes unapproachable. The trick to meeting the quintessential woman is to realize that she is just like everyone else. She has flaws. She has goals and dreams. She doesn't think she's perfect. She has her own hopes and desires. Men fail to realize these things, which leaves the woman on the pedestal. Realize these things and she comes off the pedestal, making her approachable.

How is the quintessential woman different from the dream girl? The dream girl is someone a guy typically has no chance of meeting— she's a movie star, a model, a famous singer. The quintessential woman can be met because a guy doesn't realize she exists until he sees her in real life. She's there, in front of him. He can meet her. Think of Robin Williams' character in *Good Will Hunting*. He recalls the story of how he met his wife to Will. Instead of going to see one of the most historic World Series games of all time, he slides his ticket over to his friends while he stares at a woman sitting at the bar. "Sorry, guys; I gotta see about a girl."

He had seen his quintessential woman. The quintessential woman is very approachable. The dilemma with meeting her doesn't rest with her, it rests with the guy too mesmerized to recognize that as great as she is, she is still human.

I cannot stand the bitter friend. Lots of times women travel with a bitter friend. This woman has no business being out. She is typically rude, jealous, short-tempered, whiny, and unapproachable, the life of the party. What creates a bitter friend? There are several factors. First and foremost, she has a severe lack of self-esteem. Second, even deeper, she doesn't like herself. She believes she is hopelessly unattractive. Ultimately, she believes she has nothing to offer and becomes more and more bitter about it.

What drives me absolutely nuts about the bitter friend is that she doesn't do anything to change what she doesn't like about herself. She could take some classes to develop a skill. She could dress better, wear makeup more appropriately, ask her friends for advice. There are literally dozen of things she could do to make herself happy. Instead, when friends offer her advice she bites off their heads. She goes out with her hair looking like she just spent hours tumbling in a dryer. She doesn't socialize. She insults guys who try to talk to her.

It's very hard for someone like me to swallow such a poor attitude. There are plenty of things I'm not happy with about myself. I'm skinny and have a big nose. I'm not a good athlete, even though I love sports. I developed confidence and a strong sense of humor to deal with my

Ichabod Crane features. Being bad at sports never stopped me from forming or joining teams in various sports leagues. I've developed skills and won dozens of titles. What I lack in athletic ability, I make up for in leadership and people skills, which helps to keep the various personalities on a team focused on the prize and not on killing each other. These results help make me a happy person with lots to offer.

The pain and resentment the bitter friend feels is reflected in everything she does physically. She rarely uncrosses her arms. She rolls her eyes all the time. She is gruff and barks at people. She doesn't laugh. Her friends are her crutch. The bitter friend hangs out with pretty women friends because they attract men. She lives vicariously through these friends. Eventually, though, she rains on everyone's parade. She gets angry with her friends for wanting to leave with a guy or for not hooking her up with one. She either disapproves of all the guys the women meet when they go out, or she likes them, too, and makes her friends feel guilty that the guys like them instead of her.

Pretty women hang out with bitter friends because they feel bad for them. Also, bitter friends make a good excuse to ditch a guy if they're not interested. It would be best if women left their bitter friends at home, where they would be forced to make some changes for the better.

How can men defeat the bitter friend? If she is loud and obnoxious, call her on it. Ask her why she came out, just to ruin everyone else's good time? A lot of times in a group of women, the bitter friend is really the friend of only one woman. The other ladies can't stand her either, and don't like being around her. They appreciate a guy saying something. Usually, calling a bitter friend on her bitterness will quiet her up or her make her leave.

What if the bitter friend is quiet, as was the case with Veronica's? Before making a move, a guy needs to ask the bitter friend, in front of the woman he likes, if she is having a good time. Does she need anything? Is everything okay? She'll utter something inaudible under her breath but acknowledge that she's doing fine. Tell her that's good and then take the other woman aside for a second. Get her number, ask her out, invite her home, whatever it is that is sought. When the bitter friend tries to interfere, it will be in vain; she's been defused before she could explode. She just said she was fine, how can she now suddenly be upset or sick? It will be obvious that she is merely jealous and lonely.

I've followed both of these practices with bitter friends and they have worked every time. I only wish I had practiced one of them the time it mattered most. Mmmm, Veronica. I became an atheist that night.

 **Quickie**

Sports leagues are some of the best places to meet people. Not only have I dated several women I met in sports leagues, I've also met most of my friends in them.

One tip: The leagues have sponsor bars that offer discounts on drinks and food. If playing, go to the sponsor bars as often as possible. It's the easiest place to socialize at.

Not very good at sports? The leagues offer lots of social divisions, where people play primarily to meet people. Actually, some of the sports offered are purely social sports, such as kickball and dodgeball.

The more competitive leagues offer a chance to meet competitive players. Few things are sexier to me than a pretty woman who excels at sports.

Don't have your own team to sign up? Not to worry; leagues allow people to sign up as individuals. They put these individuals together on what's called an independent team. That's how I got started years ago. From that first team I went on to recruit and form my own teams.

Don't want to play sports, just want to meet people? The leagues also offer social events. In Chicago, Chicago Sport and Social Club excels in social events. They are also branching out to other cities. Sports Monster leads the way throughout the U.S. and has even added a dating element to their organization.

Refereeing for sports leagues is another good way to meet people, especially for women. One female ref told me she met a ton of guys refing volleyball on the beach. She told all her single friends who wanted to meet guys to sign up to ref. Don't worry athletes, Sports

Monster does a great job training their refs and only the most experienced work the competitive leagues.

I can attest to female refs meeting guys. I had some of the best sex of my life with a Sports Monster ref. Visit www.sportsmonster. net for more information (on Sports Monster, not on some of the best sex of my life). Chicago Sport and Social Club's website is www. chicagosportandsocialclub.com. Players, a league available only in Chi-Town, can be accessed at www.playerssports.net. Finally, Windy City Field House, a privately-owned field house full of different sports in Chicago, can be accessed at www.windycityfieldhouse.com.

The Bitter Babe

OKAY, WE'VE DISCUSSED THE BITTER FRIEND, BUT WHAT ABOUT THE BITTER babe? The bitter babe is very different from the bitter friend. She is pretty and fed up with men and dating. Any woman can be a bitter babe at some point in her life.

A few years ago I was at a charity fundraiser thrown by an organization called the 20/30 Club. The club was started years ago by a bunch of young male professionals who wanted to meet more women, as well as help charities. They formed an organization that uses worthy causes and social events to bring professional singles together. Two great activities killed with one stone; what a great concept. The fundraiser was held at a bar called Jack Sullivan's, which no longer exists, which is too bad because I did pretty well with women at that bar. (Every guy has a few bars where he has good success meeting women, and a few others where he can't even get women to acknowledge he exists.)

One time at Jack's, Steve and I ended up standing next to a group of pretty coeds who were looking for some action. They started pulling up each others shirts and flashing one another. It's pretty easy to hook up with a woman when all a guy has to do is say, "Nice breasts." Clearly, God—angry that I was successful with women at Jack's—caused the bar to be closed.

I went to the charity event at Jack's with a few buddies. We were all looking to meet someone, not to hook up with, but to date. We arrived early enough to commandeer a table and chairs. We were there for only a few minutes when a pretty redhead and blonde walked into the bar. They walked past us and headed upstairs. I noticed the redhead glance back at me a few times. The two women set up shop near the railing of the second floor. They people-watched patrons on the first floor from their post. I caught the redhead looking at me a bunch of times within the first twenty minutes. I sized her up: very pretty, early thirties, 5'7", good body, nice tight butt. Her breasts were a little more than a handful, which I liked. Her bright blue eyes were the kiss of death. They lured me in all the way, especially with their contrast to her long red hair.

She scanned the room relentlessly. She scrutinized guys. She seemed a little annoyed and crossed her arms repeatedly. She didn't laugh or smile. I decided to remain at my table for the night and not hit on women. Bad strategy to meet the redhead, right? Wrong. Different types of women need to be approached using different tactics. A lot of guys use the same tactic to meet women. They go out, they approach a woman, if she's not interested or has a boyfriend, they move on to the next one. The weakness with this tactic is that women notice when guys hop around from one woman to the next. This offends lots of them and is a huge turnoff. It only works for trixies, vain women, and girls with low self-esteem.

These three types of women have a strong need to feel like they are the most desirable woman in the room. If a guy hops around and gets positive attention from the women he approaches, he will pique the competitive interest of trixies and other women with low self-esteem. When he selects one of these girls, she feels like she has won out over the other girls. This is important to her. Confident women don't need such an ego boost. They don't care to talk to a guy who is so obviously on the prowl. (Incidentally, if a guy hops around and is shunned by most of the women he meets, which is often the case, girls with low self-esteem will hardly say a word to him; they don't want to be associated with other women's rejects.)

This explains why confident beautiful women, referred to by some as "tens" (I'm not into the whole numbering system), sometimes date physically less-than-flattering guys. They know they are stunning and they have nothing to prove, so they don't have the trixie competitive nature. They don't need other women to be jealous of them in order to feel complete. Instead, they can simply go out with whomever they wish, as in the case of Nikki Cox and Bobcat Goldthwait.

Why don't I like the numbering system? It's inconsistent. A ten to one guy is often a seven to me and vice-versa. What's the criteria?

The system is too subjective to answer that question. Lots of guys give women with big fake breasts high numbers. I don't find anything attractive about fake breasts and give these same women low numbers. Lots of magazines rate Halle Berry as the prettiest woman in Hollywood; I prefer Claire Forlani. It's no secret why. Compare their eyes and remember my big weakness with women. Mostly, numbering is insulting to women. Instead, I just describe the woman and guys can assign her a number based on their own preferences, if they so wish.

The redhead wasn't a trixie. She didn't show signs of low of self-esteem. She watched various guys operate and seemed to criticize them to her friend. Every now and then, she glanced in my direction. What did she see when she checked on me? A guy just hanging out with his friends. I talked only to the women who were near us or who approached me. I was not on the prowl.

A lot of guys checked out the redhead but she was not approachable. She did not look like she was out to meet anyone. One guy did manage to talk to her at length. He was big, probably 6'4" with a solid build, about my age, twenty-eight. He'd talk to her for a while then go hit on younger women. When that didn't pan out, he returned to her until other young trixies caught his eye. He'd go talk to them and then return. Eventually, he reduced his hopping around to just the redhead and one young trixie. Who would be the one lucky enough to nab him? Through it all, the redhead kept checking on me. I waited patiently. The big guy's tactic wasn't going to work on her, so I didn't concern myself with him. My friend Steve showed up and I pointed out the big guy while making fun of his tactics, which is exactly what the redhead was doing with her friend. I knew she'd see me doing it, too.

It was really funny. The big guy was treating the redhead and the trixie the same. This is one big flaw with a lot of the books that give advice to guys on dating—they treat all women the same. The advice they give is geared primarily toward meeting, and typically nailing, shallow, pretty women. But, they insist that the advice is good for all women. They basically lump all women together into one mold. Unfair. That's like suggesting all baseball players are the same just because they play baseball. Certainly not true; some are better hitters, some pitch, some field better, and so forth. It is the same for women, which is why the key to success starts with observation and has little to do with following a set procedure.

The bar thinned out as closing time neared. The redhead stood alone, still watching people over the rail. Her friend was busy talking to some guy; the big guy was talking to the trixie. It was time to make my move. I headed up the stairs and walked over to her. I didn't say anything but instead leaned over the rail, looking where she was looking. I waited a few moments before speaking, "You've been up here all night watching people. So tell me, what are we looking at?"

She pointed to different patrons, "Well, that guy wants to go home with her, and she likes him, and that big guy there looks like a boring fuck anyway, and that guy there is gay and doesn't know it."

The "big guy" she referred to was the one who had been hitting on her earlier. She went on about him, "He just wants to pick up some young woman. The whole thing is pathetic, all these people trying to lie their way into bed. I'm so sick of the dating scene. If you wanna fuck me, just say you wanna fuck me, you know?"

Direct and honest. I like that in a woman. It's a sign of maturity and confidence. I caught a glimpse of Steve approaching out of my eye. He arrived just in time to hear "If you wanna fuck me, just say you wanna fuck me." He shook his head in disbelief. I could have said I wanted to fuck her. A lot of guys would have, but that was the wrong way to go. She'd know I was just saying what I thought she wanted to hear, and that would annoy her.

She was hurt that the big guy was going after a younger edition and she wasn't going to put up with that shit. What did she want? To be fucked? To leave with the big guy? She wanted a victory; not a victory as in a guy, but rather a victory in the form of being one up on men. I was happy to give it to her; she deserved it. In response to her fuck-me line, without missing a beat, I gave my reply, "Wow. You've stumped me. No one's ever stumped me, but you just did."

She smiled, "Really?"

We spoke for about ten minutes. She was very bitter. Along with being upset at the big guy and with dating in general, she was overworked at a job she hated, angry with a guy she was "kind of dating," and upset with her family. I needed to change her focus to find success.

"Would you like to dance?"

"There's no dance floor."

I stepped into her, "There is now."

She smiled again and I put my arms around her. Steve and I took a few turns dancing with her before he left. After he was gone, she and I began to kiss. Her name was Lisa. Soon the bar began to close. I walked Lisa outside. She did not say goodbye to the big guy, who had since been ditched by the trixie.

I wanted Lisa. She stirred me up and I found her to be a breath of fresh air from the trixies saturating the bars I had been to recently. When we got outside, she immediately hailed a cab. I figured she'd jump in with a quick blurb that it was nice to meet me and drive away. Instead, she opened the cab door and looked at me, "So, are we going back to your place or mine?"

Wow, what a wonderful surprise! I lived closer, so we headed to my place.

Cab drivers probably make their most money picking up a couple headed for a one-night stand. I gave him twenty dollars for an eight-dollar ride and we got out of the cab. A guy on the verge of getting lucky doesn't want to wait for change. That's just more time for the woman to change her mind. He wants the cab gone as soon as possible, before the girl has a change of heart and decides to take the cab home. Guys about to have one-night stands make for big tips.

Inside my place things got busy pretty fast. We sat on the futon, where I removed Lisa's shirt and pants as we made out. She was wearing a sexy black thong and black bra. After a while I went for the bra. She pushed me away and instead tore off my clothes. She was really into biting. She took hard bites at little pieces of skin on my chest, followed by great big bites of chunks of skin. I literally thought she was going bite my nipples off. It was quite painful. She went down on me. My immediate fear was that she would bite me down there, too. (She didn't, thank goodness.) Something told me this was as far as it was going to go—a blowjob. I wanted more, so I had to make a move.

I stopped her from sucking on me (there's something a guy doesn't do often), and went back to trying to remove her lingerie. The bra came off easily but when I tried to remove the panties, she held them on by the waistband. I licked her crotch. I had found this to be a good way to get panties off when women hesitated to remove them.

It worked like a charm. She gasped and let go of the waistband. I slid the panties off her. I was very glad I did. She had the best shave job I've ever seen. Her bush was this perfect, little narrow triangle, not too big, not too small. She was a natural redhead. I rolled her over and bit her sweet ass for a while, then rolled her onto her back. Her butt was pretty mushy upon touch, which was a little disappointing but I managed to cope. I slipped a condom on and prepared to enter. She suddenly went limp. Her eyes closed and she lay absolutely still.

"Lisa? Lisa? Are you okay?" I whispered.

She nodded and muttered.

"Do you want me inside you?"

She nodded again and muttered. She was clearly out of it, or faking, angry that I had removed her panties under false pretense. It could also have been the alcohol and work stress that suddenly gave her fatigue. She lay there, practically asleep. I thought about it. She was right there, lying naked before me. She wanted me inside her and I seriously thought about it. It would have been so very easy. My faculties weren't one hundred percent either, as I'd had lots to drink myself. I rubbed against her to see if that would bring some life into her. She murmured as though she were in a dream, "Mmm. That feels good."

I pushed in just the top of the tip. Nothing. I backed away. She wasn't kissing back, she wasn't moving; she wasn't doing anything. *Is this date rape?* I loomed over her for a good ten minutes, trying to make up my mind if I wanted to do her or not. She was so beautiful, lying there naked. Also, I had to pee badly, which is impossible while sporting wood, so I needed to finish to take care of that.

I decided that it would be inappropriate and for the first time I could see how a guy could do such a thing under certain conditions. The idea of banging a girl lying dormant held little interest to me. The idea of doing Lisa lying there completely naked in front of me—with a little more than a handful of perky tits and the best shave job I've seen—held lots of interest to me. I debated another ten minutes. A battle of will and hormones was raging and will was on the verge of defeat. Finally, though, I acknowledged that I just couldn't bring myself to do it. I pulled the futon away from the wall and opened it. I took off my condom, to help keep the hormones from resurging a more effective assault, and lay down beside her.

I watched her sleep most of the night. When it got cold, I threw a blanket over us and cuddled up against her. She was responsive and cuddled back. Every now and then I removed the blanket to look at her some more, then replaced it. I didn't take care of my pee problem. I was afraid that if I solved the dilemma on my own, she would wake up and want to fuck. I'd have wasted a great boner, which would have been a huge disappointment to me and my hormones.

I spent about eight hours with a full erection, much longer than the suggested length Viagra warns about in its commercials. I didn't know such a thing was possible. I couldn't sleep, what with the naked woman beside me and my current state of excitement. I suppose I could have left her and gotten into my own bed but that didn't even occur to me at the time. When lying next to a beautiful naked woman, not much occurs to a guy. Even if it had, getting into my own bed would have seemed like wasting a perfectly promising nude woman and no guy is going to do that.

So I lay there, for eight hours, in erotic discomfort. It was torture. God was doing some of Her best work on me. She knew I wouldn't take care of business myself and She had made me drink all those beers to fill up my bladder. Then She knocked out the naked woman, leaving me in a frenzied state. That Bitch! Lisa woke up in the late morning with a raging migraine. I assured her we had not had sex.

"You know, you could have. I wanted to, but I think I'm glad you didn't."

"I don't think it would have been any good for me with you just lying there. Sex to me is kind of an everybody-participates sport."

I walked her out and waited for her to get into a cab. I hurried back home and took care of unfinished business. After that, I took the most satisfying pee of my life. Aaah!

I learned three things from Lisa:
• Any guy can end up in a position to date-rape someone.
• Be gentler with women's nipples.
• There is a right way to pick up the bitter babe.

I never imagined that I would ever be in a position to date-rape someone. I was that night, though, and it took every bit of discipline I had to restrain myself. Hormones are extremely powerful, especially when they travel in groups numbering over three times the normal amount. There are different types of date rape. One type is exactly what it's called, the rape of a woman by her date. Another type is the one I faced. It's the type of rape where a woman no longer has the faculties to consent, usually because she's drunk.

I think this type of date rape is quite a double standard. If a guy and girl are both drunk off their asses and they have sex, she may not be held accountable for her actions, while he could be charged with rape. If a woman isn't responsible for consenting to sex because she is drunk, how can a guy be responsible for engaging in sex if he is drunk, too? Realistically, I don't know how many of these cases are tried. Fortunately for both men and women, there is a naturally built-in safety switch: A guy too drunk to think clearly is almost always too drunk to get aroused.

Prior to my night with Lisa, my idea of date rape was a scenario in which the woman is drunk and the man is sober. In such a scenario, clearly the man is abusing the woman. I quickly dismissed this misconception when I found myself sprawled over a nearly passed-out woman, thinking *Oh my God, this is date rape.* It's far more likely that both the guy and girl are drunk. Date rape is another good reason to stay away from drunken women. If a guy is inebriated and takes a drunken woman home, he is likely to engage in sex with her. He could be charged with date rape. Just like drunken women who go home with strangers, this guy has put himself in the unwise position of being unsafe. The best play for him is not to take her home in the first place.

I've been tough on some women's nipples. After nearly having mine ripped off in a set of gnashing teeth, I learned to be gentler with nipples—not too gentle, because that's no good either—but definitely gentler.

The bitter babe is tricky to pick up and can be a lot of work if approached incorrectly. She is worth the time, though, as usually she is not in the mood to play games, so a guy can refreshingly be straightforward. I actually learned how to hook up with bitter babes prior to meeting Lisa, but since I was successful in those stories, they have no business in this book. The quandary with the bitter babe is two-fold. First, she can be any type of woman, which needs to be determined to have a chance with her. Second, she is skeptical and critical of men. She needs to be approached carefully.

I like showing the bitter babe a good time. I feel like I am giving her some things she really needs, namely some good treatment, sex, and respect. Bitter women are mostly bitter because they have been dissed a lot, they feel disrespected. There are often times, though, when I pass bitter women over because I just don't have the desire to sit still for a long time or have the patience to deal with their bitterness. They can be a lot of work and take much energy.

The best way to approach a bitter babe is not to approach her. Let her observe. Watch how she responds. If she keeps looking over, she is intrigued and interested. She can't figure out the behavior and that piques her interest. Go over and talk to her. If a guy doesn't behave the way a bitter woman expects him to behave (in short, if he doesn't behave like a guy), he may have a chance with her. Bitter babes aren't looking for a male; they're looking for an anti-male. I have the bite marks to prove it.

 **QUICKIE**

I WORKED WITH CEDRIC THE ENTERTAINER, RICHARD JENI, AND ROBERT Schimmel at different times. All three guys were very cool and liked my act a lot. All three had a tendency to go over their mic times (they stayed onstage longer than expected), resulting in shows running overtime. This introduced me to a lot of women.

When a show runs overtime, the audience for the next show ends up forming a long line, which often winds down the block. Lines are great places to meet people. I met a lot of women, not to bang, but rather to play tennis with, go out with on a dinner date, and so forth. Hey, it was either that or sit in a hotel room all day. Comedians can't have a social life if they're shy.

Lines put people in close proximity of each other; one doesn't have to noticeably walk across a room to make introductions. They create an easy common-denominator.

"Can you believe how long this line is? I've been here since Tuesday...of last week."

They give people time to work on each other. They're much quieter than a crowded club, making it easier to hear and have a conversation. They provide a reference for approaching each other again once inside. Best of all, the other person can't get away without losing place in line.

It's not just lines; being outside in general can be an effective strategy to meet people. For example, hanging outside establishments in areas that have banned smoking indoors is a great way to meet smokers. They have to come outside to smoke. This leaves them alone. There are no friends around to circle wagons. It also creates another easy common-denominator. Of course, this is all assuming one doesn't mind kissing an ashtray. (It's pretty nasty. I know. I've kissed an ashtray. Actually I licked it. Hey, I was three, it was raining outside, I was bored, my dad left his dirty ashtray on the coffee table, I wanted to know what the smoking fuss was all about...do the math.)

With Friends Like These...

AFTER COLLEGE, I WAS STILL A VIRGIN. I WASN'T TOO CONCERNED ABOUT IT. After all, anyone could have sex, but how many people could live their dreams and have the career they really wanted? I was on the verge of doing that, which is where my attention was focused. Besides, I had done plenty of things and been naked with several women, mostly in the shower. Also, it's not like I hadn't had my chances.

I was eighteen the first time I saw breasts. I was walking offstage in Fon du Lac, Wisconsin, when a thirty-something woman tore open her blouse, "You make my nipples hard."

I got the hell out of there. Another time I was nineteen playing in West Virginia. The gig was at the nightclub in the hotel where the comedians stayed. After the show a very pretty, short, twenty-six-year-old woman approached me. "I just got divorced, I'm double-jointed in the hips, and I was wondering, do you like it when women get a little rough? Like with spanking and stuff?"

I danced with her for a while. She was definitely double-jointed in the hips. She could move those things like no one else I've ever seen. She kissed me.

"Want to go up to your room and shower together, then find out how I really like to move my hips?"

I did want to go. The other comedian was in his forties and kept telling me to take her upstairs and sleep with her. A bunch of local-yokels wanted to kick my ass for gaining the interest of one of their women, so it was probably best for me to get the hell out of the bar. God yanked my chain, though. She placed another pretty woman in the club who looked just like a babysitter I had a crush on when I was a kid. I wanted her more than the divorcée.

God knows something about me when it comes to both life goals and women: I never settle. If I want something in life, I go after it full-throttle. I don't always achieve it, but knowing that I put everything into it satisfies me just the same and I can move on to the next goal.

I am the same with women. A lot of guys will settle. They'll pick up anyone who will sleep with them. They'll date anyone who will date them. This inevitably leads to all kinds of problems, from getting rid of her in the morning to trying to shake a crazy girl from a relationship. When I'm out, I'm not looking to meet twenty women to increase my odds of getting laid. Rather, I try to meet the one woman I'm attracted to the most. Sometimes her personality doesn't hold my interest or she's an idiot, so I move on, but once I've found one I like who is interesting, I focus on her. Or, if there isn't anyone else, I just hang out. In short, I make a choice. Lots of guys don't make a choice.

It is sincere to make a choice. It demonstrates that I am not interested in a woman's T&A, I am interested in the woman herself. Instead of hopping from one woman to the next, I take my time with just one. If things go well, I ask her out or invite her back to my place, depending on how I see her. There are some women I can see dating, while there are others I don't want to date but I can see sleeping with them. I act accordingly. Usually the woman has different ideas, which is fine. I didn't fail. I went after the best woman and she declined. I'd rather go home alone and jerk off to her image then go home with someone who wasn't my top choice. I only fail if I don't go after the woman I want to meet the most.

God knew I would want the babysitter-look alike more, so She dangled her before me. The look alike was, of course, not interested, especially after witnessing the antics between myself and the divorcée. The divorcée settled for a local-yokel. She left with him while I worked on the babysitter-look alike. She left as well and I went back to my room alone.

There were plenty of other chances to have sex, all of which I declined. Women have no idea how to react when a guy turns them down. They're simply not used to that kind of rejection. Some cried, some punched me, some called me names. It was very interesting; knowing I could have sex seemed to satisfy me.

Once I even had Jenny Jones hit on me. She was a judge for a talent competition I was in to appear on the *Tonight Show* when I was nineteen, the same competition where I met Jimmy Pardo. All the acts and judges took a group photo together. Jenny stood beside me. She kept grabbing my butt and apologizing; then she asked me what I was doing later.

Why didn't I have sex? I wanted my first time to be with someone I was dating. The problem was I had never dated anyone, and with a promising comedy career ahead of me, it didn't look like I would be anytime soon. At twenty-one, I decided to give up on dating anyone. Instead, my first time would be with someone I liked a lot and would date if I wasn't a traveling comedian.

After my college graduation ceremony, I said goodbye to my family, who all headed back to Chicago. I got in my car and drove to the Des Moines Funny Bone to begin a three-month tour. I was the emcee for the show. The feature, Marc Rubben, was a ventriloquist who owned an emu farm, and the headliner was a guy named Dan Whitney. Dan was very busy working on a character he played on a weekly Florida radio show. He called the character Larry the Cable Guy. Today, of course, he is a very popular act and his first movie, *Larry the Cable Guy: Health Inspector*, was released in 2006. Dan is another really good guy who works hard and deserves his success. It is good to see him doing well. The three of us were quite an eclectic group and we had fun. Both Dan and Marc ribbed me like I was their younger brother. They also teased each other, as Dan took a lot of shots at the ventriloquist, both on and offstage. He kept telling the crowd that Marc slept with his dummy. I refereed some between the two.

The second night of the show my good friend Paul, whom I've known since age twelve, drove out to catch my act along with his college friends from Iowa City. I was nervous having a friend at the show but I quickly got over it. Immediately upon walking onstage, I saw a beautiful brunette sitting up front with some friends. She had long hair, mesmerizing eyes, a great smile, perfect teeth, and a hot body. She's exactly how I envisioned my future wife. I completely forgot about my good friend Paul and focused on her.

I don't recall how it happened, but halfway through my set I wound up sitting with her and her friends, eating pizza. I sat there, eating a slice with the mic in my hand. I was supposed to be performing, of course, so I had to at least acknowledge the crowd, "People, I need a few minutes here. Talk amongst yourselves."

Dan and Marc were busting up in the back. They couldn't believe it. Emcees were supposed to be nervous and often scared to be onstage. They did not halt a show to hit on some babe. I asked her a few questions. She was a coed named Stephanie.

"What perfume is that you're wearing? It smells good."

She and her friends laughed and blushed. I grabbed another slice for the road and jumped back onstage. The crowd thought it was great. She was the one; I was going to lose my virginity with her. After the show, Paul and his friends assaulted me immediately. They formed a group around me. I couldn't see past them. I kept moving my head back and forth, trying to look beyond them while trying not to be rude. I saw Stephanie waiting to talk to me with two of her friends. I figured I'd wait five minutes, then go over to her. That would keep me from looking rude to Paul's friends. It was the worst decision of my life. Stephanie left after four minutes. I looked everywhere for her. Nothing. Extremely bummed, I left the club with Paul and his friends. I blamed them for fucking it up for me.

When I got back to the condo, I found out leaving with Paul and his friends was the second worst decision of my life. Dan and Marc told me that Stephanie hadn't left; she had just walked her friends out to their cars. She returned, looking for me, and Marc told her I had already left. She then thought she had just been part of the act and left very upset. D'oh! God had screwed me again! I think I drove poor Dan and Marc crazy, pining over Stephanie for the rest of the week.

I didn't meet anyone else who I wanted to be the first for the next year. (Remember, I never settle.) I did work in Akron, Ohio, at Hilarities with a very cool act from the South, the week after he made his *Tonight Show* debut. His name was Tim Wilson and he was both an accomplished comedian and musician. Tim was a Georgia Boy and I made some extra cash working with him. I had noticed a lot of emcees went out to bars after shows and drank away their weekly earnings. In an effort to avoid this problem, I bought a Sega, which I took with me wherever I went. The only game I had was football, which came with the system. Tim took to the game and got annoyed that he kept losing to me, so he bet a dollar on each game we played to inspire himself to win. I won a little over twenty bucks off him for the week.

While in Akron, Tim and I both spoke to a booker out of St. Louis named Al Canal. Al was booking the Funny Bones across the country at the time and we happened to talk to him just after he was in a bad car accident. (Thankfully, he fully recovered without complications.) Al was not in the mood to worry about booking clubs, so he filled up his calendar with a bunch of dates for Tim and me. Again, timing played a huge role.

Tim and I wanted to work together again but we could only match up on one gig. We booked a week together for two months later at the Funny Bone in Arlington, Texas, just outside Dallas. That's where I met a waitress named Heather. She was a blonde with long hair and just a touch of sexy Texas twang in her voice. She was twenty, 5'7", with a great pair of legs and the best butt I've ever seen. She was slightly self-conscious about her small breasts, which I thought were very nice. She also had pretty eyes and a broad, warm smile, along with a sexy sarcasm.

Heather and I took an instant liking to each other. We flirted and chatted as often as we could, although it was a little tricky, what with her having to deliver drinks all the time. She and her roommates threw a small party Saturday night after the show at the house they rented. We got a lot of time to talk there.

It was great. Someone challenged me to a game of chess. I told Heather, who was wearing short shorts and a t-shirt, that I needed a partner. She sat on my lap as I played. We were both barefoot and we played footsies with each other throughout the game. My opponent sucked and I got off to a great start. Realizing the game was going to end quickly, I threw it. I didn't want Heather off my lap anytime soon. Shortly after we finished playing, Heather went off to play hostess. A guy I had met earlier, who had been hugging Heather off and on all night, came over to me. His name was Frank.

"So, whaddya think of Heather?"

"She's great; lots of fun, really smart."

"Yeah, she is. We've been dating for a year now."

What?! They were dating?! I didn't believe him. The end of the night rolled around and I decided I wanted Heather to be my first. I was nervous as hell. I couldn't come up with anything. I decided to just tell her I really wanted to stay and that I hoped she felt the same way. Heather came into the room, "Did you have a good time, Ian?"

"Absolutely."

I was about to deliver my irresistible line when Frank appeared on the landing upstairs. He yelled down, "Hey Heather, are we sleeping in your room or your roommate's room tonight?"

She gave him a questioning look, "My room."

They *were* dating! I couldn't fucking believe it. God had gotten the better of me yet again. I said goodnight and headed back to the comedy condo.

The weather in Texas is insane. Shortly after I got home from the party, out of nowhere, it began to hail. There wasn't any rain, just hail. Huge balls of the stuff pummeled people and their belongings. Pieces got as big as softballs; not the wimpy twelve-inch sized softballs people catch with a glove, but the sixteen-inch sized Chicago ones that break fingers when they come off the bat. People were killed by the hail. Killed by hail! If someone gets killed by hail, God simply didn't like him. Imagine…this poor schmuck lives life perfectly. He eats all the healthy foods, doesn't risk sleeping around, never smokes, doesn't do drugs, drives ten miles below the speed limit, and wham! God kills him with hail. She just didn't like him. Poor schmuck.

The next day, Sunday, I went outside to find that my car had been hammered. There were dents all over it. One very large piece of hail had landed in the middle of the windshield. I knew the exact size because it left a perfect imprint of itself, outside of which were a series of circular cracks. It looked like the ripple effect of a stone-thrown-into-water had been frozen onto my windshield. Another piece left the lower corner of the windshield on the driver's side nearly shattered. I could literally push the windshield at that spot in and out; it moved easily. One of my tires had been pierced by yet another piece of hail. I didn't really think about the hail damage, though. I was still too pissed about what had happened at Heather's party to pay much attention.

That night was the last show of the week and I went out with the staff afterward. Once again, Heather sat on my lap. She drove me back to the condo. I looked at her, "I have a real problem. I really want to kiss you."

"I really want you to kiss me."

We made out for a while.

"You know, Heather, I really wanted to stay last night."

"I really wanted you to stay last night."

What?! With her boyfriend there?! What kind of girl was I dealing with? Just what the hell kind of things went on in Texas?!

"What about Frank?"

"What about Frank?"

"He told me you guys were dating."

"What...he did? Ohhh...you know, he called me today to apologize for saying some silly things last night. He was drunk and said he might have said some stuff to you that didn't make sense."

That asshole. He cock-blocked me. While Heather was completely clueless, it was obvious to me that Frank liked her but was too much of a chicken shit to make a move. What had he meant when he referred to sleeping in her room? Heather had previously coordinated efforts with her roommates and friends for my anticipated sleepover. Frank and another guy always crashed at her place after parties there. The two guys would sleep in Heather's room, while Heather hoped she and I would stay in her roommate's room, as the roommate was spending the night at her boyfriend's. The icing on the cake was that Heather had asked her good friend Frank if she should invite me to stay or wait for me to make a move. He told her to wait for me. Of course, he knew how I would interpret things when he asked her where "they" were staying for the night, especially after I heard "they" would be in Heather's room. Very clever.

I invited Heather in but she had a final the next morning. We made dinner plans for Monday night (I had to stay in town an extra day to get my tire fixed), and she headed home. The next morning Tim headed back to Georgia and I had the condo to myself. I got my tire fixed and planned the date. It was a lot of fun. I rarely got to have a normal date as a comedian, so I really enjoyed putting it together. I had no idea what I was doing. Good thing I watched a lot of sitcoms. They became my reference.

I bought flowers and the ingredients for spaghetti, as well as a bottle of wine. Heather came to the condo and was very pleased to be on the receiving end of such romance. She was stressed out about finals, so she lay down on the floor after dinner and I gave her a massage. At that time my older sister was a masseuse (she's had a lot of careers), and I applied some techniques I had learned from her. Heather kept sighing and didn't protest when I removed her bra.

"Mmm, that feels so good, mmm."

"Most tension goes to the butt. Want me to massage there?"

To my delight she said, "Yes."

I massaged her voluptuous butt over her jeans. She threw me a curve ball when she suddenly rubbed herself against the carpet twice while murmuring, "Mmmm."

Damn my lack of experience! If only I had been the guy back then that I am today, I wouldn't have asked if I could touch her butt, I would have just done it. And I wouldn't have left her jeans on for the butt massage; I would have removed them without asking. (If she protested, I would have left them on, but I would have at least made the move.) When she rubbed herself against the carpet that would've been it. I would have rolled her over and whispered to her, "I can take care of that, too." We would have then made incredible love.

Unfortunately, I was not that guy back then. Instead, when she rubbed herself against the carpet, I stopped massaging her butt and just watched it pump the second time. *Wow.* She slid on her bra and sat up. We made out for a long time. She was by far the best kisser ever. She had this seductive way of gently sucking on my lower lip as she ended some of the kisses. No woman since has ever kissed me in that manner, despite the fact that I have used the method on them and they love it. Go figure.

We talked about her spending the night. She had an early final the next morning for which she still needed to study. I had to leave that same day to begin the drive to my next gig, which was in Denver. We knew that if we wound up in bed, we'd want to stay that way for the night; I don't know how we knew, we just knew. We decided it would be best for her to go home, taking a moment to again relive the tragedy of me not spending the night after the party. Damn that Frank! I walked her out to her car, which was parked only fifty yards from the condo. It took an hour to get there, though, because we kept stopping to kiss every two steps. I held her hand the whole time. It was the first time I felt like I was on a normal date. I loved it and didn't want it to end.

I kept in touch with Heather. Her father worked for a big airline, so she got to fly for free. She talked about flying up to Chicago, while

I worked hard to book another gig in her area. I got one, booked for five months after we met, at Hyena's in Fort Worth, sister city to Dallas. It was a low-paying isolated gig, but I wasn't going for the show. Heather and I wanted our moment and we were going to have it. In the interim, I was afraid Heather was going to lose interest or even worse, begin to think I had a woman stashed away in every town, that she was merely my "Dallas-Girl." My sisters didn't help in this regard, as they both kept telling me I needed to keep letting her know she was special.

I decided to say things to Heather I thought she wanted to hear. I told her I'd date her if I could, that I wasn't meeting any other women on the road. Two months after we met, I even sent her roses. (I couldn't be there, so I felt like I needed to do something.) Sending roses was apparently far more complicated than I realized. My sisters explained it to me, "If you send red, it will look like you're in love with her. Pink is like a softer kind of love. Yellow means you just want to be friends. White means peace."

Jesus fucking Christ, wasn't there an "I like you" color? How could there not be one? Why do women need to add such complexities to everything? Don't they realize that men aren't going to know any of this, that they will be reading into signals the men never knew they sent? I was about to give up on sending roses when I discovered one last color. "What about peach? Can I send peach?"

My sisters gave me the clearance to send peach roses. *Yeah!* I had something simple written on the card, like *Thinking of you.* Heather was out of town when the roses arrived. Her roommates accepted the flowers and when she returned home, she found them brown and lifeless. I had made my point, though. Truthfully, I didn't really want to send roses; I just didn't want Heather to feel forgotten.

About a month before my return trip to Texas, Heather told me a story. "This one time, I met this guy who I really liked a lot, but he was into me way too much and I knew we wouldn't end up together long-term. I moved without giving him my new address and phone number. I felt really bad about it, but I thought it was for the best."

I laughed, "Wow, that sucks for the guy."

Two weeks before I headed to Texas, I called Heather to make arrangements for getting together. Her phone was disconnected. I called a few more times. Nothing. She had long since quit waitressing at the Funny Bone, so I couldn't reach her there. I dropped her a postcard: *Hey Heather, will be out there soon. You forgot to give me your new number. Don't do me like that one guy. Ha ha.*

I never heard from Heather again. It wasn't until I was driving down to Texas that I realized I was that one guy. Heather hadn't told me a story about what she had done in the past, she had told me a story about what she was going to do, to me. I was driving all the way to Texas for no money, with no other gig booked in the area, to see a woman I wasn't going to see; a woman I wanted to be my first time.

Upon arriving in Texas, I frantically called every club within four hundred miles, trying to recoup some of my losses. I found an open emcee slot for the following week at the Comedy Corner in Oklahoma City. Although I was featuring at the time with headlining gigs scattered here and there, I took it. I should have just swallowed my losses and driven back to Chicago. The gig was horrible. The crowds were small and the other acts were two paranoid Texans. They were convinced that communists were taking over the U.S. government and needed to be stopped. They carried weapons of mass destruction in their shared pickup truck (shotguns and rifles, loaded with everything from bullets to rock salt—yeah, people actually use that stuff).

They kept spouting off about things to look for to spot a government turning communist. Apparently there is some sort of list that exists and they followed it to the letter. I only remember two of the five things to watch for: a government that removes all resistance and disarms its citizens. The two guys actually carried laminated cards listing the rules. According to them, the Democrats were communists because they wanted gun control laws. I pointed out that Republicans must be the true commies because by having no gun control laws, they were allowing so many deaths by guns that eventually the public would not resist at all when the government banned them. (Rule one: remove all resistance.)

This did not sit well with them. I had challenged their belief system and my argument made sense. They didn't know what to do or which party to endorse. Somehow I don't think either party really wanted their endorsement. I found it hilariously ironic that these two paranoid guys chose comedy as a potential career (they both had day jobs—traditional employment—and did comedy on the side).

To make matters worse, the club owner was a bitch, undoubtedly an angel of God sent to further disturb me. She gave me the wrong directions to the club the first night. They weren't even close to being accurate and I arrived late. At the end of the week, she refused to pay me for the first night because I had been late, even though I had still done my set, and even though it was her fault I had been late.

The next day I waited for Tweedle dee and Tweedle dum to leave for home. I then carried the TV out of the condo and put it into my car. I pawned it for the exact amount I had been stiffed, a trick I learned from another comedian. Harry Hickstein used to carry stuff right out of clubs when people stiffed him. No one even tried to stop him…with good reason. He was well over six feet, had large hands and a big build with a large gut. He looked like a biker, complete with an unkempt yellow beard that hung down to his belly button. His deep gruff voice could drown out a monster truck's engine. Yup, Harry could take just about whatever he wanted. In reality, he was a great big teddy bear and a really good guy.

I felt bad for the future comedians who wouldn't have a TV at the condo until the club replaced it, but then Heather felt bad for me too, so who gave a fuck? Thankfully, it was the only time I got stiffed (although one time I did have to stalk an agent at her home to collect my money). I was glad I took the TV; I later learned that the owner gave the wrong directions every week to new emcees. It was her way of making them late to save herself a little cash. What a bitch.

I learned seven things from Stephanie and Heather:
- Momentarily ditch friends as needed.
- Never go out of your way for a woman.
- Never book gigs just to see a woman.
- Don't tell a woman what you think she wants to hear.
- Leave romance for dating.
- Take advice from women about women with a grain of salt.
- How to deal with a woman's friend when he wants to be more than her friend.

I should have momentarily excused myself from Paul and his friends in Des Moines. I could have taken that moment to talk to Stephanie, introduce myself to her friends, and let them know I'd be right back. Everyone would have been happy and Stephanie and I would have had a very memorable night. In future situations that's exactly what I did, which led to the ultimate guy's fantasy for me one night in Atlanta.

I had subbed in for a feature one night in Columbia, South Carolina, at the Comedy House Theater. The owner of an elegant restaurant was in the crowd. He was so impressed with my show, he invited me to his restaurant for a free meal the next day. A year later he was scouting locations for another restaurant in Atlanta, where he saw that I was opening for the popular comedian Brian Regan at Punch Line. He came out to catch the show.

I noticed a pair of strikingly beautiful blonde twins during my set and used them for one of my talk-to-women bits. After the show they came over to me. Just before they arrived, the restaurant owner surprised me. He started going on and on. He was a really nice guy who had given me a five-course meal for free, so I didn't want to be rude. On the other hand, I could see the twins standing right behind him, waiting to talk to me. I thought of Stephanie and momentarily excused myself.

I talked to the twins and told them about the situation. They were at the show with dates anyway, so they just gave me their number and invited me over for a late-afternoon lunch the next day. They left and I went back to the restaurant owner. Everyone was happy. The next day I went to the twins' place for lunch and had a wild time. I arrived to find them both wearing the same yellow summer dresses, the kind that makes a guy go crazy. They didn't wear them for long. It was like a dream. Every now and then I still wonder if it wasn't a dream.

I went out of my way for Heather. I took a gig just to be near her. I sent her flowers in an effort to be romantic. I kept telling her the things I thought she wanted to hear instead of the things I wanted to say. Had I told her what I wanted to say, I would have kept things light and just flirted, which would have led to her being my first time, which is what I desperately wanted.

And then I took all the advice my sisters gave me as law. It turned out they were dead wrong. Each woman is different. While it's helpful to get advice from women about women, take it with a grain of salt. They are all different and they are not all on the same page.

I am still disappointed that I did not get to sleep with Heather. I wanted to share that with her and spend the night in each other's warmth. I would trade the night with the twins for a night with

Heather if I could, that's how much she meant to me. Of course, had it not been for Heather's friend Frank, Heather and I would have had that special night together. I hated him. I had never hated anyone before but I hated him.

Truthfully, I was jealous of Frank, as well as disgusted by him. He liked Heather. He had the chance to date her, to tell her how he felt, to see her all the time. Did he do it? Nope. He was a coward. So instead, he pretended to be her friend. He hung around her all the time. He gave her bad dating advice and cock-blocked. When she wanted me, he went to great lengths to ruin it for her. What kind of friend is that? He wasn't a friend, he was an asshole.

I had but a brief window of opportunity with Heather. I wanted her and I told her. I took that risk. I wasn't a coward. I could never date her, though; that opportunity wasn't afforded me.

I met a lot of Franks after that. Dozens of beautiful women I met seemed to have at least one guy friend who hung around all the time but who really wanted to date them. I call it Ross Syndrome, after Ross in *Friends*; he exemplifies the wanna-be-dating friend.

A lot of women like to date guys that start off as friends; they think it's endearing. They are flattered that the guy took so much time to know them and be near them. They wrongfully assume that he isn't looking to just get into their panties. His long commitment to the friendship is evidence of this. Bullshit.

Examine Ross as an example. Ross would have nailed Rachel anytime, anywhere, had he had the guts to make a move. Instead he endlessly pined away for her. He gave her bad dating advice, cock-blocked, and didn't give her messages from guys she'd met. He used friendship as a guise to be near her so he could block out other guys, learn everything about her, and hopefully take advantage of her when she was most vulnerable. He never appreciated the friendship because he was too busy using it to his advantage.

When Ross did date Rachel, he couldn't believe it. He didn't believe it would last, so he tirelessly worked to keep her. He was supportive in everything she did, as long as it served his purpose. He became jealous, protective, and eventually overbearing. When she got the job of her dreams, was he happy for her? Nope. All he could see was that the job put her in contact with an attractive guy, and that she had less time for him. Boohoo, poor Ross.

The most important part of both friendships and relationships is honesty. The wanna-be-dating friend isn't honest in the friendship, indicating he won't be honest in the relationship. He has extremely low self-esteem. The longer he's been friends with the woman, the higher he cranks up the pedestal on which he's placed her—completely unfair to her. He's been imagining what it would be like to sleep with her for so long, she stops being a woman and becomes a trophy. If they date, he eventually loses interest in her, which is why he is the guy most likely to cheat.

These guys ruin women for real men. Women can't figure out why their good friends changed after they started dating. When they catch him cheating or they break up, they are crushed because they've not only lost a boyfriend, they've also lost a good friend. They become hardnosed skeptics of all men. They think *if a friend could treat me this badly*...Instead of identifying the problem, they decide that their next boyfriend needs to be someone who they're friends with even longer than they were with this one. This only opens them up to guys with even lower self-esteem, who take longer to make a move, and will end up hurting them even more.

Realize something, ladies: Guys who pretend to be your friends in order to date are not true friends. They are low self-esteem losers. When they finally admit their feelings, or make a move when they smell vulnerability, get rid of them. Kick their asses to the curb, no friendship, no dating, nothing. Stop talking to them. They'll be upset but who cares? They've been nothing but disrespectful liars since the beginning and that will never change. Losing a friend will leave a void, but that void will fill with time.

Guys, dealing with a Ross is easy. First, he's identifiable by the fact that he'll never leave the woman alone with an interested guy. Or he'll say something to the guy when she's not around to make it appear as though he's dating her. Simply call him on it, right in front of the woman if necessary, "Dude, so how long have you liked her? Are you ever gonna tell her?"

Remember, he's a coward with low self-esteem. He'll be embarrassed and want to get away as soon as possible. He doesn't want her to know he's interested; that ruins his well-developed plan. He'll pull her aside in order to get her to leave with some badmouthing,

"That guy's a total jerk. You want him talking to your friends like that? Let's get out of here."

Let her go but beat him to the punch, out of his earshot.

"I'm sorry, my friend needs me for a second. I'll be right back. By the way, he doesn't like me."

"No problem, I understand. Trust me, though; I'm a guy, I know he likes you. I can prove it. When you get over there, he's going to badmouth me and say you should leave with him right now. He does it all the time, right? Tells you not to go out with this guy or that guy? He likes you."

She'll defend him, "He's not gonna try to get me to leave."

"Betcha a drink."

"Okay."

All the bases are covered. If she agrees to leave with him, she still has to buy that drink. Insist that she have another, too. He won't come anywhere near, instead preferring to stand back some distance. Talk her up, win her back. If she doesn't agree to leave with him, he'll be pissed, whine, and eventually storm out. Enjoy the free drink with her. On the off-chance that he doesn't badmouth you to her, she has to come back to collect her free drink. Apologize and win her over. See? All the bases are covered.

If a guy is dating a woman and she has wanna-be-dating friends, he has nothing to worry about. They won't make a move while she's dating someone; they're cowards. They will try to break up the happy couple, but as long as the boyfriend is nice and complimentary to her wanna-be-dating friends, it won't work. Being nice and complimentary to the wanna-be—while he is badmouthing you behind your back—makes you appear far more confident than he. Attacking the wanna-be is a bad idea. It makes you look weak; it fuels their fire. Also, attacking is moot; he is her friend and she's not going to change her mind about him.

If you are the wanna-be-dating friend, knock that shit off. Grow some balls and ask out the girl. Tell her something like, "I have a confession to make. I've been using our friendship to get closer to you in the hope that we will date. I realize this is wrong and unfair. Plus, it's been torture watching you suffer in other relationships."

Go on to discuss things. How does she feel? Everyone will be happier and relieved, which will build confidence. Wanna-be-dating friends badly need confidence.

Now, women, getting back to the *Friends* analogy, it is important to differentiate between Chandler and Ross. Chandler didn't like Monica throughout the friendship and then, when he did realize he liked her, he told her and took action. Chandler showed confidence.

Confident guys make good friends. How can a woman spot the difference in her friends? A confident guy tells a woman he likes her or makes a move shortly after he realizes it. He either asks a woman out, they end up becoming friends because she's not interested in dating, or they were friends and he suddenly finds himself liking her. So he acts accordingly to find out if the feeling is mutual. Consider two different guys who say these two different things to a woman:

"You know, I've recently found myself having feelings for you that go beyond the friendship we have."

"You know, I've liked you for a long time, pretty much since we met and became friends."

The first guy is confident and a keeper. He's honest and could make a good boyfriend. A woman should kick the second guy to the curb, even if she has feelings for him. He's dishonest and non-confident. He will only bring pain and misery. Trust me ladies, get rid of the wanna-be-dating friends. They account for the single biggest problem with the dating scene. Do not perpetuate the problem by dating these fools. This only encourages such behavior and creates more of them. Lose 'em; happiness depends on it.

 Quickie

One percent of the male population can maintain their erection after orgasm. I looked it up. Why? The first woman I slept with asked how I could go three times straight.

"What do you mean?"

"What do I mean? When guys are done, it goes limp."

I had no idea; I didn't discuss orgasms with other guys. I thought nothing of it but after having several girlfriends comment on it, I did some research. Again, this is just another example of why it can be very beneficial to talk about sex with partners.

Apparently, I'm in that one percent. I keep my erection after orgasm. There do seem to be some tricks to it, though. The first time or two I'm with a woman, I may not maintain because of the newness of her. It is extra exciting to see someone naked for the first time, as well as to touch her. (I'm a lights-on kind of guy. Surprise, surprise, eh?) If I'm extremely attracted to her, though, I do keep the erection. Once we become lovers, keeping the erection after orgasm is very common.

Women, you don't have a guy in that one percent of the male population and you want to keep his erection lasting as long as possible? Stop making all those sexy noises! That drives us to finish faster.

"Ooh, mmm, yes, aahh, thsss, harder, faster, slower, easy, yes, yes, YES!"

It drives us crazy! We love those sounds and when we hear them, we can't help but push toward the finish line. Want it to last longer? Then shut up, already! Better yet, try yelling out unsavory things.

"I hope I got rid of that toe fungus!"

"I have a yeast infection!"

"I hope my BO isn't making your eyes water!"

The guy will go longer, seriously, I'm not kidding. Unless, of course, he is totally turned on by stinky women with yeast infections and toe fungus, in which case he'll finish immediately. Sorry about that; my bad.

Wild Times

GETTING DITCHED BY HEATHER SENT ME INTO A WHIRLWIND. I DECIDED there was no more waiting around; I didn't need a special connection. The next hot woman I met was going to be my first time.

I met her in Ashland, Wisconsin. I'm no longer sure of her name. I guess that's weird, for a guy not to clearly remember the name of the first woman he slept with, but I've always marched to a different drummer. Besides, what does it really matter? She was a hot brunette with long hair, in her mid-twenties. She wore a pretty summer dress and sat up front at a show—a kick-ass one-nighter—and heckled along with her friend. I quickly put her in her place, and after the show she made it clear she wanted me to put her in her place back at my place…only not quickly this time. The three of us went to a diner to hang out. I think it was the only place open. We ran into her wanna-be-dating friend, who was there with two of his buddies. The six of us were the only customers in the place.

There was a jukebox and she selected some songs. Her wanna-be came over to our booth and tried to cock-block. He didn't stand a chance; I was now armed with plenty of knowledge and practice. I barely let him say a word to her.

"Hey, how are you? You guys—"

"You know, I don't wanna know how you are. I wanna know how you dance. Come on."

I grabbed her and pulled her out onto the floor.

"There's no dance floor here."

"There is now."

No sooner had we started to dance when he tried to cut in, "Excuse me, I'm gonna cut in."

"You live around here?"

"Yeah."

"Well, then you have all the time in the world to dance with her. I only have tonight, so save your dance for tomorrow."

"Excuse me? I—"

"We're dancing; tell her you like her on your own time."

I turned her away from him and we glided to another spot on the floor. He stood quietly, trying to figure out his next move. He started to walk over. I whispered into her ear, "You know what else I want to know?"

"What?"

"How you kiss."

I kissed her, just as he reached us. We started to make out. I really didn't need to push it that far, but it was less about him and more about Frank (Heather's wanna-be). I wanted to hurt him, to rob him the way Frank had robbed me. In fact, at that moment, he was Frank in my mind. The idiot stood beside us, still trying to cut in, "Ah, excuse me...excuse me..."

She let him have it, "What? What do you want? We're busy; I'll talk to you tomorrow."

He looked like his heart had just been ripped out. He waited, not knowing what to do or say, and then walked away. We danced for a little longer, then she decided she wanted to go skinny dipping. We drove her friend home, then headed out for some naked swimming. Damn, Lake Superior is freezing, even in the heart of summer. Eventually we found our way back to my hotel room, and I "became a man." I also got an education in talking dirty.

I took my pants off while she lay naked beneath me. She looked up at me, "Do you know how badly I want you to fuck me?"

"Ah...pretty badly."

I was completely caught off-guard. She kept going, "Do you like me pink and wet?"

"Yup."

I didn't even know what the hell she was talking about. Don't worry; eventually I caught on and threw my own dirty talk back at her.

I always appreciated it when a small-town woman hooked up with me. The smaller the town, the more I appreciated it. Small-town residents have to deal with a completely different set of problems than big-city dwellers. One of these problems is that there are no secrets in a small town. When a small-town woman left my hotel in the morning, the employee at the front desk just itched to tell someone. I caught a few of them making calls when I returned from walking girls out to their cars.

"You won't believe who I just saw leaving a guest's room."

I guess there's just not much else to do in a small town but be a busy body. I buried a lot of wanna-be-dating friends, even if I wasn't interested in the women. I just called them on it. I knew the women would be happier knowing these guys liked them. In fact, some of the women confessed they liked the guys, too, and they ended up dating. I was a matchmaker. For others, it didn't go quite so well.

My favorite idiot was a guy in Seymour, Indiana, a small town very close to Kentucky. A lot of the residents had southern accents. (The town may sound familiar because it's John Cougar Mellencamp's hometown.) I was in my mid-twenties at the time and there was a very pretty nineteen-year-old emceeing the one-nighter, which literally took place at the town hall. She aspired to be a comedienne and I liked her passion.

I had no interest in the girl. She was naïve and wide-eyed, more like a sixteen-year-old than a nineteen-year-old. She asked me a lot of questions about comedy while the feature was onstage (I was headlining), which I was happy to answer. Her idiot wanna-be-dating friend and two buddies approached me when she went to get some water. He actually told me that they had just gotten engaged. He had the foresight to realize I might question why she wasn't wearing a ring. He told me he was letting her pick it out herself the very next day. The damn fool. She returned before he left; of course the first thing I did was congratulate her.

"Congratulations fer what?"

"For what?"

I saw him swallow hard.

"For your engagement, of course."

She had no idea what I was talking about and shredded him, "Ah never wanna talk to you agin!"

She stormed off. I shrugged at him and he ambled away. It would have made a great Southwest Airline commercial. "Wanna get away?"

Armed with the aforementioned hard-learned lessons, I did well with women. I didn't sleep with many of them (remember, I never wanted sex to become routine, like brushing my teeth), but I did plenty of other things, and I did sleep with the ones I really wanted. Of course, I still had my failures. Why wouldn't I? God was still against me. I met a stripper in a small Texas town one night who was actually very hot. Outside of her, I've never met an attractive stripper, which is just one of the many reasons I've never been to a strip club. She was a tall, leggy blonde who came out to yet another one-nighter. I got a few soft kisses from her but couldn't seal the deal. I couldn't seal the deal with a stripper! That's like a Kennedy not being able to start a car while he's drunk.

Another time I was in Baltimore, playing one of the best clubs in the country, Slapstix. I always had great shows there and Baltimore audiences rocked. Near the club was a washtub bar. A washtub bar is a pretty simple and lucrative concept; they hire several hot women to wear the smallest bikinis they can fit into and stand in various places throughout the bar, behind washtubs full of ice and beer. The bar made a killing.

All of the washtub beauties were grad students, save one; she was a lifer. Every year I played Slapstix and went to the washtub bar a few nights after shows. All of the bikini models would be new each year except for her. The first time I saw her, she was the hottest woman there. She wore a small, sexy zebra-striped one-piece suit, the middle of which was gone, leaving most of her flesh exposed. Her hair was long and black. I couldn't get my feet to walk away from her. At one point I asked her to hold a test tube shot. She had nowhere to put it, so she told me to slip it between her cleavage, which was an awesome, natural C cup.

Before I knew it, I was doing test tube shots from her cleavage. One after another, I buried my face between her breasts and pulled out a shot with my mouth. The best part was it didn't cost me a dime. (Okay, that really wasn't the best part.) A bunch of fans from the comedy show paid for the shots. They wanted to do them themselves but were too nervous, so they kept paying to watch me go down. Hey, what choice did I have? The show must go on…Each year I returned, her breasts got bigger and bigger, her lips fatter and fatter, and her hair blonder and blonder. She got less and less attractive. The last time I went to the bar, I couldn't even bear to look at her. Her breasts were so big they arrived everywhere she went an hour ahead of her.

That last same visit to the bar, I also met a very pretty newbie, wearing a lime bikini. She was a blonde with short hair who stood about 5'5". She also had some nice natural C's. We got to talking and she mentioned she was doing some house-sitting in Cumberland, Maryland, the following week. I was going to be passing through Cumberland that week on my way to some college shows in West Virginia. She invited me to crash with her one night, so she wouldn't die from boredom.

"Will you be wearing that bikini?"

"Absolutely; they have a nice pool and a hot tub."

"I'm there."

I arrived at the house the next week. She answered the door wearing the bikini and invited me in. She walked around the whole time in that thing, blowing me kisses. She cooked a tasty dinner. We retired to the living room, where she sat beside me on the sofa. "I want to read a little bit first."

She lay down, placing her legs onto my lap. I began to stroke them, which distracted her reading, so she decided to flip and instead rest her back on my lap. After a while I began to softly rub her belly. She cooed and soon I was rubbing her breasts while I kissed her. I started to untie the strings to release her wrongfully imprisoned breasts when the doorbell rang. She sat up and called, "Hello?"

"Hey, baby; it's me!"

She jumped off the sofa, "I'll be there in a minute!"

She checked herself in the mirror and wiped my kisses from her mouth. She looked over at me and whispered loudly, "You're my cousin!"

She answered the door. A guy twice my size stood in the doorway.

"Oh my God, what a nice surprise!"

"Hey baby, I knew how lonely you were, so I thought I'd surprise you."

He picked her up in a big bear hug and gave her a kiss. She introduced me—her cousin—to her boyfriend. How nice of him to stop by. Instead of having sex with a hot little number, I got to sleep downstairs on the sofa and listen to her and her boyfriend have sex, off and on throughout the night. Good one, God, good one, especially with the timing. God plops the girl's boyfriend on the doorstep after I get all worked up and bothered, but just before I was about to see and have any real fun with her breasts. I would have left except I still didn't have contacts and couldn't see to drive safely at night. *I really need to get contacts* I thought as I listened to the bed bounce upstairs and her cry out her boyfriend's name.

Another time in Texas I met a very pretty model, almost my height. She had short dark hair. We went out to a club. When we decided to head back to my motel, a bunch of guys tried to keep her from leaving with me. I figured it worked once before, why not again? I slung her over my shoulder and carried her toward the exit. She had no complaints until we got to the door and she happened to check her bare neck, "Oh my God! My grandma's necklace, my grandma's necklace! Put me down, you idiot!"

Apparently her necklace, a family heirloom passed down generation to generation from her great grandmother, had fallen off while I was carrying her. It's amazing what bouncers will do for a babe that they won't do for other women or men. They stopped the music, turned up the lights, made an announcement, and everyone searched. I knew I had to be the one to find it or I was done. Remarkably, I did, in only ten minutes. It was near the exit. I went from zero to hero and we went back to my motel, whereupon getting out of the car she screeched, "Oh my God, oh my God! My purse, my purse!"

Oh my God! Well said. We went back to the club for her purse— which one of the bouncers was holding for her—and she ran into some of her girlfriends, who were just leaving. She turned to me, "You know, there's just been too many signs that this isn't meant to happen."

She said goodnight and left with her friends.

In Tucson, Arizona, where I worked with the hilarious Chris Fonseca, I secretly left Laffs Comedy Corner with a tall, beautiful brunette with long hair and big, full breasts. The club owner had been working on her for months but she was not interested. She took me to a dance club, where there was a long line to get in. I realized I had forgotten my ID. She insisted that I would not be able to get in without it and didn't want to give me a chance to try. Instead of grinding on the dance floor—which would have led to some great sex—we wound up in a quiet bar trying to carry on a conversation. It didn't work, and as Chris astutely pointed out later, I had blown my chance with her. He was right. I tried to get her to go out with me again later in the week but she wouldn't. All we shared the night we did go out was some soft kissing.

Mostly, though, I did well. I got plenty of dates and more when I wanted. I didn't do romantic things unless I got into relationships, I didn't go out of my way for a woman, and I never booked shows just to see one. If I returned to the area, I would call and she was either still interested or she wasn't. I didn't tell women what they wanted to hear, I told them what I wanted to say in the way they wanted to hear it. The difference? Consider Heather: I guessed at what to say to her—instead of saying what I wanted—based on my own concerns and my sisters' advice, not on anything she did. Now consider Julie: I told her what I wanted to say, the way she wanted to hear it. I reacted to what she did and said; I did not guess. I was successful with Julie, not Heather.

I also followed all the other lessons I've listed, like keeping things light and flirting a lot, not just during the initial meeting, but through first dates as well, even when women tried to be serious. Women call this "being mysterious." Oo-ooh. Dating articles and books always advise men to be mysterious to get women, but they don't typically define it or state why it works. Basically, being mysterious meant that women had to work to find out anything real about me. It didn't mean that I had a cool job, strange habits, or that I disappeared to somewhere unknown for hours at a time.

I don't know why, but having to dig to learn about a guy appeals very much to women. Ever notice how the conversation after sex can be very real and intimate? People are most vulnerable at that point. I had women sleep with me just because they wanted to reach that honesty with me, to get some of their questions answered. This is one reason why being mysterious can lead to more one-night stands and sex earlier in a relationship. Really, this strategy is misnamed mysterious. A better name would be evasive. All I did was dodge questions while making jokes.

"What are your goals, Ian?"

"Well, after I finish this beer, I plan to kiss you."

The woman would laugh, "I mean your long-term goals."

"Oh, well, sex isn't out of the question, if you play your cards right."

Again, a laugh. That's what women call mysterious. Men call it evasive. I've learned that's a key difference between men and women; we both call the same things by different names. It creates some basic fallacies. It would help both men and women to realize these fallacies, but most don't. One fallacy is that women are excellent communicators while men suck at it. The truth is men are good communicators. When something is on a man's mind, he decides whether it is worth mentioning or not. If it is, he communicates it directly; if it's not, he lets it pass.

Women are horrible communicators. They can't decide if what's on their minds is worth mentioning or not. It gets under their skin. If they decide it's not worth mentioning, it might still come out later, oftentimes in an argument. If a woman does decide something is worth mentioning, she communicates it indirectly. She hints at it. Her guy may even have to ask, "Honey, what's wrong?"

"If you don't know, I'm not going to tell you."

Sound familiar? What do people really mean when they say men are bad communicators? They mean men are horrible at reading emotions, both their own and women's. A man may be upset and not know why. He may not know what he's feeling. He may have a hard time assessing his lover's emotions. This is why women will often give men the "if you don't know" line. Women are much better about reading their own emotions, as well as their lover's.

I also learned that women like boldness. I got bolder and bolder with them. One time I made a date with a woman named Lynn, who lived in Michigan. I was passing through on my way to Canada and had met her a few weeks before while on vacation. She had just broken up with her fiancé and was temporarily living with her older brother. The plan was for me to crash at their place for the night.

The date was pretty lame. She was very quiet and I ran out of things to talk about, which says a lot. At one point—after five straight minutes of agonizing silence—I attempted to both break and acknowledge the awkwardness with a joke, "So...do you floss?"

"Yes."

We went back to silence. Back at her place, we just sat around, doing nothing. She was quite beautiful, with long blonde hair, a sexy smile, blue eyes, a very sweet ass, and big, full breasts. She stood around 5'5" and was twenty-three, three years younger than me. When it came time to call it a night, I prepared a place to sleep on the floor. Lynn slept on a futon beside me. Her brother slept in the same room; they hung a blanket from the ceiling each night to divide it. They had two dogs, which I thought might bother me while I tried to sleep, but after I lay down, it looked like it wouldn't be a problem. I was only on the floor for a few minutes when Lynn invited me into bed with her.

I didn't know what to make of being invited into her bed. Was it an invitation to fool around or just to keep me out of the dogs' reach? I lay beside her and tested the waters. I stroked her back over her shirt. She didn't give any response at all, positive or negative. I slid my hand under the shirt and stroked her back. Again, no response. I worked my hand lower and lower. I dropped my hand down to her butt and slowly began to rub it over her shorts. No response. I decided to get daring. I listened for movement from her brother's side of the hanging blanket; shit, he was still awake. I didn't care. I decided to slip my hand between her shorts and panties.

Oops, she wasn't wearing panties. She grabbed my hand and pulled it out of her shorts. I went back to caressing her ass over her shorts. She didn't object. My hand soon found its way down her shorts again. This time she left it there. Her butt was nice and cool. It was very round and firm; it felt extremely good. I began to whisper into her ear and give her soft kisses on the cheek. I rolled her over, rubbed her stomach, and then slowly slid my hand up her shirt. She softly sighed. She had an exceptional pair of breasts. Surprisingly, her nipples were small, very small considering she had such big breasts.

I pulled her shirt up over her breasts and fell in love with her nipples. When she got excited, they formed these perfect little hourglasses, which were just the right size for sucking easily. I didn't have to open my mouth wide or anything (I'm pretty lazy). It was effortless and very fulfilling for both of us. We fooled around for a while. Whenever her brother coughed or stirred, we got quiet. After a moment, we would start up again. We came very close to having sex before we stopped.

My boldness gave a whole new meaning to PDA. I played mini-golf at the Mall of America with the emcee the week I worked Acme in Minneapolis. Acme was perhaps my favorite comedy club in the U.S.—an absolute blast with fabulous crowds. The emcee was a short, pretty, thirty-one-year-old brunette with short hair and big breasts. I liked her a lot simply because she was a talented comedienne. I was twenty-three at the time.

The golf course was crowded and we were getting bored. Each hole we had to wait for like six families ahead of us to putt. Behind us was a line of six or seven other families, waiting for their turns. It was ridiculous. There wasn't anything else to do, so we started to kiss between holes. After a few holes it got hot and heavy. My hands found their way up her shirt while hers stroked my crotch outside my jeans. I could hear the disgusted families chatter behind us. She kept stopping me, noting that parents were getting upset. I would make some rude, witty comment loud enough for the families to hear, but not directly to them.

"Ian, Ian; come on, we need to stop."

"I'm trying to teach these kids something."

She'd laugh and we'd resume groping one another. At one point I actually removed her bra and slid it out from under her shirt. One of the fathers went to get security. His wife had a small rack.

"Oh my God, that guy went to get security. We're going to be banned from the Mall of America."

"No we're not, just give him your bra. Tell him his wife will grow into it."

She laughed and we went back to business. Eventually, most of the families quit playing and we breezed through the back nine.

Another time, in my late twenties, I was out with my friend John at a bar in Chicago called The Irish Oak. They have live Irish folk music, which is a nice change of pace from rock music in bars. I was hoping a particular group would be playing but they weren't. I asked around to see if any of the other patrons knew what nights they played the bar, but none of them did. John started to talk to a woman standing near us. Her friend was a beautiful brunette with long hair, in her early twenties. She was tall and had a very nice body, along with deep brown eyes. I innocently asked her if she knew anything about the band I liked.

"Sorry, don't know them; I'm not from here."

"No? Where are you from?"

"I live in Ann Arbor, Michigan. I'm about to start law school there. This is probably my last weekend out for a long, long time."

Ann Arbor is home to one of the best law schools in the country. I wasn't looking to meet anyone that night, but with her falling onto my lap, how could I waste the opportunity? I knew instantly that she was looking for one last wild night before heading into the study dungeon for the next few years. The four of us headed a few blocks away to El Jardin, a Mexican restaurant and bar with a racy dance club upstairs. I danced with Amber—the law student—for a little bit, but she seemed totally disinterested. We went and sat down, leaving John and her friend on the dance floor.

Things were going very badly. Amber hardly said a word to me. She wouldn't even look at me; but, she hadn't left. I was desperate to break the tension, so I did the only thing I could think of; I turned her head toward mine and kissed her. To my surprise, she immediately reciprocated. Things got out of hand pretty fast and we were asked by a bouncer to leave. We found John and Amber's friend on the dance floor and we all left. As we walked back to the girls' car, I kept slowing Amber down. I'd stop her and we'd make out for a while. Her friend would eventually yell from ahead and we would resume walking. We reached their car, which was parked on a residential street, and I pulled Amber aside. "I want you to come home with me."

She shook her head. "I can't."

"Sure you can."

"No, I can't."

She refused to come home with me. I figured what the hell, I was going to get what I could while I could. I suggested we sit on someone's lawn. It wasn't long before she was completely topless and I was on top of her. I pulled her jeans halfway down and slipped my fingers inside her. This was not a quiet street. Every few minutes, people heading home from the closing bars walked by. They catcalled and whistled.

"That's a nice move."

"Can I get on when you're done?"

"Ooh, me next, me next!"

I looked over at Amber's friend every now and then, who couldn't quite see what was happening because I was blocking her view with my body. She eventually called to us, "Here, why don't you guys sit in the car for a while, while we go for a walk?"

Amber agreed to that. I put her clothes back on and we got into the car. I gave her one last chance but she still refused to come home with me. Within a few minutes she was naked, sitting in the driver's seat. I sat in the passenger's seat with my pants half-off. She didn't want me inside her and she wouldn't go down on me, so I fingered her while she caressed me. Cars honked as they drove past. A few passing taxis stopped and watched for a while. I finished and pulled up my pants, then helped her put her clothes back on. It was none too soon. Her friend returned with John just as I zipped up Amber's jeans. John and I said goodnight to the girls and walked home. I told him what happened and asked him a question, "Why didn't you talk to Amber? Why her friend?"

He shrugged, "I figured I didn't have a chance with Amber, so I went after her friend."

Remember what I said about settling and assuming? Being bold and getting used to rejection? John screwed up big time. Had he approached Amber instead of her friend, it would have been him getting honked at by cabs. She was out to let her hair down in a big way and John missed out because he didn't try to talk to her. His loss was my gain.

In my mid-twenties, I met another comedienne at yet another great comedy club, Yuk Yuks in Edmonton. (All the Yuk Yuks—a comedy club chain in Canada—rock.) She was an open-miker who stopped in to catch the pros' sets. After the show, she held my hand as we walked through the parking garage to her car. She was in her mid-thirties, blonde with short hair and a firm body. We started to kiss. She stopped me, "I'm married."

I was past the point of no return. We made out for a while. As things progressed, she got less and less married.

"I don't think I love my husband anymore."

"We haven't really spoken much this entire week."

"We're actually separated."

She put an end to it when I suggested we get into her car.

"I can't do this."

"Okay; I understand. If you change your mind, you know where to find me."

I tuned and began to walk away.

"That's it?"

"What else is there to say?"

She showed up again at the last show of the week. We went back to my hotel room. She told me she and her husband were definitely separated. We got naked but she would only let me screw her in the butt. Afterward, noticing that I was still saluting, she gave me a hand job. It took forever. I kept pushing and pushing, "Think of how long this is taking. I could be inside you this whole time. Wouldn't that feel good?"

"Mmm, I was just thinking about that."

She resisted, though. After I finished, she informed me that when she said separated, she meant that she and her husband slept in separate beds in the same room. I was angry about this and sent her home. I didn't give her cab fare or even walk her to the door of my room, let alone outside to the street.

I learned five things from these events:

- Always carry ID.
- Talking is not always necessary.
- I was capable of doing things I promised myself I would never do, namely having an affair.
- The key to good anal sex.
- Why women like jerks.

Always carry ID. Had I had mine in Arizona, I would have had some great sex. Instead, I ended up boring the poor girl with monotonous conversation.

Talking is not always necessary to build rapport and have sex. This was quite a novel discovery for me. My entire life revolved around talking. It was my job. It was how I got bookers to give me work. It was how I got free stuff in exchange for comedy passes to shows (like oil changes, car washes, taxi rides, games of laser tag, horseback rides). Talking was how I kept in touch with my family and friends. Most importantly, it was how I maintained a social life. When I hit a new town, I hung out in the tennis ball aisle of Sport Mart, where I got pickup games against people buying balls. I introduced myself to strangers who arrived at restaurants at the same time as me, and joined them for lunch. Talking was everything. It was a big shock to learn that I could get women naked without having to say more than a few words. Since then, I've had sex with several women who I went on dates with and had almost no conversation. I've fooled around with bunches of others.

I never thought I could have an affair. It simply wasn't possible. I would not sleep with someone's wife. Yet, I did. True, she told me her marriage was all but over, but I knew she was lying. I knew she let me do her only in the butt because she felt guilty. Worse, I was mad at myself for being with her and I took it out on her. I'm sure she felt very small and alone leaving my hotel.

The married woman talked me through our sexual encounter. The key to good anal sex is to move extremely slowly; slower than slow-motion. It's the best way to keep the woman from being uncomfortable or feeling pain. Lotion can help, but it isn't necessary and the sex still needs to be performed slowly.

Why do women like jerks? Ah, yes; the age-old question men ask themselves. Actually, women probably ask themselves the same question. We've already covered why trixies and women avoiding accountability like jerks.

It's not just women who like jerks; it's everyone. Being around a jerk is like going to a movie. We get to step outside ourselves. We get to watch somebody say the things we want to say sometimes, do things we wish we could do, and generally not care. Wouldn't it be nice to just not care for a change? Caring can be such a weight. Jerks free us. We either get to watch them amuse us or they involve us in their antics. When we tire of them, we simply stay away from them, until the next time we need a jerk-fix. Jerks are kind of like nieces and nephews that way. I love playing with my nieces and nephews, but when they completely wipe me out, which they often do, I take them home and leave, free again from their antics. Basically, Jerks are novelty acts. When the novelty wears off, we have no use for them. Jerks have a huge need for us, though; they always need an audience. One can't be a jerk without an audience.

Women are drawn to jerks sexually for the same reasons. A jerk will push a woman to test her boundaries. Maybe he'll get her to have sex in a public place, or have a threesome, or suck on her tits fifteen feet away from her brother, on the other side of a blanket. This is why women at certain ages are more apt to be attracted to jerks than women at other ages. Coeds and women just out of college are often doing a lot of sexual exploration; a good time for them to be with jerks. Women just getting out of bad or frustrating relationships, especially long-term ones, also seem to be attracted to jerks.

The problem women run into with jerks isn't with the jerks; it's with themselves. Women often aren't honest with themselves. They tend to confuse what they wish they wanted with what they actually want. Check out Match.com sometime. Almost every woman on the site lists boldness as a turn-on. I know that's accurate because I've seen boldness work with women time and time again. Scores of women also mark brainiac as a turn-on. Bullshit. I have yet to see a single woman respond favorably to a brainiac. These women *want* to be attracted to brainiacs, so they mark it down, thinking a brainiac will contact them and they will talk to him, and then fall for him. It's not going to happen. They are being dishonest with themselves.

It's the same thing with jerks. Women think they can emotionally detach themselves from the sex they have with a jerk, and thus not be hurt by him. They believe they can kick him to the curb whenever they so desire. Inevitably, they become emotionally attached to him, though; it's simply how women work. Emotion is a big part of sex for women, while it isn't necessarily for men.

Women then find themselves in the difficult position of trying to make the jerk something more than a novelty act, also known as trying to "change the guy." That's a tough trick and once again, the women are not being honest with themselves. They started off telling themselves they didn't care if the jerk just wanted sex, that's all they wanted, too. Later, they find themselves trying to change the jerk because they care deeply for him, which is what they told themselves they didn't want. They confused what they wanted with what they wish they wanted. Women wish they could be emotionally detached from the sex with a jerk, but they can't. The result is an invention called chocolate.

QUICKIE

GET A PRETTY WOMAN'S NUMBER? CALL HER FOR DATES, ONLY TO GET THE runaround from her time and time again?

"Oh, I'm not sure what's going on this weekend, yet."

"I'm not sure, yet; I'll get back to you."

Does she still keep in touch, though, and return calls or emails every now and then? Frustrating, isn't it? What's a guy to do?

Tell her when and what the date is going to be but ask her to choose the place. It works; I've done it many times.

One time I met a pretty woman on the beach. We started swapping emails and I decided I wanted to get to know her better. I called her up and asked her out. (Always ask a woman out for the first date in person or over the phone. It's fine to use email to make arrangements, but not to ask her out.)

She was busy and didn't know when she would be free. I went through this a few times; I would ask her out, she would give me the runaround. She kept returning my calls and emails, though, so she was interested in me in some capacity. One day I sent an email just asking her what she was up to for the week.

Not sure, yet, how about you?

I replied, *Well, Thurs. I'm having dinner with you, 8pm. Where are we going?*

Her reply?

Wow, you really blew me away with that. Okay.

We went out and had a nice time, although there wasn't much chemistry. We still keep in touch and are friends. Telling her we were going out worked. She simply needed that little nudge. She's an attractive woman and probably gets asked out a lot. I needed to separate myself from the pack. It was also a bold move.

Just FYI, I tried the brainiac thing with a few women, just to be sure it's not a true turn-on. I emailed them all the following statement: *The square of the hypotenuse on any right triangle is equal to the sum of the squares of its two legs.*

Nothing. Stick with boldness.

man in the mirror

Dom Irrera—a big name in comedy—was very good to me. I worked with him twice, once in Florida and again a few months later in St. Louis. He is the only other act I know, besides myself, who can eat right before a show. Most comedians are too anxious to eat right before they go onstage but that was never a problem for Dom or me. At the end of our week in St. Louis, he walked up to me, "Hey, good working with ya. Is there a club you've been trying to get in with for a while, that you haven't been able to?"

"The only club I haven't been able to get in with is Punch Line, out in San Fran."

"Cool," he shook my hand and left.

Punch Line was the premiere club in the country at the time. They had a room in San Francisco and another in Sacramento. If an act headlined Punch Line, he was practically guaranteed headlining work anywhere. I had been trying to get in with them for a year without any luck. A few days after my second gig with Dom, Punch Line called me, "Sorry we haven't returned your calls; we have a lot of acts, all of them big names. It's very hard to break in here. We've heard good things about you, though, and we'd like to book two weeks, one in San Fran and the other in Sacramento."

Just like that I was in. I knew Dom had put in a good word for me. If he hadn't, I'd still be calling Punch Line today, nearly ten years later, still without success. The kicker was, they booked me to headline. I was expecting to get an emcee gig the first-time-around, feature if I was lucky. I got the headliner spot…well, at least during the week. Punch Line headlined top talent during the week. On the weekend, a big name act came in to headline, while the weekly headliner moved down to feature. The week I worked Sacramento the slated weekend headliner was Damon Wayans.

Outside of Joan Cusack, I have never met a happy celebrity. They were all nice, genuinely good and friendly people, but they weren't happy. They all gave me the same advice, "Cherish your anonymity while you can. It's something you don't miss until it's gone, and once it's gone, you can never get it back."

Celebrities are constantly hounded. Fans always want autographs. Businesses want endorsements. The media waits around every corner, ready to pounce, hoping they'll fuck up something. Imagine living life as carefully as possible not to make a mistake, knowing that it would be blown out of proportion, exaggerated and twisted, maybe even never forgotten. Not exactly comforting, is it?

Additionally, celebrities are responsible for a lot of peoples' well-being. If their show gets cancelled or they make a career change, a lot of people are out of work, not just them. They have agents, publicists, managers, business managers, roadies, hair stylists, and all sorts of people who make their sole income off them. That's a lot of pressure to put on one person. Imagine losing a job and having to fire some of these people. Hell, I got so busy touring, I hired a business manager to pay all my bills and make some travel arrangements, just to help keep my head above water. I felt bad letting him go when I quit the road, and I wasn't even his only client. Celebrities' affairs are so complicated they often become the only client for their employees.

So, it's easy to understand why most of the celebrities I met were not happy. Damon Wayans was no exception. The green room was stacked high with videos of his movies; the club's staff had brought them in for him to sign. He had to remember which boxes went with which names. Every local comedian, professional and amateur, stopped in to suck up. They harassed him constantly, "Can I get you a drink?"

"Want some water?"

"Do you need anything from the store?"

Once he sneezed and one of them left the green room. He returned a few seconds later with a napkin from the bar, which he handed to Damon, "Here ya go."

They all wanted favors in return for their sucking up.

"Can you get me in with your agent?"

"Can you make a call to get me in with the Improv in Hollywood? I'm sure with a call from you they'd give me mic time."

What most people forget when they get around celebrities is, celebrities are people, too. They have needs and desires just like everyone else. Few people take a moment to hear their gripes; instead they bombard them with their own. Everyone assumes fame brings complete contentment. I treat celebrities just like I treat everyone else. It makes for very interesting conversations. They have a lot of good advice, which makes sense; they've reached an extremely high level of success. I ask them how they're doing, how their trip was, where they're headed to next, what projects they're working on, and so forth. Damon was not in the best of states when we met. His career was in a slump.

"This industry is unforgiving. I was making five million a picture. I made a few bad movies, my next film I'm making twenty grand. I'm paying my own way to New York to film my scenes."

That's quite a pay cut. His dating life was in a slump, he was divorced, and he was having trouble bonding with his son. Every time Damon took the little guy somewhere, like to Disneyland, he was bombarded by fans. This made it hard for him to get quality time with his son. He handled it all very well. He didn't complain, he took everything in stride, he knew it went with the territory. The second to last night of the week, another celebrity comedian—and good friend of Damon's—showed up at the club. I won't reveal his name because I'm going to write some unflattering things about him, and mudslinging is not the point of this story or book. For easy reference, let's call him Chuck.

After the show, Damon, Chuck, a few guys who had been sucking up hard to them, and I piled into Damon's limo. We headed out for some major partying. It was quite eye-opening. We pulled up along convertibles full of sexy young women and told the limo driver to tell them where we were going. He would roll down his window each time, tell the car overflowing with T&A who was in the limo, and then tell them where we were headed. I was flattered that he mentioned Damon, Chuck, and me each time. "Damon Wayans and Ian Coburn are in this limo."

The girls all assumed I must be important. I suppose the driver did it because while everyone else had been busy sucking up to Damon, I had taken time to chat with him. He must have appreciated it.

As we neared our destination, the driver called ahead to let the staff know we were near, so that they could make all the necessary arrangements. Shortly thereafter, we arrived at some fancy club. There was a huge line of people waiting to get in, winding down the block like a snake. (In California, people seem at home standing in long lines. I've seen lines to get into a club reach numbers over a hundred. Perhaps it's the nice weather. Not so much in Chicago. In Chicago, if there are more than twenty people waiting to get in, most people just head to another club.) Everyone was well-dressed, as the club had a strict dress code, and there were a lot of hot women. We pulled up in front of the club. Bouncers radioed each other, "The Robin has landed." What were we, spies? We waited while the bouncers pushed the inquisitive crowd back and cleared the entrance. They opened the limo door for us and we filed out. The crowd went nuts. They started to scream and wave. It was ridiculous; all this for getting out of a limo. The bouncers looked at us, "Gentlemen, who would you like to see from this line in the club?"

We looked the line over and selected a dozen or so of the prettiest women. The bouncers retrieved them. It was unbelievable. The "chosen ones" ditched their friends, boyfriends, and even fiancés to join us. We waited a few minutes until all the women in the convertibles we had invited arrived. Damon gave the order, "Let them in, too."

"No problem, Mr. Wayans."

We went into the club. The bouncers cleared a wide path before us, leading us back to a large roped-off section, where we sat down to be treated like kings. One by one, every important person affiliated with the club came by to greet us. We met the night manager, the day manager, the general manager, the publicity representative, the special events planner, the owner, and so forth. All of them invited us back any time.

"Even if Mr. Wayans isn't with you, come back whenever you want. Everything will be on us, including accommodations if you need them. We have several suites upstairs."

I replied, "Cool. Is there a password?"

"A password? No. Why?"

"No reason."

Damon chuckled; he knew what I meant. So much for the club's empty invitation. If I had shown up the next night, they wouldn't have recognized me. I bet they wouldn't have let me wash crud off their windows. It was all simply part of sucking up to Damon and Chuck, which is why I made a joke about whether there was a password. A group of comedians hitting on women would make a great reality show. Imagine the guy who can talk to anyone in any situation and spin words as needed. Now take him to the nth degree. Now multiply him by three, the typical number of comedians out together after a show. It's like a nature program. The males work to impress the females, each trying to outdo the others. Women love wit and confidence, and the comedians give them heavy doses of each. When most guys go out, they split up the women they meet, each targeting a different one. Why do that, when—if a guy plays his cards right—it's possible for him to get more than his share? A comedian's attitude is more along that line of thinking. He better be good; the least competitive comedian is the loneliest.

I was good. On some nights I made dates for the whole week, while the other acts couldn't even get digits. One time I made out with a woman before saying goodnight to her and her friends. I went back to my hotel room and her friend called me from the lobby twenty minutes later. She came up to my room.

The night with Damon and Chuck was effortless. We filled up the roped-off area with invited women. Most of them figured I must be someone important. They didn't want to admit they didn't know who I was, so they pretended they had seen me on TV. I had made several television appearances but I doubted any of them had actually seen them.

After we tired of one batch of girls, we sent them out of the roped-off area and the bouncers brought us a new group. We met four separate groups of women in this manner. Unfortunately, I had no interest in any of them. They were lost in a world of makeup, fashion, and gossip. Some of the local suck-up acts made dates for the following week. Damon and Chuck had a tougher time. They would be heading back to Hollywood in two days, so they weren't looking for dates, they were looking to get laid. So far, they were striking out.

The night wore on and we decided to leave. On the way out,

Chuck, in an all-out-last-Hail-Mary effort, hit on a girl who had been standing near the roped-off section all night, hoping she would be invited in. She was obviously disappointed each time we passed her over for other girls. She was thrilled at the offer and agreed to come with us to Sacramento's equivalent of Denny's. We hung out there for an hour or so, poor Damon being bombarded with questions while Chuck worked on the woman.

"What was it like to work with Bruce Willis? What's he like?"

"What other celebrities do you know, bigger than you?"

That's another downside of being a celebrity. People always seem to want to know about the bigger stars they've worked with. There's always a bigger star. It's insulting. That's like me meeting a woman and asking if she has any available pretty friends.

When it came time to leave, we waited by the exit while Chuck worked on the girl. She would not leave with him and he had to settle for making out with her in the booth. When his tongue tired, he joined us to leave. She was very excited because he told her he'd leave her six tickets at the box office for the next night's show. She had to promise to stop by the green room afterward.

The next night was the last show of the week. Damon finished signing the stacks of videos and we waited with his friend in the green room after the show. A bouncer came in and talked to Chuck, "There's a woman out here who says you asked her to stop by after the show. Can I bring her in?"

"Where is she? Is she just outside the door?"

"No, I made her wait back near the bar."

Chuck got up and looked out the green room door. I could see the girl from the other night standing at the bar with several of her friends. She was very animated.

"She looked better when I was drunk. Tell her I don't know who she is."

He sat back down.

"Yes, sir."

The bouncer left to deliver the message. I stood outside the green room to see what would happen. I watched the bouncer tell her in front of her friends. She was devastated. They pointed and teased her, "I knew you didn't know him! Let alone make out with him!"

"Come on; tell us how you really got the tickets."

She started to bawl. Talk about a Southwest Airline commercial. "Wanna getaway?" More like, "Wanna be dead?"

I returned to the green room, thinking I could help her. I sat down and waited for a moment before speaking to Chuck, "That girl from last night is crying. Her friends are all teasing her, saying they knew she was lying about meeting you."

I figured upon hearing such news, he'd go fix things. Instead, he just shrugged. "That's life."

I learned five things working with Damon Wayans:
- I prefer the girl-next-door type of woman.
- Even celebrities struggle with women.
- What I looked like in the mirror.
- I never want to lose my anonymity.
- Balance is the key to happiness.

Most of the women I met after shows or at clubs were dolled-up hotties, or obnoxious, obese women. Those are the types that typically have the conviction to approach acts. The girl-next-door women are too shy and composed to fight their way through the other women to talk to acts.

I didn't mind meeting beautiful, made-up, sexy women or obese ones. Nothing happened with either because neither appealed to me. The made-up women bored me with talk of fashion and questions about what celebrities I had met. They wore too much makeup; who knew what I would have awakened next to in the morning? Knowing God, probably a guy with a beard named Pete. The obnoxious, obese women were annoying. They tried too hard and usually spent their time ripping on the pretty ones. They didn't seem to understand that it wasn't a good idea to point out women who were skinnier and prettier than them. This was actually their pick up strategy.

"Oh, look at her; that skinny little tramp with big tits. You know they're fake. She probably puts out right away."

Think so? Thanks, I'll go over and talk to her. Have a good night.

Plus, I've never been attracted to obese women. It's nothing intentional, I simply don't feel any chemistry, much like how I feel about Asian women. There are plenty of women who aren't attracted to me because I'm skinny. That's simply how chemistry works. I have heavy friends who are all very nice and sweet, not obnoxious or rude. I just don't like being around obnoxious, rude women—heavy or slim.

What I dreaded were the moments when I would meet heavy and dolled-up women at the same time. That was always disastrous and I always wished I had a gun, so I could blow my brains out. The sexy women always arrived first. The heavy women then barged in, interrupting them. That's where the trouble began.

"Excuse me, we were talking to him."

"Oh, I'm sorry. I didn't see you, Miss Skinny Tart. Why don't you eat a sandwich? Then maybe people could see you."

"Well I would, but it looks like you already ate them all."

It was frustrating, sitting there caught in a pointless weight battle, while watching the girl-next-door women leave the club. D'oh! Usually I just waited for the right time to quietly sneak away. Sometimes, though, I snapped, "I can save you guys a lot of time and arguing; none of you have a chance."

I realized I prefer the girl-next-door types. They tend to be very pretty without the obsession over makeup and fashion. They have lots of other topics they like to discuss; some even play sports.

Everyone assumes celebrities can have whatever they want, whenever they want it; including women. Not true. I watched both Damon and Chuck strike out repeatedly.

Chuck was an utter ass. How could someone treat another person with such indifference? And why? Was he punishing her for not sleeping with him the night before? I don't care how much fame or fortune a person has, no one has the right to treat a person with such horrible disregard. Who would do that? What kind of man would make out with a woman one night, then deny knowing her the next? What kind of man would make her cry and humiliate her in front of her friends? What kind of man would...undress a woman and suck on her tits fifteen feet away from her brother on the other side of a blanket? What kind of man would screw another man's wife in the butt? Fondle a naked woman on a lawn or in a car for the entire world to see? Point to women at a club to have them brought over, then send them away when he decided he didn't like them, as though they were cattle? Apparently me.

Meeting Chuck was like looking at the man in the mirror. I did not like the reflection. There is a thin line between being playfully obnoxious to get acts of intimacy from a woman and being a jerk. I had crossed that line. How? When? I don't know. I only know that night I didn't like myself. I decided to make some changes. The first thing I did was to try and right Chuck's wrong. I caught up to two of the girl's friends in the parking lot. "Hey, I was with them the other night. She does know him and they did make out."

They didn't believe me.

"Thanks for trying to help her, dude, but we know it's not true. She does this from time to time; tells crazy lies. We'd only believe it if it came from him and since it's not true, that's not going to happen."

I couldn't fix that but I could change myself. The first question I had to answer was: Why did I behave like a jerk? Simple; it worked. Men behave like jerks because it works. Among the previous reasons we've discussed as to why women like jerks, there is yet another.

Some women feel the need to change a man. I think it helps them separate themselves from other women; it gives them an identity. I had women want to sleep with me, who said all kinds of things which told me they thought they were going to change me.

"After a night with me, your life will be changed forever."

"I bet you'll quit the road after one night with me."

I never slept with any of these women. I felt that there was something inherently wrong with them. These are the type of women who tend to become bitter and angry with men when they fail to change them. They are needy and obsessive. Frankly, these women remind me of the chick in *Fatal Attraction*. No thank you; I'll pass.

Anonymity is something I'm not willing to lose. As a popular name on the comedy circuit, I had my share of people stopping me on the street for autographs and buying me free meals and drinks. This was always very flattering and I didn't mind in the least. I also had my share of weirdos, women who harassed me, drunk people calling me at four in the morning to tell me jokes they just heard, and a few people who wanted me to jumpstart their comedy careers. Imagine dealing with that a hundred fold. And then there's also the media, who would bother my neighbors, friends, family, as well as dig through my garbage. That would be annoying, having to worry about what was in the trash before throwing it out, in case a reporter could find something in it that could be made to appear scandalous.

The key to happiness is balance. That's why so many celebrities aren't happy; they don't have balance. And that's why Joan Cusack is happy. She has a solid career, a family, and resides where she is unmolested by adoring fans and media. She has balance.

I decided I no longer wanted to work the road. It wasn't giving me balance. I couldn't date, I couldn't see my friends, I couldn't see my nephew (I only had one at the time; now I have three nephews and two nieces), I couldn't play in any sports leagues, and I couldn't write screenplays, as there wasn't enough time between traveling, booking gigs, and gigging. Writing screenplays was fast becoming what I really wanted to do.

Quickie

WOMEN OFTEN COMPLAIN ABOUT MEN WHO SLEEP WITH THEM, THEN NEVER call again. They assume that these men were only after sex. In some cases they are right; in some cases they are wrong.

Hormones are powerful things. Believe it or not, there are times when a guy thinks he really cares for a woman a lot, only to find out after sleeping with her that he doesn't. He's been duped by his hormones. He doesn't want to lead the woman on, so he doesn't call. There was nothing intentionally misleading about his actions to be with the woman.

The truth is, sometimes men can't tell the difference between really having feelings for a woman or when it's just our hormones going crazy for her. What's a guy to do to get clarity? I met a comedian once who had a simple foolproof test. Masturbate. If a guy wants to call a woman immediately after jerking off, he really cares for her. If he has no desire to call her after jerking off, he doesn't. He might still try to sleep with her, but at least he knows it's purely hormonal.

Of course, this helps men but not women. How can a woman know if a guy is really into her or if it's just hormonal? She just has to roll the dice. Or, when he calls her, she can simply ask him, "Hey, did you just finish jerking off?"

If he did, great news; he really cares for her.

The Bonedigger

THE FIRST THING I NEEDED TO DO WHEN I QUIT THE ROAD WAS MEET PEOPLE. I had several friends who still lived in the Chicago area, but most of them were in the burbs. I needed to meet people in the city, where I lived. I did have three good friends who lived in my neighborhood and figured that was a good place to start. They got me into a weekly open-volleyball night at a church. They also invited me to pub crawls and happy hours organized by churches' young adult groups. I soon learned that there were lots of functions to hit in Chicago.

I went to events organized by the 20/30 Club, by various churches, by sports leagues, and by social clubs organized by people just looking to have fun. The largest social group by far was the PPC Fridge Door, run by a guy named Jeff Fujimoto. This guy was a real party animal; he had events going on almost every night! There were also bars that held various events, like Bar1Events, who owns several of the best bars in Chicago. Four Corners Taverns boasts another great group of bars. Some bars affiliate themselves with professional sports teams or colleges. Both Durkin's and Joe's, for example, are jumping Pittsburgh Steelers bars. There were also social businesses, such as Highlife Adventures and Eight At Eight, not to mention things like speed dating. Chicago itself hosts a variety of festivals. It was great and I started to meet a ton of people.

I met John and Jessie playing volleyball. We noticed that a lot of people played volleyball on the beach in the summer, mostly two against two (two's). So the three of us went down to the beach together to find out how it worked. A lot of the courts would accept a "challenge." This meant that we could challenge the match and the winner of the game would then play us next. We started to go down and challenge games regularly.

Around the same time, I heard about volleyball leagues. I signed up as an independent with Chicago Sport and Social Club, where I met a guy on my team named Mike (Mike and I now play tennis together regularly). As I met more people, I formed teams to sign up with Sports Monster. Before long, I was playing in several volleyball leagues. I met a ton of people amidst these various venues.

The following summer an inspired Jessie bought a net. He went down and set it up on the beach Sunday mornings. Then the fucker called me at eight in the morning to see if I could come out and play. I hadn't had a Saturday night off in years (the busiest night of the week for comedians), and I was making up for lost time. I was driftwood on Sunday mornings.

"Hey, Ian, it's Jessie. I'm down at the beach. Ready to play?"

"Fuck you."

Click. I went down to the beach closer to ten...like two-thirty in the afternoon. In the interim, Jessie had met two guys, Rex and Rich, who had two nets. We combined forces and as the weeks went by, we invited more and more people to play with us. Before long we had our own small group and someone coined a nickname for us, SOB's, short for South of the Boathouse. (We set up our nets just south of a boathouse on North Avenue Beach.)

Rex and I also met another group of players who set up on Saturdays. They flew a Ferrari flag to mark their nets for easy locating. We invited some of them to join us on Sundays and vice-versa. Soon the two groups intermixed and we SOB's began to fly a smiley face flag to mark our nets. In a few years the group became very large. Two of the Ferrari flag players—Eric and Dennis—branched off and formed yet another group. They merged with three other groups and became quite large themselves.

A few of us were invited to play in a volleyball tournament organized by an even larger group called the Bonediggers. We quickly spread word about this awesome tournament and it grew to include more than a hundred participants.

During the winter I played volleyball inside, where I found a floor hockey league in which to play. (Shut up, floor hockey is too a sport.) I had been dying to play some floor hockey and was thrilled to find a league. The only problem was, I didn't know anyone who played. So I talked a bunch of volleyball players into playing. It was ugly...very,

very ugly. Five minutes into a game our opponents would be up seven to zip. They would pull their goalies. We lost games twenty-something to one or two every week, even though the other teams played most of the time without a goalie. Our team did have fun, although one of our players insisted, "The girls on the other teams are mean!" I'd call him a wimp—except he was right.

Actually, the first hockey goals we scored, were scores for the other team. Santo, our center, won the very first face-off. He panicked in the rush of the other team, turned around and shot the puck back at our own net. Our goalie, Jaime—can't imagine why he was not anticipating a shot from a teammate—watched it go between his legs. The other team was up one to zero before they touched the puck. Santo won the following face-off...and did the same goddamn thing! Our opponent was now up two to zip and they still had not yet touched the puck. Jaime yelled at Santo, "What are you doing?"

"I figured you'd be ready this time!"

When I say we were bad, I fucking mean it. But during the first season, I met enough players from other teams to form a floor hockey team to play on another night. One of these players told me about a girl, Shannon, who wanted to play. When we got a team together, we signed up for a Sports Monster league. I later joined a group who played open hockey on Saturdays, as well.

Dating-wise, things were going well. I was going out with plenty of women, although I wasn't meeting anyone I was really into. There were a lot of two-week flings. I was getting tired of "playing the game" (incorporating all the dating techniques I've mentioned). I decided that when I met a woman I really liked, I would not play the game with her; instead, I would just say and do whatever I felt.

The first time I called Shannon was to see if she wanted to play on the hockey team. I gave her the details, such as the cost and location.

"Okay, Ian, got it; thanks."

I expected that to be the end of the conversation.

"So, are you from the area?"

"Yeah, Oak Park, originally. I've been traveling a lot until recently, though."

"Where to?"

Next thing I knew we had spoken for more than an hour. It was a good conversation. The next time I called Shannon was to tell her the time of the first game. (My computer back then was a Commodore 64, which apparently did not get email, so I had to call team members with game times.) The same thing happened—we chatted again for an hour.

I didn't notice Shannon when I met her; I didn't notice anyone. There were only four teams in our hockey league, and I was afraid we were going to lose players because of it. So I spent a lot of time just trying to collect all the money to cover the cost of the league, go over some strategy, and make sure we had enough people to play every week. Who had time to notice anyone? I kept calling each player on the team every week to remind them of that week's game time. And every time I called Shannon, we spoke for over an hour. She had a sexy voice and a charming laugh. It finally occurred to me that I liked this woman. I decided to ask her out.

The following week I paid attention to her when I went to the game. She was very pretty. She had blonde hair that hung down over her shoulders, which she wore in a ponytail for the game. She had pretty eyes, a warm smile, and a good body. She was around 5'4". What all the other guys had noticed about her on Day One of hockey season were her big breasts. They were big; too big for my taste, typically, but somehow on her they looked great. Normally I prefer brunettes with medium-sized breasts, but I was willing to bite the bullet and settle for a blonde with big breasts. I should get a Humanitarian Award.

Later that same week both Shannon and I went to a Super Bowl party, thrown by one of the players on our team. She and I spent most of the time talking to each other and I don't know what happened in the Super Bowl, except that Baltimore won. She drove me and one of my friends home. I liked her a lot and looked forward to not having to play the game with her. The next night we had hockey. After hitting a bar with the team following the game, I nabbed some time alone with Shannon as we walked to our cars. I asked her out.

"I knew you were going to ask me and I was thinking about it."

Uh-oh, women thinking; never good. She had already analyzed us dating before I even asked her out.

"I recently broke up with the guy I thought I was going to marry. I'd like to go out, but I think it would be a bad idea right now."

I didn't know what the hell to make of that. It was a game. Anytime anyone answers a yes or no question with anything other than "Yes" or "No," it's a game (my friend Adam taught me that). She had given me nothing to work with; was she interested or not? She could have told me to ask her again in a month, or that she would let me know when she was ready to date again. I gave her a chance to clarify, after showing an appropriate amount of empathy for her breakup.

"Okay, well, do you want me to ask again sometime or no?"

"Oh, definitely; definitely ask again sometime."

All right, she was interested. Of course, I had no idea how much time was in a "sometime." One week? Two? A month? When her first child was born? I also anticipated that her ex would jump back into the picture. If she had thought she was going to marry him, it probably wasn't going to be a clean break. I kept seeing Shannon at hockey and she subbed for us a few times in volleyball. We also flipped a Frisbee around a couple times. Real exciting stuff. We invited each other out a few times but our schedules never matched up or one of was sick; there was always something. She kept me wondering.

"Want to go see Phil Collins in two weeks?"

"Can't, Ian; I'll be out of town."

Okay...again, nothing to work with; she could have said she would love to go but couldn't, or "No thank you." She was playing, making sure she kept me on the hook. Even her friends got in on it. One night I met some of them and they all said that they had heard "so much about me." At the end of the night one commented to me, "Nice meeting you, Ian. I'm sure I'll be seeing a lot more of you."

While Shannon played, I did not. I told her I enjoyed talking with her and hanging out. I remarked that it was funny I hadn't noticed how she looked when we first met. I could see in her face that she didn't believe most of what I said. She was used to having guys go gaga over her breasts and I wasn't. Clearly, as far as she was concerned, I was up to no good.

As anticipated, Shannon got back together with her ex about a year after I met her. Perhaps I had been her backup plan in case they didn't get back together. He did not care for me and I told the team to start looking for another player; no way was he going to let her play with us anymore. Sure enough, shortly thereafter, Shannon stopped going out with the team to bars after games. She stopped playing with us. I stopped hearing from her. Then, about a year later, she called me out of the blue. I instantly knew she and he had broken up again. Sure enough, they had.

Shannon did not rejoin the team, but rather subbed for us when one of our other women couldn't make it to a game. During this time period, I went out with a couple of different women, but again, no one who really got to me. Shannon was the only woman I had met in Chicago who had really gotten to me. She was smart, sarcastic, athletic and fun. There were a lot of red flags with Shannon which I chose to ignore. She said she liked to be friends with a guy before dating him. Yikes, we know what kind of guy that lands. She didn't like to play sports at which she didn't excel and didn't like to try new things. She didn't give straight answers when asked out. I felt that she had been interested in me at one point but wasn't anymore. Still, I asked her out again one night when she drove us to a bar after a game.

"So, Shannon, I've been trying to figure out what it is about you. I finally have. You make things better by being there. I'm asking again."

She looked completely uncomfortable, which, in turn, made me uncomfortable. Again, she gave me some vague answer instead of "Yes" or "No." I decided she wasn't interested; even if she was, I had reached the limit of my tolerance. I kept in touch with her for business as usual to sub for hockey.

Another year passed when suddenly Shannon freaked out. I saw her at floor hockey one night, where she was playing for another team. She was very distant. I called her the next day to see what was wrong. She didn't answer and I left a message. The next day Shannon sent me an email. It wasn't rude or chastising, but it was weird. She asked that I never email or talk to her again. She basically implied that I was infatuated with her and was just being a friend to get close to her. What the hell was wrong with this chick?

Unbeknownst to Shannon, she had done the worst possible thing she could have done. She accused me of being the very thing I loathed: the wanna-be-dating friend. I replied to her email, said that was fine, and told her I would be sending her a long letter, which I did. I was trying to save the friendship, although I knew it would be in vain. Why bother? It's easy to be a friend when the waters are calm; the true challenge is to be a friend when the waters are rough. If our friendship ended, it wasn't going to be because I couldn't sustain rough waters. In the letter I surmised that a lot of guys had cheated on her. Knowing she liked to be friends first, I knew the type of guys she dated.

I also included a poem with the letter that I had written about her one night to clear my head. The point of the poem wasn't to woo her; it was to give her comfort. I told her she could whip it out the next time someone cheated on her and she would feel better. That's a good gift to give someone. A week after I sent Shannon the letter, I learned through the grapevine that she had broken up with her latest boyfriend. Yes, she had been friends with him prior to dating. And she caught him cheating on her. That clinched it; no doubt I had infuriated her by being right. Few things piss a woman off more than a guy being right. I was certain she would never contact me again, which she didn't. Too bad, we could have been good friends.

Shortly after Shannon ended our friendship, I met Vanessa on the beach. She was the friend of a woman who came down to watch us play volleyball on the Ferrari flag nets. Vanessa immediately took to me. She asked when I would be playing volleyball on the beach again. I told her; she showed up on that day by herself to watch. She asked me to walk her home. I asked her out and she gave me her number. After speaking a few times on the phone, we hit Guthrie's. The date was just okay; she was far too quiet for my taste. I asked her out again, though. I know that people often get nervous on a first date, so I reserve judgment until a second date. She said she'd like that. After we spoke a few more times, she said she didn't think it would be a good idea to go on another date. I replied, "Okay, no problem. It was nice meeting you."

Vanessa then said she'd like to be friends and invited me to a party she was throwing at her new condo several weeks later. Parties are always good places to meet people and she probably had some cute friends, so I accepted her invitation. A few weeks passed. I completely forgot about the party. A friend of mine, Vishal, who knew some of Vanessa's friends, reminded me. He didn't know where she lived and I couldn't remember, so I called her. "Hey Vanessa, it's Ian. How are you?"

"Good, how are you?"

"Pretty good, thanks. I was just calling to get your address again for the party tonight."

"Oh sure, no problem. Can I call you right back? I'm on the other line."

"Sure."

Vanessa called me back a few minutes later, "Hi, it's Vanessa. Um, Ian, I don't think it's a good idea for you to come to the party, given our history and everything."

History? I instantly knew she was some kind of nut job. *Stay away, stay away!* Someone that delusional was bound to cause trouble.

"Okay. Have a good party."

"Thanks."

No sooner had I hung up than the phone rang again. It was Vishal. "Dude, what happened? I just got a couple calls from some of Vanessa's friends. She's freaking out about you coming to the party."

All this over one lousy date? Good thing we didn't go out twice; if we had, she probably would have sued me for alimony. I told him what Vanessa had said and washed my hands of her. Eight months later—again, eight months—I went down to the beach to play some volleyball. I found out that Vanessa had been telling people all kinds of crazy things, among them that I had crashed her party and was constantly harassing her to sub for my volleyball teams. It was a pain in the ass, but along with help from some friends I resolved the issue. It probably helped that Vanessa was a horrible volleyball player and my friends knew that I would not ask a poor player to be on one of my teams; the games were far too competitive for her skills.

At a party after one of the Bonedigger tournaments (they host three every year—two in Chicago and one in Denver), I met a very pretty woman. (After each tourney, everyone goes home and showers, dumping five pounds of sand into their tubs. My tub maintains a thick, sandy paste throughout the summer because I'm on the beach so much.) She had a sweet ass and was a becoming redhead. We went out a few times and had some nice intimate moments. I thought it could go somewhere but then she started to fade away. She stopped returning my calls. She was too busy to get together. She kept saying the same thing, "I don't want to be defined by a relationship."

I had no idea what she was talking about but I figured it out. She didn't have a job. She was living in the burbs but wanted to live in the city.

"Okay, I think I've figured this out. You're afraid that if you get into a good relationship, that will be the only thing going well in your life and thus would define you. You don't want that."

"Right. Thanks for understanding, Ian."

"Do you wanna just be fuck buddies, then?"

"No, I can't do that because I like you too much and it wouldn't work."

The kicker was she had decided to date another guy. Since she didn't care about him that much, she felt that she could end the relationship at anytime; she wouldn't be defined by it. Huh? This was an odd bit of reasoning and I thought maybe she was just letting me down easy. I surveyed a bunch of women friends and volleyball players to get their thoughts on the matter. Surprisingly, almost all of them or their friends had made similar decisions at some point in their lives. It made perfect sense to them.

Other than these three glitches, dating has gone pretty well for me. Of course, I still have my funny moments; after all, God is against me. My most memorable one occurred when I decided to meet one of my neighbors. I live in a courtyard building and a woman moved in across from me, who was very pretty and had a body women would kill to have…men, too. I spoke to her a few times; she was very friendly. I decided to make a move. I told my friend, Mike—the guy I play tennis with—that I was going to go over to her place with a six-pack and see if she wanted to throw down a few. He insisted that I take wine instead. Against my better judgment, I went over to her place with a bottle of wine. I knocked on her door.

"Who is it?"

"It's Ian."

She opened the door, "Hey, how are you?"

"Good," I held up the wine, "Just wondering if you'd like to share a glass or two."

"Oh, you know what? I don't drink wine. I'm more of a beer kind of gal."

D'oh! I made a mental note to punch Mike in the face the next time I saw him.

"I'll take the wine, though; I have a friend coming into town tomorrow and she loves wine."

What could I do? She had me and she knew it. I gave her the wine.

"Thanks, have a good night."

She closed the door and I left.

I learned sixteen things over the past few years of my life:

- There are lots of things to do in cities and towns outside of dating.
- A solid base of friends is good for a healthy dating life.
- Strange things can happen when you don't play the game.
- The most important time to play the game is when you really like a woman.
- Don't let a woman keep you on the hook as her backup plan.
- Women are bombarded with the notion that all men do is lie.
- Don't get back together with exes; make the breaks clean.
- Tell women what they're used to hearing.
- Friendship is not of the same importance or value to each person.
- Some women are just nuts.
- There are people who will fabricate stories without a thought to the impact of those stories.
- Women think differently than men.
- Women will knowingly date the wrong guy or a guy in whom they have little interest.
- It's good for a man to have women friends.
- It's harder to be a woman than a man.
- Never listen to Mike.

There are tons of things to do in cities and towns, which create ample opportunities to meet women and make friends. At first glance, it may appear as though there is little to do socially, especially in towns, but with some effort, plenty of action can be found. Towns have festivals and events throughout the year, as part of their effort to maintain a young population that is critical to their futures. As a touring comedian, I was often part of towns' efforts to provide entertainment for their communities.

It's clear that I have a lot of friends and a strong social life. This enables me to make better choices when it comes to dating and one-night stands. I have a solid support system and I don't need a woman to make me feel good about myself. I have plenty to do when I'm not dating or getting laid. I have friends who don't do much socially. They date or sleep with whoever comes along, just to have a social life. The results are always disastrous. A solid base of friends is good for a healthy dating life. I cannot emphasize this enough. It takes time to build friendships. It's a step-by-step process, as I tediously detailed at the beginning of this chapter. Be patient.

Shannon is a perfect example of what happens when you don't play the game. I was way too open, not at all evasive (mysterious), didn't flirt, I was nice, and when I had a few chances to make a move, I didn't. The results were ridiculously disastrous. When a guy really likes a woman, he doesn't want to play the game; he wants to share with her right away. For example, he wants to tell her his goals and aspirations, while finding out hers. It is at this point that the guy needs to play the game more so than at any other time. Once you have her, you can switch gears and share. Although it will go against every fiber of your being, you must be patient and play the game. If you don't, you are almost certain not to get the girl.

Both men and women will keep each other on the hook (or line) as a backup plan, especially in a saturated market like Chicago. Shannon kept me on the hook, most likely while she waited to see what would happen with her ex. If people suspect they are being kept on the hook, they need to address it immediately.

"Look, my guess is you've put me on the back burner while you wait to see what happens with someone else. I don't like being second choice, so let's plan a date or good luck with that other person."

I've had several successes with this approach. It's a confident statement that forces people to make a decision. No matter what the outcome, I don't waste any time trying to figure out where I stand. How can people tell if they are being kept on the line? They get vague answers to invitations for dates that never include a "Yes" or "No."

"Would you like to do something this weekend?"

"I don't know yet, I have to get back to you."

"Possibly, I have to see what else is going on first."

"That might work. Call me later in the week."

These answers are intended to keep someone on the hook. Answers that aren't intended to keep someone on the hook include a "Yes" or "No," usually followed by a question.

"Would you like to do something this weekend?"

"Yes, but I don't know if I can, yet. Can I get back to you?"

"No, I can't this weekend. Are you around next weekend?"

"No, I don't think so. Thanks for asking."

Just to complicate matters, sometimes people aren't leaving you on a hook; rather, they are "letting you down easy." In truth, they're letting themselves down easy; they avoid answering honestly to get out of an uncomfortable situation. Most of what we do as people, we do for ourselves under the guise that we are doing it for others. How can you spot the difference between being kept on the hook by someone who is somewhat interested, versus being let down easy? A person keeping you on the hook stays in touch to reset the hook as needed; contact is initiated by both the "hooker" and the "hookee." A person letting someone down easy does not keep in touch; all contact is initiated by the hookee.

Women are bombarded with the notion that men will lie anytime they get a chance. I wrote this book in part because I found so many of the dating resources available to women preach this folly. Women's magazines and books don't encourage women to believe men. Instead, they encourage women to pretend to believe men. Then, when the men are unaware, women should decipher whether they are lying or not by using such proven scientific methods as interpreting their bodies' sleep positions and noting how they brush their teeth. One book for women suggests that wives who catch their husbands cheating should ask them to make lists. The lists would note all the things the wives could do to fill the empty voids their husbands are feeling. Once these voids are filled, the husbands will no longer cheat.

The overall message is that men lie and women should just accept it. What a bunch of bullshit. There are plenty of men who don't lie. Women should not put up with lying men. Kick them to the curb.

I've seen a lot of people get back together with exes. In some cases it's a constant boomerang. Why? Comfort. It's tough to lose someone who's been such an important part of daily life. It's even tougher to get back into the dating scene. So, couples often find themselves on-again, off-again, as they use each other as crutches. The result? They are not out doing what they need to do most—meeting new people, one of whom might be the right person. Don't get back together with an ex. Remember, there's a reason there was a breakup. While I've remained good friends with all my exes, I've never gotten back together with them. I make a considerable effort to avoid it.

People see themselves the way the world sees them. They are used to being treated in a manner that coincides with that way. For example, Shannon has big breasts. Guys stare at them so much she wears only high necklines and crosses her arms in front of herself as often as possible. Although it annoys her, it is important for a guy who approaches her to comment about her breasts at some point. She's used to hearing it and guys need to tell women what they are used to hearing.

One of my biggest mistakes with Shannon was not noticing her breasts. Think about it. Every time she turns around she finds herself staring at an ad, article, TV show, or movie telling her that men lie. She knows she has big breasts. Guys comment to her about them all the time. She overhears men discussing them whenever she's out. I came along and never mentioned them.

In Shannon's mind, not only was I a lying guy, I was a bigger liar than most. I pretended I didn't notice her breasts. *Did I think she was stupid?* Instead, I pretended that I was into her because she made things better by being there. *Yeah, right; try my breasts make things better by being there*, is probably what she thought.

This is why it is important for men to tell women what they are used to hearing. Don't tell a beautiful woman she's smart, or a smart, homely woman she's beautiful. Why? To them these praises come off as nothing more than bad pickup lines. They are simply more lies that the media warns women about. This is why many men believe women don't want to hear the truth.

The reality is Shannon is desperate to hear praise about anything but her breasts. The dilemma for men is getting her to believe such praise. The solution is simple; throw in some comments for her breasts along with the other praise. It would have been much better if I had said the following to Shannon, and then pointed at her breasts, "You know Shannon, you make things better by being there. And I don't just mean because of those."

Simple. She would have stayed in her comfort zone. She would have believed me because I brought up what every guy notices.

She also would have been pleased that for once someone noticed something besides her overachieving rack. I blew it with Shannon by being honest. How's that for irony? Remember, tell women what they are used to hearing and what they want to hear in the way they want to hear it. It's the only way to slip the truth by them. It's like feeding a baby food. The only way the baby will eat is if there are all kinds of airplane noises along with loopy moves with the spoon.

I highly value friendship. Not everyone shares the same view. There are people who go through friends like someone with the bird flu goes through a box of Kleenex. They don't respect friendship. Shannon obviously did not respect our friendship or me. When she had a problem, she didn't address it, she let it fester. She misjudged my intentions. When I tried to find out what was wrong, she simply ended the friendship through a cowardly email. Our friendship was based solely on her discretion and whims. I try to avoid being friends to people with such a poor understanding of friendship.

There are people who will fabricate stories to fuel their self-importance, without care or regard to the impact such lies will have on the lives of other people. The trouble Vanessa's lies caused me is a good example.

Women think differently than men. I did not realize how differently, until the woman from the Bonedigger turned me away because she did not want to be defined by a relationship and her attitude was considered quite reasonable by other women. A guy without anything good going on in his life would be thrilled to find a good woman. It is during such troubled times that it is best to have a strong support system—such as a good catch—on which to lean. Plus, it's a good indicator that she is into the guy, not his money or stature.

Women will knowingly date the wrong guy. I knew they would date the wrong guy from time to time. But until the Bonedigger girl, I had no idea they sometimes did it knowingly. This is one more reason why relationships can be so confusing and unfulfilling. The wrong guy doesn't know he is the wrong guy. Wouldn't it be better to just not date or to have a fuck buddy, rather than to date the wrong person? Or to date someone for the wrong reasons?

A lot of my friends are women, many of whom are very attractive. Lots of guys won't be friends with women. I've had guys comment to me, "If you can't fuck 'em, what's the point?"

Women offer all kinds of good insight into the thought process of other women (although remember to take their advice with a grain of salt). Also, attractive women catch the attention of other attractive women. I meet women much more easily when I'm out with other women than I do when I'm out with men. I know when to cut the strings, though; if I ever find myself falling hard for a friend who isn't interested, I take a break from her until I can handle being just friends. If I can't handle it, I stop keeping in touch after telling her why.

Being a woman is much tougher than being a man. Women get all kinds of mixed messages from society. *Be pretty. Be smart. Slim is sexy. Big is beautiful. Have great sex. Women who sleep around are sluts.* It never ends. To complicate matters, most of the resources available to women are geared toward men. They hold women responsible for many things, while they hold men accountable for very little. These resources encourage women to work very hard for little gain, while they encourage men to work very little to gain a lot. Look at the covers of women's magazines. What kind of articles do they advertise?

Why Can't You Keep a Man?
Give Him What He Wants
Make It So He'll Never Leave You

This is a lot of pressure on women, combined with articles on how to use makeup to look like a goddess, how to trim down, how to fit into a smaller dress, and so forth. The magazines are full of half-naked photographs of pretty women. These things are all geared toward men, not women. Now look at the covers of men's magazines.

Summer Blockbuster Movies
She Wants to Cheat...with You
How to Land Her in Three Sentences

Not much pressure. The magazines are full of half-naked photographs of pretty women. These things are all geared toward men. No wonder women like to avoid accountability; there's a ton of pressure on them from society to bear the weight of accountability when it comes to dating. Comparably, society puts little pressure on men to bear the weight of dating. If a guy leaves a woman, it's her fault. If a woman leaves a guy, she didn't do a good enough job either changing him or accepting him. It is always the woman's fault that the relationship did not work. It is never the man's fault.

Of course, women put some of the pressure on themselves. For example, no straight guy would ever buy a magazine full of sexy pictures of men. If magazines want to sell to men, they need to have sexy pictures of women. Why women would buy magazines full of pictures of sexy women is beyond men's understanding. It's simply one of the ways we think differently from each other.

Accountability is yet another reason why women will date jerks. The general consensus is that, if a woman dates a good guy and they break up, it must be her fault. She couldn't keep him. Or she didn't change him. If she dates a jerk, though, it's his fault and everyone knows it. Better to date the jerk. Who needs the pressure of keeping a man? Or the embarrassment of losing one?

QuicKies

ENJOY DATING. IT'S SUPPOSED TO BE FUN. TOO MANY PEOPLE DON'T HAVE fun on dates. Disagree? How much time on a date is spent on the cell phone, ignoring the date? How many people go to lunch for a first date, so that it's short if it sucks? (Lunch is not a date.) Put a half-effort into dating and that's all that will be received in return. Have fun and the date will be fun.

The grass is always greener somewhere else. Women with small breasts complain that men only want women with large breasts. Women with large breasts complain that men don't listen to them; they just stare at their breasts. I wish I had a bigger build. I have well-built friends who would trade their builds for my sense of humor. Instead of complaining about what's lacking, accentuate and use what's abundant.

There is a ridiculous notion that men should avoid women with cats, especially when they are in their thirties (the women, not the cats), while it is fine to date women with dogs. Truthfully, it is better to date women with cats than women with dogs. Women with dogs have too many excuses available to them and require extra work.

"I have to go home and walk my dog."

Is she telling the truth or does she just want to end the date early?

"I have to go home and walk my cat."

Obviously, the woman is not interested. This is a great line women with cats should use to get rid of unwanted guys. It's crystal clear and non-confrontational. Who could ask for more?

If a guy dates a woman with a dog, guess who gets to walk the dog? And the prettier the woman, the uglier and smaller the dog. I once saw some poor schmuck walking some pocket-sized creature down the street. I say creature because it couldn't have been a real dog. It looked like a gremlin fucked a rat.

That guy is dating a gorgeous woman or he is very, very gay, I thought. He could have salvaged both the dignity of men and dogs if he had just shoved the damn thing into his pocket, so no one had to see it. I have never seen a guy walking a cat.

Loose Ends

WE'VE REACHED THE END OF THE BOOK AND THERE ARE STILL MANY unanswered questions. Why do guys like younger women? Why can't women find a good guy? Why don't men like foreplay? Where can one find good gremlin-on-rat porn? All right, all right; calm down.

People take dating for granted. There are a lot of walls out there in the dating world that people build around themselves. The irony is most people don't need them, they simply choose to build them. They assume there will always be someone to date, that they will get a chance to hit on the beautiful woman at the bar on another night, and so forth. Some will wake up alone one day and wonder how they let it all slip away.

When I was a comedian, I had a legitimate reason to struggle with relationships and put up walls. I was never in one place very long. I had only one night, one chance, whereas other guys had lots of years and dozens of chances. Mentally ill people legitimately struggle with dating, as do physically limited ones. The rest of us? We simply take dating for granted. I've spent years learning how to get over, under, and around built-up walls. Some I've even torn down. I'm glad to have the skills and I don't take dating for granted.

Women in their thirties often complain that men like younger women. They assume it's because gravity hasn't affected these women yet and because they have smoother skin without wrinkles anywhere. Men do like younger women but not so much because of their looks. It's because they have fewer walls, are less bitter, and have more fun.

Women have a tough time meeting good guys because they practice silly techniques to pique a guy's interest. These techniques only work on idiots. It doesn't help that the advice available to women is often poor. I flipped through ten dating books for women at the bookstore, for research purposes. Some of the advice in the books is good but most of it is ludicrous. More than one book advises women to never return a guy's call. If a woman doesn't return a guy's call she is only going to meet two types of men. One has no one else to call; no other options. The other one calls occasionally whenever he runs out of T&A; he needs a new ass to tag. Are these the kinds of guys women want to meet? Return calls, ladies.

Some books tell women not to communicate their feelings when their men take them for granted. Instead, they should hint and drop clues. Wonderful; we all know how much men love to play guessing games. If a woman doesn't bring up an issue near the time it occurs, her man will never believe it was that much of an issue, that she is just being melodramatic when finally—after hiring several detectives to work around the clock—he discovers why she's upset. Think of men as dogs; if they crap on the floor, the owner has to spank them right away or rub their noses in the crap to get them to realize they've done something wrong.

My absolute favorite advice to single women in one of these books is that guys associate cinnamon with love; therefore, women should bake a glob of gooey, cinnamon pastry before a guy comes over to pick them up (it doesn't need to be edible). He will smell the cinnamon and love will be on his mind.

Bake cinnamon before a date? Sure, after getting all dolled up and putting on just the right outfit for the night, baking is what every woman wants to do. Fucking insane. What happens next? The date goes bad and the woman sits there pissed all night, mad that she wasted time baking for such a lame date. The guy doesn't know why she's upset; all he knows is that she didn't offer him any of those delicious cinnamon rolls she was baking when he picked her up. Bitch.

Why don't men like foreplay? Foreplay is more time for women to change their minds or sober up. Also, the longer the foreplay, the shorter the sex. Men get more and more aroused during foreplay. They finish faster when there's foreplay, especially the first time they're with the woman. Personally, I like a lot of foreplay the first time I'm with someone. I like to take my time and get her more and more aroused. I just hope she realizes that when I finally get inside her, it will only take a few pumps for me to finish because of that foreplay.

Dating is a game. Men can say they don't want it to be, women can deny it. That doesn't change anything. It's a game. To date, one has to play; it's not a choice. If people don't play, they don't date. The only choice is who to play with and a hope that he or she wants to play as well. Follow the advice I learned the hard way, pay attention, and enjoy each other. Life isn't too short for games…it's too short for losing games.

As for good gremlin-on-rat porn, hey, I'm not into that. My advice is to google it.

About the Author

Comedian-turned-screenwriter Ian Coburn was one of the most highly sought standup acts on the comedy circuit throughout the nineties. He opened for acts such as Drew Carey and Damon Wayans before headlining himself. He still boasts the industry record 106-straight weeks on the road. Ian has written two feature length screenplays for hire along with nine of his own. He writes fast, knocking off some topnotch scripts in less than a week. His manager is currently negotiating the options of two of his scripts while he is developing a third with Davis Entertainment (*Predator; Flight of the Phoenix; I, Robot*). Ian is also under consideration for a staff writing position on a newly pitched television series. His scripts have won screenwriting contests, including HSI's competition. Please feel free to visit www.iancoburn.com for more information.

Share your own dating disasters and see a comedy
video at:

www.godisawoman.net

Printed in the United Kingdom
by Lightning Source UK Ltd.
124655UK00001B/213/A